THE TEST MATCH CAREER OF
SIR
JACK HOBBS

CLIVE W. PORTER
Foreword by JOHN ARLOTT

SPELLMOUNT LTD

For Marion with love

In the same series:

The Test Match Career of Geoffery Boycott
by C D Clark

In preparation:

The Test Match Career of Colin Cowdrey
by Derek Barnard

First published in the UK in 1988 by

SPELLMOUNT LTD
12 Dene Way, Speldhurst
Tunbridge Wells, Kent TN3 0NX

© Clive W. Porter 1988

British Library Cataloguing in Publication Data
Porter, Clive W.
    The test match career of Sir Jack Hobbs.
    1. Hobbs, Jack, *1882-1963* 2. Cricket
    players–Great Britain–Biography
    I. Title
    796.35'8'0924   GV15.H/
    ISBN 0-946771-61-8

Design by Words & Images, Speldhurst,
Tunbridge Wells, Kent
Printed in Great Britain by
Anchor Brendon Ltd, Tiptree, Colchester, Essex

FOREWORD

Because Clive Porter is such a thorough cricket student, this is more than an account of Jack Hobbs' Test batting. It gives the background to his innings and many relevant details of his, and other people's, performances outside the representative game.

This is a study of the man whom his fellow professionals so justly called 'The Master'. No one can compare him with W G Grace, who, of course, picked up cricket in its primitive state and created the modern game. Sir Jack, though, can be accepted, as even the Australians believed him to be - the finest batsman of modern times: in cricket, praise from the ranks of Tuscany is the highest there can be. Certainly Sir Donald Bradman was a more prolific run scorer, but he was a good wicket batsman. He was never able to say, as for instance Sir Jack Hobbs could after the fourth Test in Australia of 1907-08, that a score of 57 - made out ot a total of 105 on an Australian 'sticky' - 'I still think [it] is the best innings I ever played.'

This was a master, indeed; he faced, dealt with and scored prolifically off, the bowlers of the world over 30 years on all types of pitches. That period is significant in that he did not by any means play for 30 seasons: he lost four years to the First World War, best part of another to the two-day-match season of 1919 and yet another to illness. He suffered, too, several injuries that kept him out of play, while for some years he was rarely free from migraine.

Towards the end of his career, he certainly wished he had scored the other two centuries that would have given him 200 in first-class cricket. He said, though: 'It doesn't worry me but it does seem to worry my friends.' Also significant was the fact that he would never count in his records the two centuries he scored for Patiala in India which would have taken him to that figure. He dismissed them with: 'They were exhibitions, not serious games - the Maharaja just wanted to print them on the walls of his pavilion.' The fact is, though, that he might have had those, and many more, centuries if he had wanted them, in his great days. He once said: 'You see, if Sandy and I had put 150 or so up on a good Oval wicket there was no point in carrying on: there were good batsmen like Tom Shepherd, Andy Ducat, Mr Fender [to his dying day he called amateurs Mister] and a lot more to come. So I used to have a go at some hardworking bowler on the other side - usually one of my old mates - enjoy myself and give him a chance to get me out.' Mr Porter's statistics are revealing and valuable but they do not show - indeed, they could not - just how often Sir Jack was out in the sixties and seventies having a go.

There are also many hints of the important fact that this was essentially a good man: honest, modest, gentle, devout, but without the slightest suggestion of priggishness. When they were both in their old age, and Lady Hobbs was extremely frail, it is accurate to say that Sir Jack forced himself to live so that he might look after her - which he did as tenderly as a woman - because he feared that, if he was not there to take care of her, she would be put in a home. When she died he just simply relaxed and died himself. It is true to say that if he had never made a run or excelled at any sport, those who knew him must have seen him as a great man because of the unmistakable nobility of his character.

John Arlott

CONTENTS

Foreword by John Arlott
Acknowledgements

ACKNOWLEDGEMENTS

This account of Sir Jack Hobbs' Test career lays no claim to being a full-scale biography. The events of his private life are but briefly touched upon. His cricket for Surrey and other sides, including the Players, is covered, as are his opponents and colleagues but within the context of the Test matches and series. The book does seek to provide a comprehensive survey of his performances at the highest level. A minimum of three, and in many cases several more sources have been consulted for description of each of his Test innings. I hope the portrait emerges of a great batsman and a great cricketer, a man almost universally loved and admired. The reasons for this combination of affection and veneration should also become clear.

The book would not have been possible, however, were it not for the kind and valuable assistance of the following who, through correspondence, the provision of material or in interview gave freely of their time:
Sir George Allen, Maurice Allom, Leslie Ames, the late Bill Bowes, Sir Donald Bradman, F R Brown, Jack Burrell, the late Jim Coldham, Geoffrey Copinger, C L R James, Fred Jeavans, Tony Mitchell, Gerald Pawle, Godfrey Prior, Jim Swanton, and R E S Wyatt.

My task was made much simpler by the helpfulness and efficiency of Brian Taylor, Reference Librarian and his colleagues at Maidstone Library, and of Anne Atkinson, Area Librarian and all the staff at Meopham Library.

Especial thanks are due to John Arlott, for his encouragement and his generous Foreword, to my Editor, John Bright-Holmes, for his constructive and cogent comments and to my wife, Marion not least for her excellent typing but, most of all, for her loving support.

Permission to quote from *Wisden*, *The Cricketer*, *The Times*, *The Oxford Illustrated History of Britain* (OUP) and *Overthrows* (Century Hutchinson) is gratefully acknowledged.

The illustrations for this book came from the Author's collection and the ILN Library. Every effort has been made to trace present copyright holders both for copy and photographs. The publishers apologise in advance for any unintentional ommision or neglect and will be pleased to list the appropriate acknowledgement in any subsequent edition of this book.

CWP

Note:
In the text the score is given as '61/1' for brevity's sake, meaning '61 runs for 1 wicket'. A bowler's figures appear as '6/91' meaning six wickets for 91 runs. In addition, the accepted style of using an asterisk (*) to denote a 'not out' innings has been followed.

1 The Man and his Technique

I saw Jack Hobbs in 1933 when he scored 221 for Surrey against the West Indies. It looked when he began as if he already had 200. When he had made 200 it looked as if he could make 200 more. What impressed me most was not his technique, although he was a super batsman, but his mastery of all that he was doing. One example will show this. Griffith had a man at mid-off and Hobbs was pushing ones and twos through the gap in front of square on the leg side. The bowler moved the mid-off across. Immediately Hobbs moved out - he didn't jump - and banged the fast bowler twice for four through the mid-off. In the same over as he had moved him, the bowler was compelled to return the fielder to his original position.

(C L R James in an interview with the author, 1986)

Jack Hobbs was a cricketer whose consistency was equalled only by his charm. He graced the first-class game from 1905 when he played, on his debut, against W G Grace, until 1934, in which season he played against Don Bradman and he made the last of his 197 centuries, a record that seems unlikely to be broken as long as the current structure of cricket is maintained.

What made Hobbs so very special? A combination of great natural ability (he never had any formal coaching), a sound technique and an abstemious way of life all contributed. As he matured none of these attributes altered. Twenty-two years old in his first first-class game, he developed his cricketing qualities until his retirement when he was fifty- one, an astonishing age by the standards of today when it is unusual for first-class cricketers to play beyond their fortieth birthday.

Hobbs' firm foundations were unshaken by the ageing process. It is said that after 1914 he was never quite the player he had been before the Great War. He took this view himself. Perhaps it is as well to be reminded that he scored 65 centuries between 1905 and 1914 in his more brilliant period and a further 132 between 1919 and the end of his career.

At the crease he was a fine example of cricket being a sideways-on game. His left shoulder led into the drive. Brave, consistent and capable batsmen of a later era, such as Ken Barrington of Surrey and Dennis Amiss (Warwickshire), made many runs using the so-called 'two-eyed' stance with a square-shouldered approach; in its extreme form (as exemplified by Northamptonshire's Peter Willey) this is not so very far from the 'French cricket' position. From there, however, it is impossible to play the classical

1

off-side shots that were such an integral part of the poised elegance of Hobbs' repertoire. He may have been somewhat chest-on to the bowler in his stance, but he moved into the traditionally correct position by the time the ball was delivered.

There seems to be sufficient evidence to suggest that he did score more slowly in the post-war period but this is a relative statement and has to do in part with different philosophies of play and field-placing. He was no slouch even in his senior years. He struck the ball with a full swing of the shoulders but such were his timing and balance, he rarely seemed to be striking as a hitter of the ball. He would smooth it away just as Colin Cowdrey of Kent was to do in later years when sweetly on song. He stroked it as a stylist, unaffected, unselfconscious, unpretentious, but with a simple beauty; and he used the full face of the bat.

Hobbs was blessed with an athletic build and the sense to take care of it. Loose shoulder and strong flexible wrists remained his assets throughout his career. But the physical attributes alone are not enough. From the outset it was clear that he had not only a wide variety of strokes but, what was more important, the temperament and judgement to make the most of them. That he was an intelligent, discriminating cricketer is evidenced by the number of runs he scored. He made the most of his opportunities and talents on all types of wicket. This may perhaps only be said with such certainty of W G Grace and Victor Trumper although such moderns as Gary Sobers (West Indies), Barry Richards (South Africa), Greg Chappell (Australia) and Vivian Richards (West Indies) have rarely looked to be at a disadvantage in unfavourable conditions.

Hobbs was a comfortable batsman at the crease. There was no angular awkwardness, no sign of anxiety or inner turmoil. Apparently relaxed and at ease, his composure was remarkable. He stood with his feet rather close together, with his weight evenly distributed. His footwork was supreme and therein lay the key to his success. Hobbs did not dither in what was once delightfully - and accurately - described by Ken Barrington as ' two-man's-land.' As a result of his balance, he was able to go right forward or right back with equal aplomb.

His backlift was straight, over the middle stump, not angled to slips or to point. The fullest possible face of the bat came down equally straight to meet the ball. But it was a full and proper backlift, no half-cocked lackadaisical affair which passes for a backlift in some present batsmen's hands. Hobbs was never seen in an ugly, awkward, cramped crouch. Standing, with bat upraised, at his full height, he was able to judge the length of the ball early and keep his options open until the last moment. If the ball had been given too much air, he would be ready for the drive. On the other hand, an uneven bounce could be dealt with passively - if such a word may be applied to so impassive a batsman. The bat would then rest on his shoulder and not be lifted aloft, as is sometimes seen today. With his high

2

backlift Hobbs was prepared for an attacking stroke but he was quick enough in mind, eye and body to adjust for defensive purposes.

His technical mastery was such that, as a general rule, it was not necessary for him to hit against the spin or across the line of the ball. He could place the ball quite wristily at need but his driving of the good length ball was his glory. He stood upright and stroked through the line with panache and perfect timing. This particular gift, his timing, coupled with his strong wrists, would put the ball away to the ropes, all along the ground. He was well aware that this method was safer than using a cross bat, especially if an unexpected bounce brought the ball up sharply. The chance of a catch, square on the leg side, was much reduced by the use of the straight bat.

He had the skill to dictate terms to the bowler because of his capacity to score heavily off good-length bowling. Hobbs' readiness to attack, to wrest the initiative from the bowler, was a constant feature of his play. He could jump out to drive or walk out confidently to destroy the effectiveness of a good-length ball by turning it into a full toss. His swift powers of adjustment enabled him to defend when necessary but his first thought was to score from, not merely to stop, the ball. He thus frequently compelled the bowler to drop short which gave Hobbs the chance to demonstrate his expertise with the cut. If the bowler tried a different line but with a similar length he would be forced away on the leg side with a firm snap of the wrists. Hobbs was not afraid to loft the ball in attacking the bowler's field but he was always aware of the danger this might involve and quietly capable of altering his mind in the middle of a shot, if the ball were not quite 'there' for hitting, and producing instead a controlled, defensive stroke. The alternatives, scotching the spin or stunning the speed, were equally within his compass. He might be at full stretch and literally using every inch of his reach but he would remain in command.

He was just as effective when dealing with the short-pitched ball. A formidable square-cutter, he used his wrist power with authority and speed. Hobbs' facility with the late cut to the ball slightly more pitched up provided a demonstration of his neat footwork. In dealing with these deliveries he would go right back on his stumps with his right leg. This naturally made the ball shorter and from there he could dispatch it efficiently, at the angle of his choice, through the slips. Unusually, he slipped his right hand down the handle when moving into position but this movement in mid-stroke, so to speak, which could have been disastrous for the ordinary player, hampered him not at all. Indeed, it gave him great control enabling him to keep the ball down. He was, almost invariably, on top of the shot.

Not all the bowling in his time was obligingly delivered on or outside the off-stump for the batsman's convenience. To the good-length ball on his legs, Hobbs would move out in order to turn it forward of square leg.

* * *

Jack Hobbs, the eldest of a family of twelve children, was born in

Cambridge on 16 December 1882. Humble circumstances gave him few material or social advantages but he described his childhood as a happy one and there is no reason to doubt him.

It was when his father gained employment by the University as a professional net bowler and umpire, that the boy's association with Parker's Piece began and his love of the game. School teams were a rarity for the elementary schoolboy of that period. He played cricket for a choir. He played cricket for a church side. Leaving school at thirteen, he became, like his father, a college servant and played cricket for a local club. He made his mark and in 1901 he scored 30 for Cambridgeshire against Hertfordshire.

The following year, Tom Hayward, one of the great players of the period for Surrey and England, and a Cambridge man of high renown, was so impressed by the batting of Hobbs that he said he would put him forward for a trial at The Oval. At about the same time, a friend, wanting Hobbs to have a second string to his bow, wrote to Essex extolling the young man's virtues. Essex never replied. On such small events do whole histories turn.

Hobbs was duly called to Surrey's trial in 1903, succeeded, was offered terms and spent the next two years obtaining the necessary residential qualification. He made his runs for the Colts, for Surrey Club and Ground, and for Cambridgeshire. At the age of twenty-two, in 1905, he was more than ready for the first-class game.

The influence of Hayward was, not unexpectedly, considerable. The senior man was a prolific scorer, a fine technician and no mean artist himself. Hayward's style was most correct. In that Hobbs bore a strong resemblance but he was faster on his feet than his guide and his attacking prowess was of a different dimension. Tom Hayward's contribution to Surrey and England cricket was a great one. 43,551 runs at an average of 41, with 104 centuries, give solid evidence of his quality. Hobbs was to learn much from Hayward.

On 27 April 1905 the following assessment appeared in *Cricket*, the major magazine of the period on the sport. As a prophecy it was not very wide of the mark. With only slight first-class evidence at his disposal, the anonymous writer deserves credit for his prescience:

Hobbs the young professional who made a most successful first appearance for Surrey on Easter Monday is qualified by residence. For Cambridgeshire last season he had an average of 58, his highest scored being 195 while he took fifteen wickets, at an average of 20.33. He is a batsman who may go a long way for, with a variety of strokes, he plays with confidence and in an excellent and business-like style.

That first appearance was against the Gentlemen of England, who included W G Grace at the age of fifty-seven, took place on 24, 25 and 26 April 1905. He opened the batting with Tom Hayward with whom he was to open for the County until the First World War, although they were to be so partnered in Tests in just one match.

4

His first entry in the Surrey scorebook:

c Townsend   b Beldam 18

is not an impressive one, but Hobbs shared with Ernie Hayes the top score in what was a rather out-of-touch display by Surrey on their own wicket which, at this stage of the season, was less than true. They were bowled out by Beldam and Brearley before lunch on the first day. Knox with 5/39 then kept the Gentlemen of England's lead down to 29.

When Surrey went in again, Hayward and Hobbs played such fine cricket that they put on 81 in the hour before the close of play: Hayward 29*, Hobbs, very much the junior partner in terms of experience, had made 44*.

In the morning they completed the first of their forty century partnerships before Hayward departed. Hobbs was eventually caught at square leg trying to pull Walter Brearley who, in a friendly way, advised the newcomer to cut out the shot. His 88, made in two hours, was top score in a total of 282. The game, much interrupted by rain, ran quietly to a draw. *Cricket's* generous appraisal of Hobbs' performance was shared unequivocally by *Wisden* who called it 'an emphatic success'.

A week later, Hobbs made an even more substantial impact. At The Oval, in his first Championship game, against Essex, he scored 155, his first first-class century and the highest score for either side in the match. *The Times* commented: 'a masterful innings including a variety of strokes and marred by only one chance at 80. There should be a great future before Hobbs in the cricket world'. Hobbs' three hours' stay showed him to be master of the situation as well as of the Essex bowlers. They included Buckenham (genuinely fast) and Tremlin (fast-medium) who were to be instrumental in the only defeat that summer, outside the Tests, of the touring Australians. The variety of Hobbs' strengths was at once apparent. It was equally clear the he could hit hard (this was particularly evident after he had passed 100) and that he had a strong defence. The contemporary view was accurate: 'He can keep his head and does not seem to be a man who will be ruined by the flattery which is the undoing of so many promising young players.'

Surrey's five-wicket win owed much to Hobbs. His 155 was made out of 249 while he was at the wicket. Three all-run fives, and nineteen fours, give some idea of the certainty with which he placed his strokes. He was not flustered by the early loss of two partners and a 175-run third-wicket stand with Baker (53) lasted only 100 minutes, a signal that Hobbs could be a fluent and fast-scoring player. Lord Dalmeny, the Surrey captain, took the unusual step of awarding him his County Cap at once.

His only other century of 1905 (102 at Leyton) was scored swiftly against Essex, once he had played himself in quietly, and it helped to secure another five-wicket victory. Mention must be made, however, of his first meetings with the Australians. He played in both Surrey's matches against the tourists. In May, a week after his 155, he top-scored in the first innings total of 225. Cotter, a dangerous fast bowler, with whom Hobbs was to have several stern contests in international matches, made the ball rise nastily but neither he nor the guile of Armstrong and Laver disconcerted Hobbs. The Englishman did enjoy some good fortune: he was missed on 14 by Armstrong in the slips and by Noble at point when 42. He looked set for a century until he fell to a brilliant piece of fielding. His own account of the dismissal appeared in *My Life Story*. He was not entirely happy with the decision and makes that clear even thirty years after the event. While Hobbs was going for a second run, 'Clem Hill threw the ball in from the boundary and although almost square with the wicket, hit the stumps. I was out for 94. Even today I still think that I just got home in time, but it was a magnificent throw.' His innings lasted two-and-a-half hours, included thirteen 4s and was made out of 167/4. This fine effort brought him loud applause for only five centuries were made against the Australians that year outside the Tests. The very capable Reggie Duff had the distinction of being Hobbs' first wicket in first-class cricket on the following day when, later, the teams were presented to the Prince of Wales, Prince Edward and Prince Albert.

This game was drawn but a weakened County side was defeated in the return fixture. Hayward and Hobbs put on over a hundred for the first wicket but the latter, after the dismissal of his partner, seemed to lose his way. He took an hour over his last six runs before being caught in the slips by Trumper off Cotter for 58. This was probably due in no small measure to Armstrong's tactics. He bowled well wide of the leg stump to a seven-two field. The only fielders on the off-side were at cover and in the deep. Never a stodgy player at any stage of his career, Hobbs, like any other mortal, could get curiously bogged down on occasion when apparently well established. The remarkable thing is that this happened so rarely. It nevertheless comes as a surprise, such is the power of the legend of his command at the crease; but this was, after all, his first season.

Perhaps his most exciting innings of the season was played at The Oval against Middlesex. In a low-scoring game, the fast bowlers, Knox for Surrey and Mignon for the visitors, had much success. When Surrey required 168 to win in the fourth innings they had to achieve the highest total of the match. Hayward (82*) and Hobbs (75*) knocked off the runs in a little over two hours, the last 90 runs being made off 16 overs. Hayward struck twelve fours and Hobbs eleven. The latter had some more luck as he was missed at slip before scoring and at mid-off when on 33. *The Times* commented: 'on a wicket on which the bowlers had up to that time carried everything before them, it would be difficult to find a performance of more merit.'

As the rigours of six-days-a-week cricket sapped his stamina, Hobbs did not maintain his promising start and was later moved down the order. Even so Hobbs completed a most satisfactory first season with 1000 runs at an average of 25. *Wisden* was complimentary about his prowess. He was 'the best professional batsman Surrey have brought forward in recent seasons. Easy and finished in style, he is particularly strong on the on-side.' There were, however, two criticisms. It was said that he 'developed a tendency to play too much with his legs'. The use of the pads was regarded as an accepted part of the batsman's defence to the ball pitching outside the off-stump and breaking back. At that time, according to the Law, he could only be out leg before wicket 'if with any part of his person he stops the ball which in the opinion of the umpire at the bowler's wicket, shall have been pitched in a straight line from it to the striker's wicket and would have hit it.' This was not changed until late in the year of Hobb's retirement from the first-class game, 1934, after the 'Bodyline'controversy. No doubt the criticism was fairly made, but the wonder is that Hobbs made so many runs, and few of them slowly, through the seasons if he were prone to use this negative technique.

The second criticism Hobbs himself felt was unfair: ' he should endeavour to brighten up his fielding.' He had spent much of his summer at third man or elsewhere in the deep. He tired; he 'threw his arm out'. On occasion he laboured. His improvement over the ensuing years was spectacular. As a result he ranks as one of the very best cover-points in cricket history.

From humble origins Hobbs was reaching towards heights social, professional and international which he could never have dreamed of in his Cambridge Council schooldays. In *My Life Story* he writes of having an 'inferiority complex to a marked degree'. His later achievements are, in the light of that self-assessment, all the more remarkable.

2 Early Years and Test Baptism, 1906-08

Hobbs began his career approximately halfway through the 'The Golden Age.' In his survey of the game immediately preceding the First World War, *The Golden Age of Cricket*, Patrick Morrah describes the quality of that period:

It is tempting to think of the Golden Age as an era of unbroken sunshine, of sparkling strokes and sparkling weather, elegant spectators in top-hats and frilly summer dresses, with background music of popping champagne corks; joyous cricket played in a spirit of harmonious good will. The temptation must be resisted. The period 1895-1914 had its fair share of dismal summers; there were acrimonious disputes and instances of regrettable behaviour, just as there have been throughout cricket history... Nevertheless there was unquestionably something golden in the cricket itself which is not paralleled in any other period of the game's history, and taken as a whole the sporting nature of the play was worthy of its quality. Close study of the Golden Age confirms that it did not belie its name.

The influence and example of W G Grace with his technical mastery were strong. Just as the art of batsmanship had developed so the quality of first-class pitches had improved. The wickets began to give the batsman a fairer chance than he had hitherto enjoyed because they were faster and truer. Stroke-playing rather than self-defence became the order of the day. The public-school tradition was already significant and well-coached young amateurs made the transition from playing-fields of Eton and elsewhere to the first-class scene with ease and elan, with style and dash, with flair and grace.

The cricket of this period may have been a less sophisticated game but it was a thing of beauty and despite the passing of the years, it remains in the folk memory a joy for ever. Not all the fielders could bend and pounce with the athleticism of those of the 1980s. The field placings were less defensively minded than those of the present time. Bowlers were not encouraged to bowl the 'dot ball'. Batsmen were not expected to play for their averages. This was the climate in which the aspiring professional had to learn his craft, but it would be a mistake, indeed, an injustice, to see the Players as the plodders holding their teams together with a dull, painstaking approach while the Gentlemen stole the show with their glamorous style. The professionals were expected to put bat to ball and the best of them were no slower in their scoring than their amateur colleagues. Many of them, however, found it a struggle to break into their Test side when competition came from such amateurs as Archie MacLaren (35 Tests), Charles Fry (26), Stanley Jackson (20), Gilbert Jessop (18), Ranjitsinhji (15), Pelham Warner (15), Reggie Spooner (16), Reggie Foster (8), Lionel Palairet (2). Even so the professionals did find their place among that elite company. Hayward, for example played as many Tests (35) as Foster, Spooner, Palairet and Warner put together. Johnny Tyldesley (31), Jack Hearne (24), Frank Woolley and Jack Hobbs himself, amongst others, played a part, although frequently, if not in all cases, they had more than one string to their bow. Examples of such all-round strength were Rhodes (58), George Hirst (24), Len Braund (23), Albert Relf (13) and Woolley (64), but if these figures seem modest by comparison with the number of caps won by cricketers in more recent times, it has to be remembered that between 1900 and 1914 only 69 Tests were played by three countries. By contrast, between 1960 and 1974, seven nations competed in 268 such contests.

Test opportunities for professionals in Hobbs' time often came as a result of their availability for and willingness to tour, which, for business or financial reasons, amateurs were unable to do. Two comprehensive victories may best illustrate the point. The England batting order for the fourth Test at Melbourne in February 1912 reads: Hobbs, Rhodes, Gunn, Hearne, Foster (Frank), Douglas, Woolley, Mead, Vine, Smith, Barnes. The winning margin? An innings and 225 runs. Not much wrong with that. Only two amateurs, F R Foster and Douglas, were in that side. In June 1912 England beat South Africa in the first Test by an innings and 62 runs. The team: Hobbs, Rhodes, Spooner, Fry, Woolley, Jessop, Foster, Smith, Barnes, Warner and Brearley. In addition to Foster, there were five amateurs, namely Spooner, Fry, Warner, Jessop and Brearley. It is difficult to believe that the difference between the two sides was solely a matter of form. It would not do to press the point but other examples are not hard to find. This is not to imply in any way that the amateurs were not worth their place.

It is easy to slip into the trap of assuming that this was a golden age only for batsmen, and that the bowlers were but dutiful trundlers whose sole purpose was to serve as cannon fodder for the batsmen. In 1909, for example, the year in which Hobbs played his first home Test, eight bowlers took over one hundred wickets, at an average of under 18: Schofield Haigh and Rhodes of Yorkshire; Brearley and Harry Dean (both Lancashire); Tom Rushby (Surrey); Blythe (Kent); George Thompson (Northamptonshire) and Armstrong (for the touring Australians). Two years earlier, in addition to Haigh, Rhodes and George Hirst (Yorkshire), there were Arthur Fielder (Kent); Albert Hallam and Tom Wass (Nottinghamshire); George Dennett (Gloucestershire); Frank Tarrant (Middlesex); joined by the South African tourists Reggie Schwarz and Ernie Volger. The average cost of their victims was under 17. They included bowlers of all types. Between them they bowled fast, medium, slow, off-cutters, swervers, leg-breaks and googlies. The last were a largely new phenomenon in 1907.

In 1906, Hobbs had made four centuries (two home and two away) and scored his 1913 runs at an average of 40. However, the most important event of that year for him was his marriage to Ada Gates which took place in Cambridge on 26 September. Although it sounds sentimental, it is true to say 'they lived happily ever after' until her death in 1963.

Now the wet summer of 1907 saw one of the worst starts of Hobbs' career. One century eventually came in his twenty-fifth innings, 150* against his favourite Championship opponents, Warwickshire. Only in 1911 did he play more innings before he first passed the hundred mark. 1907 did see him carry his bat for the first of seven such occasions: 60* out of 155 against, yes, Warwickshire. The passing of 2000 runs and an appearance in the top ten of the national first-class averages were two other notable 'firsts'. 2135 runs at an average of 37 took him into eighth position. Mention must be made of four consecutive opening partnerships in a week in June with Tom Hayward: 108 and 125 against Cambridge University; 147 and 105 v Middlesex. Hobbs' scores were 72 (when, oddly, at one stage he took half an hour to score 5 when well set!), 56, 70, 65.

It was, nevertheless, not one of his great seasons and, on 1 August he was not one of the first group of professionals invited to tour Australia in 1907-08. Four of them (Hayward, Hirst, Lilley and Tyldesley) declined the terms, and this provided Hobbs with his opportunity. In addition to the professionals' refusal to tour, both Jackson and R E Foster had declined the captaincy, so it may be seen that the final side was by no means representative. The party, under the leadership of Arthur Jones (Nottinghamshire), was: Frederick Fane (Essex), Kenneth Hutchings (Kent), Jack Crawford (Surrey) and Dick Young (Sussex) with professionals Wilfred Rhodes (Yorkshire), Len Braund (Somerset), Ernie Hayes, Hobbs (both Surrey), Charlie Blythe, Arthur Fielder (both Kent), Joe Hardstaff (Nottinghamshire), Joe Humphries (Derbyshire) and Sydney Barnes (Staffordshire). It was reported, when the team departed, that George Gunn (Nottinghamshire), travelling for health reasons, 'would be available for the team'. Plagued by seasickness which was to a regular, miserable part of his tours abroad, Hobbs was in no condition to be an active participant immediately Australia was reached. He missed the matches with Western Australia and South Australia, two comfortable victories in which Jones and Fane opened successfully. In his first game, the draw against Victoria, he did little. Not selected for the New South Wales fixture, he returned against Queensland but made no impact. Both these games were won. Three innings had produced 3, 26 and 21. Jones now contracted pneumonia which was to keep him out of cricket until just before the fourth Test. Hobbs was thought little of at this stage of the tour and not unreasonably felt somewhat aggrieved by his treatment:

The impression was created in my mind that A O Jones had not the highest opinion of my capabilities and I could not help harbouring the thought that the right course would have been to play me. If I was worth sending, I was worth trying, to see how I shaped.

It does not take much imagination to understand how he must have felt when Young, the reserve wicket-keeper (previous scores 26, 25, 40, made when batting lower in the order) was pressed into service as opening partner to Fane for the game with An Australian XI. 34 runs secured him the position in the first Test.

It was not this that upset Hobbs so much as the selection of Gunn, who was not an official member of the party and who had not played for the side thus far. For the team it was an inspired selection, although Hobbs, twelfth man for the Test, could hardly be expected to see it in quite those terms. There was no quarrel between the players. Writing in 1924 Hobbs said, 'There was certainly no ill-feeling between us during the tour. As a matter of fact Gunn and I were on that tour, as today, the best of chums.' Gunn made 119 and 74, top score in both innings, and did much to take England close to victory. Australia nevertheless managed to bring off a remarkable two-wicket triumph, having still needed 89 when their seventh wicket fell. The experiment with Young (13 and 3) was not a success. More importantly, he also made costly mistakes behind the wicket. This was not the last occasion in Ashes' history when England were to make the cardinal mistake of selecting their wicket-keeper on the basis of his batsmanship and not on the superiority of his 'keeping.

Restored to his proper position, Hobbs made a timely 77 against Victoria and a further 58 in the second-class game with XVIII of Bendigo. For the second Test at Melbourne, he was selected. Over 90,000 spectators watched this slow-scoring six-day contest.

Australia, having won the toss, found runs difficult to come by. Noble (61) and Trumper (49) were most successful in resisting a sharp England attack in which the orthodox medium pace of Crawford (5/79) was outstanding. McAlister earned the dubious distinction of being the first Test batsman to be run out by a fine cover fielder as he was dismissed by 'a smart return by Hobbs'.

On the second morning, on a good wicket, Fane and Hobbs set off in pursuit of 266. Fane departed at 27 but Gunn helped Hobbs bring up the fifty before being, according to one report, 'greatly dissatisfied with the decision' that removed him lbw with the total 61. Determined to make his mark, Hobbs scored much more slowly than usual. His 50 took one-and-three-quarter hours. At tea England were comfortable: 113/2, Hobbs 59*. After the interval Hobbs batted with much more freedom. On

69 he gave a chance to Macartney at square leg before he was finally bowled by Cotter. Albert 'Tibby' Cotter, who took 89 wickets in his Test career at a cost of 28 each, deserves a special mention as he was the fastest and most frightening bowler of his day. Never afraid to pitch the ball short and bounce it at the batsman's head, he was capable of making all but the bravest 'a trifle apprehensive'. Hobbs' 83 included eight 4s and his dismissal left his side on 160/3. During his three hours and twenty minutes at the crease he had shown great patience and a very strong defence that reminded onlookers of Tom Hayward. Hutchings now went on to enjoy his finest hour in what was, in the main, a disappointing Test career. His hundred was reached in under three hours with some fine driving and vigorous hooking. Frank Laver, the experienced Australian medium-pace bowler who watched this game commented that while Hutchings had been brilliant, Hobbs' 'sound and stubborn game helped to kill the bowling'.

After England reached 382 (Hutchings 126), Australia fought back strongly through Trumper (63) and Macartney (54) who opened, and, later, Noble (64) and Armstrong (72) to set England a target of 282. 'The play often became wearisome as England played an entirely defensive game,'was the view of one reporter. It took them four hours to make 159/4 by the end of the fifth day, but the first fifty took only 54 minutes. That promising start was spoiled, four minutes later, when Hobbs was bowled by Noble. The distinguished all-rounder controlled his off-spin and his swerve well. He varied his pace deceptively and shrewdly between slow and medium. Hobbs' innings of 28 which occupied 65 minutes was described as 'patient and watchful'.

On what was to be the last day, England fell away badly to 243 for 9 wickets and all seemed lost. Barnes, however, had other ideas, choosing this moment to make his highest Test score (38*) and, ably supported by Fielder (18*) took his side to a dramatic victory. 'The ladies shrieked as each run was obtained and men stamped their feet.'

Melbourne was to be the scene of many of Hobbs' triumphs. In *My Cricket Memories* he gives a reason:

The light is beautiful; once you get used to the clear air you can see the ball like a football. The thin atmosphere prevents the ball from swerving much, except when it is quite new, save on the rare days when the ground and air are humid.

Neither he nor the side was to experience similar success in the third game of the series. The toss won, on a good wicket, Australia must have been disappointed not to make more of Fielder (4/80) and Barnes (3/60). Only Macartney (75) passed the half-century mark although Ransford (44) and Hartigan, in his first Test, with 48, gave valuable support. All out for 285, they left England with an hour's batting before lunch on the second day, in which time Hobbs (21*) and Fane (25*) put on 50. Hobbs had had the good fortune to be missed by Noble at point off O'Connor before he had scored. The opening stand was broken at 58, however, when Hobbs, on 26, was caught by wicket-keeper, Carter, off Saunders, who enjoyed considerable success against Hobbs in this series. This left-arm bowler, who had a good high action and great powers of spin also had a doubtful action. Indeed one of his own captains, Joe Darling, was moved to describe him as 'the dirtiest chucker Australia ever had'. As Saunders pushed the ball through briskly, especially in helpful conditions, he was a difficult proposition.

Fane went on to 48 while the solidity of Gunn (65), the freedom of Hardstaff (61), and the boldness of Crawford (62) took England to a first innings lead of 78. By close of play on the third day Australia were just 55 runs on with four of their best batsmen back in the pavilion. When their seventh wicket fell, they were only 102 ahead. Then came what can only be described as a great stand between a sick man, suffering from influenza which had prevented him from fielding (Clem Hill) and a tyro in his first international contest (Hartigan). During this afternoon the heat became intense: 107° in the shade, 152° in the sun. The bowlers flagged and the fielders must have been affected. The heroes of Melbourne were guilty of costly errors. Barnes put down Hill (then 22) off Rhodes. Fielder grassed Hartigan (when 32) off Crawford. They struck 243 together which still stands as an Australian eighth-wicket record in Tests. Hill, normally at number three, came in at nine. Not surprisingly perhaps, no one has hit more than his 160 batting in this position in Tests. Hartigan made 116, his only Test century.

Having fielded for more than nine hours, England were not in the best shape to seek the 249 required. Hobbs, having scored a single, was badly hurt in the stomach or groin by the first ball Saunders bowled. After lying on the ground for a few minutes, he recovered to some extent but was obliged to retire. He did not return until the total was 146/6 and was at once missed off an easy caught-and-bowled chance by O'Connor. He then struck out boldly, hitting a straight 6 and three 4s to finish on 23*, but the English resistance was generally negligible in a total of 183. Hardstaff again, with 72, and Braund (42) were exceptions. Saunders with his sharply spun left-arm medium-pacers, took 5/65. As O'Connor, like Hartigan, on his Test debut, finished with 5/40 - his best Test figures - the Australian selectors must have felt inspired.

England then had a chance to regroup and raise their spirits with a visit to Tasmania, where two matches were played, then the return against Victoria. The last-named amounted to a second-eleven side as the first team had been exhausted by a titanic seven-day struggle with New South Wales. Hobbs made runs consistently: 104 and 65; 58; 30 and 115. Two victories and the better of a draw should have restored morale.

No one could say that England had much luck on the tour although, had the catches stuck, they might have won the series. The way the rub of the green was against them may best be seen in the fourth Test. Jones, restored to fitness and the side, lost the toss and, in good weather and on an excellent wicket, Australia would surely have anticipated a substantial total. Fine all-round fielding, high quality slip-catching (by Crawford, Jones and Braund) and clever, varied bowling, especially from Crawford (5/48) and Fielder (4/54) had them out for 214. Ransford made 51 and Noble 48 but the rest struggled. At the close England were 9/0 but Reuters' comment at the end of the day was ominous: 'Light rain is now falling.'

No play was possible before lunch on the second day but a hot sun enabled a start to be made by 2.20 when the wicket was slow, although the ball was already rising quickly. Let Hobbs describe what happened:

What a wicket it became in no time! Just as perfect, but for the bowlers. A sticky wicket, and the sticky wickets in England can't be compared with it. A beast. The ball - kicks, flies, turns wickedly - does all that it shouldn't do. And Saunders, the medium left-hander whom I always thought a bit of a thrower; couldn't he make the ball do things!

I felt there was nothing for it but to go all out for the bowling, taking every risk, and I hit 57 in seventy minutes. I felt like going further too. But Noble put himself on to bowl and I played his first delivery for a break. The ball went straight, I missed it, and my stumps rattled. And that was the end of what I still think is the best innings I ever played.

Hobbs at one stage had five successive scoring strokes for four. Of the opening stand of 58 Gunn made only 13. When 47 Hobbs gave a difficult left-handed chance to Armstrong at cover-point off Saunders. The first hour of the innings brought 60 runs. Hobbs' own 50 arrived eight minutes later. Having struck ten 4s, he was the third wicket to fall at 88. The rest of the side, with no answer to Saunders (5/28) and Noble (3/11), collapsed to 105 all out.

When Australia slumped to 77/5, thanks mainly to Crawford and Fielder, England were back in the game, but Armstrong, dropped by Crawford on 44, and Ransford with a similar escape on 26 turned the course of events. They made 133* and 54 respectively, well supported by Carter (66). England finally needed 495 to win.

Gunn (43) and Hardstaff (39) alone offered resistance of any significance in the total of 186. The series was lost. Hobbs suffered the rare indignity of a Test duck. The only other instances were in his first home Test at Birmingham in 1909, the fourth Test at Cape Town in 1909-10 and at Sydney in the fifth Test of the 1924-25 series. Considering that he went to the wicket 102 times in his Test career of 61 matches, this is a remarkable achievement.

The draw with New South Wales which followed saw Hobbs fail with the bat but he did take three wickets in the match including that of Macartney whom he caught and bowled for 20. In retrospect, and in the light of events in 1909, this must have afforded the bowler some wry amusement.

In the final Test at Sydney, Jones won the toss and put Australia in. On a rain-affected, lively, kicking wicket, Barnes, with his best figures in an Ashes contest, 7 for 60, promptly put them out again for 137. Noble struck back at once by dismissing Fane for a duck before Gunn joined Hobbs for a 134-run stand which lasted 138 minutes on a steadily-improving wicket. Both showed great caution at first moving the score slowly to 40. The 50 came at a run-a-minute, however, and Hobbs' personal 50 in eighty-seven minutes. By the early close of play, brought about by poor light, they had reached 116/1: Hobbs 65*, Gunn 50*. In the dull weather of the second morning Hobbs was not able to take full advantage of a slow easy wicket. With the score 135 and having struck seven 4s, Hobbs fell victim once more to Saunders and was bowled for a faultless 72. *Cricket* commented: 'The Surrey man gave a very sound display and suited his game admirably to the changing conditions.' Gunn went from strength to strength finishing with 122* and being instrumental in securing a first-innings lead of 144.

The great Trumper whose previous Test scores had been 4, 0, 0, 0 and 10 in the first innings was overdue for runs. He needed a slice of luck to save him from another failure. When he had made 1 he was missed by Rhodes, a difficult one at short-leg off Barnes. After this reprieve he 'came good' with the highest innings in the series on either side (166), on the best wicket of the game. A glance at Trumper's overall Test record (3163 runs, average 39) will not reveal to a modern reader why it was against him that Hobbs was measured or why it was with Trumper that he was compared. They were the best beloved cricketers of their time and they had much in common.

Both were batsmen of consummate artistry who reduced the best bowlers to impotence but they did so with a smile and a grace and an ease which compelled affection as well as admiration. Their performances on bad wickets, their attacking style, their effortless timing made them kindred spirits and they were warmly regarded by colleagues and opponents.

With help from Gregory (56) and Hill (44), yet another fine second innings recovery was made, this time to 422. In each of the five Tests, their second attempt brought the Australians more runs and, in all but the first Test, substantially more. The final straw as far as England's luck was concerned (neither Fielder nor the first choice wicket-keeper was fit for this match) came with the fall of rain which made the pitch awkward again.

Hobbs was dismissed by Saunder's fifth ball, caught by Gregory at mid-off for 13. Hardstaff was troubled by a thigh injury caused when trying to stop a Trumper boundary the previous day, so Hobbs accompanied him as his runner. He must have been unfamiliar with his role or curiously immobile, as he was twice struck at square leg by Hardstaff's pull. The close of the fifth day saw England on the ropes at 117/6. Rhodes (69) batted sternly while Jones (34) fought well. Their efforts were to no avail. Saunders (5/82) led the Australians to a 49-run victory when the last England wicket fell on 229.

Before the MCC party left for home there were two draws with South Australia and Western Australia. Hobbs made small contributions of 7, 12 and 40 but finished the tour with a highly satisfactory average of 42 and an aggregate of 934 runs in all matches. He was second to Gunn (51) in the Test averages with 43. H S Altham wrote:

From that start he never looked back and when he left Australia it was with the reputation of being the great professional batsman of the near future.

It was a rare summer when Hobbs had an average under 40. 1908 was one of them. Signs that all was not as it should have been were evident in the second Championship game of the season against Hampshire at The Oval where a spectacular partnership with Goatly doubled the score from 132/5 in ninety minutes and Hobbs was said to have played 'many beautiful strokes both in driving and pulling'. He did not, however, show his usual mastery. A personal score of 161 seems to give but little grounds for criticism, but he had been missed at third man by Mead off Llewellyn before he was into double figures and offered several other more difficult chances later. In his next eleven innings his highest score was 41. He seemed particularly at fault with his timing against Leicestershire where he was twice dismissed for 23. *The Times* commented on 30 May: 'It appears that this batsman is suffering from too much cricket and a rest might be beneficial.'

The next match against Essex, although he only made 34, he looked in better shape, and his runs were 'made after the manner of Hayward - in fact the resemblance is most noticeable between the two bats'. He was nevertheless rested after the Essex match.

He returned against Nottinghamshire. He had yet to do himself full justice at Trent Bridge. His first innings of 57 was not a triumph as he frequently mistimed the ball and was out to a long hop. In the second innings, however, his 117 was, as they say, 'something else again'. With things going badly for his side, he succeeded in saving the game. Hayward, Hayes, Marshal and Crawford all went quite cheaply. Hobbs was the bastion against which the Nottinghamshire assault faltered. His runs were made out of 205/7. On the following day there was some press enthusiasm: 'Always an attractive player he was seen at his best yesterday afternoon and he is much to be congratulated on his skill, nerve and resource.'

Of his next eighteen innings, half passed the fifty mark and three of them reached the century. These were not flawless performances. Indeed, there is no reason why they should have been. Against Oxford University he made 102 but was by no means comfortable at the beginning. Missed in the slips on 5, he was later hit on the body by a short ball from Robinson. Collecting himself he put together a brilliant second half to the innings. Against the Gentlemen, however, he played the best innings of the day in making 81, being particularly severe on anything pitched well up. At Northampton, having had a good look at the bowling, he compiled 125 and it was at this time that he was being described by *Wisden* as one of the best professional batsman of his day, putting him on a par with Hayward and J T Tyldesley (Lancashire). This was an important qualification, for it was a season when amateurs such as Fry, Ranjitsinhji, Warner and Jessop stole many of the headlines. His best innings was in the defeat by Kent at Blackheath when he made 106 out of a team total of 183 on a worn wicket. In the return at The Oval he mounted a daring attack on the slow left-arm spin of Colin Blythe who, in his previous thirteen Championship innings had dismissed him no fewer than eight times. Blythe was a great attacking bowler who had a swirling loop in his delivery. He gave the ball plenty of air and kept it up to the batsman even when he was being hit. Hobbs, in this game, had some luck, being twice missed before he reached 30, by the wicket-keeper Huish and at extra cover by Marsham. There was no further flaw in 155 made out of 393 in four hours and a quarter.

It was his last big innings of the summer but he was now firmly established as a leading player. *Wisden's* choice of him as one of its Five Cricketers of the Year (actually the article was entitled ' Lord Hawke and Four Cricketers of the Year' - perhaps his lordship wasn't considered to be much of a cricketer!) was right and proper:

Hobbs makes no secret of his indebtedness for good advice and encouragement to Hayward, on whose superb method his own style of batting has obviously been modelled. From the first he was very strong on the on-side and though with increased experience he has naturally gained in variety of strokes, his skill in scoring off his legs remains perhaps the most striking feature of his play...As a fieldsman Hobbs has during the last two years or so improved out of knowledge...Very keen on the game and ambitious to reach the highest rank, he is the most likely man among the younger professional batsmen to play for England in Test Matches at home in the immediate future.

S H Pardon, Editor of *Wisden*, could not have been more accurate in his prediction - but he was nearly proved wrong by the England captain.

3 The Emergence of a Great Batsman, 1909

Cricket reported that Hobbs 'showed wonderful command over the ball and throughout his long innings did not make the slightest mistake although he was always scoring fast. It was a very masterly display'. This was in the match with Hampshire when, in partnership with Ernie Hayes, runs came at an amazing pace - 371 in two-and-a-half hours - as both made their highest scores to date. Hobbs hit exactly 100 out of 192 before lunch in one hour fifty minutes. He went on to make 205 out of 430 in three and three quarter hours giving an almost perfect performance. Hayes scored 276. In just over five hours Surrey made 645/4 - the highest total made in a day and the first occasion on which two Surrey batsmen made double centuries on the same day. C B Fry, now fully involved with the future of the training ship *Mercury*, had left Sussex. This was his first match for Hampshire, and he must have wondered what he had let himself in for.

Hobbs' timing, which had presented him with several problems during 1908, was now hardly ever at fault. His placing and forcing away of the ball on the leg side showed the skill of a great batsman. The last 130 runs of the stand came in just forty-five minutes. This was the first of Hobbs' sixteen double centuries, all of them made in this country, seven of them at The Oval. This rather gives the lie to the myth that, once he had made a hundred, especially as he grew older, he gave his wicket away, for ten of these double centuries were made when he was over the age of forty.

Cricket was to pronounce confidently on 27 May: 'Those who follow the game at all closely are unanimous in predicting that he is destined to play an important part in Test Match, as well as in Surrey, history.' This was at the end of one of the most productive and fluent months of Hobbs' entire career.

In somewhat more demanding circumstances, for example, against the Australians, Hobbs did not slow down. 'He played an excellent game, facing the various bowlers confidently and scoring off all of them freely'. His 44, top score in a Surrey first-innings total of 191, was made out of 62 in fifty minutes. He then jumped out to drive Armstrong's second delivery, hit outside it and saw his leg stump flattened by a straight ball. In the second innings Armstrong had Hobbs in trouble again. He played very shakily for a few overs, for 4 runs, before again falling to him - lbw this time. In all Armstrong was to dismiss him five times in eleven innings in 1909 and that was not the only problem he presented, as will be seen when the third Test was played. For Surrey Tom Rushby, the temperamental fast bowler, with 10 wickets in the match, and the reliable Hayward with 96 in the second innings, were the major figures in a victory which was to be the only one achieved by a county against the tourists that summer.

Hobbs enjoyed a fine game at Birmingham in the next fixture with Warwickshire against whom he was to score more centuries in the County Championship than against any other side - 14 in all between 1907 and 1933. This was the first of six occasions when he was to make two separate hundreds in the same match. His 160 came out of 294 in four-and-a-half hours; the second-innings 100 out of 182 in two hours and five minutes. Only one other such double was to be achieved away from his beloved Oval - in 1925 at Taunton against Somerset on a more famous occasion.

The Warwickshire bowlers must have been heartily sick of the sight of Hobbs by the time he had completed his second hundred of this match, for ten days earlier he had made 41, when a rare misunderstanding with Hayes led to Hobbs being run out; and then 159 in the second innings which suggested that the attack of Field (fast) and Foster (fast-medium, left arm), Santall (medium) and Hargreaves (slow-medium, left-arm) was very much to his liking. Even though he gave chances on 86, 127 and 133, he made the most of his good fortune against hard-working bowlers and tight fielding.

In this second match he played himself in quietly, getting the pace of a good wicket on his way to a first innings top score of 160. This was described as a fine innings for his side, showing nerve and skill. Second time around he was said to have played 'perfect cricket' on a still true wicket, especially after passing 50. It was just as well that he did, for Surrey could only manage a total of 197. Not many of such 'doubles' can have been scored when hundreds were so necessary to the side. Time and again, throughout his career, Hobbs demonstrated that very rare ability to make runs when all around him others, many of whom were no mean performers, were struggling.

Hobbs then rather missed the boat against Essex - he made only 99, but this innings did not show him at his best. He appeared tired after his exertions against Warwickshire. Nevertheless, he was obviously in prime form for the first Test. The contemporary view is appreciative: 'apart from getting all the runs he has this season, in itself a notable performance, what is still more notable is that they have always been wanted.'

Although his achievements in Australia had given him grounds for optimism about his inclusion in the side, this was by no means certain. No fewer than fifteen names were announced from whom the team was to be chosen, and the selectors were taking few gambles with youthful inexperience. In their list only one player could be described as being in the first flush of cricketing youth. The players and the gentlemen were: C Blythe (30), W Brearley (33), C B Fry (37), H A Gilbert (22), T W Hayward (38), G H Hirst (37), J B Hobbs (26), G L Jessop (35), A O Jones (35), A A Lilley

(41), A C MacLaren (Capt) (37), A E Relf (34), G J Thompson (31), J T Tyldesley (35), W Rhodes (31). Most of these names ring with quality down the years, but spare a thought for Humphrey Gilbert. He was bowling medium-paced off-breaks for Oxford University. A remarkable May had brought him in successive games 7 wickets (v. Surrey), 6 wickets (v. Leveson Gower's XI) and 9 against the Australians, including 8/71 in the first innings. This put him into contention, but he was not in the final selection, nor did he ever come so close again. Few would question the soundness of the judgement of the selectors (Lord Hawke, C B Fry, H D G Leveson Gower) at this stage of the summer, although they were not to be at their most decisive in a season during which no fewer than 25 players represented England. For different reasons, Brearley, Hayward and Relf were the other unlucky ones who did not play.

So Hobbs was in but it was by no means as simple or as obvious then as it seems now. Archer MacLaren was very much his own man, with very decided views. He was not leaping at the opportunity to have Hobbs in the side, despite the Surrey man's prolific start to the season. Long afterwards he wrote:

I remember so well H D G Leveson Gower, a member of the Selection Committee coming to me and saying, prior to the First Test, played at Birmingham, that he was certain young Hobbs was a fine batsman and that he felt sure I would be pleased with him, and that he was anxious for him to be included in the England Eleven. I knew nothing about him then but I replied that it was good enough for me, after listening to the Surrey skipper's description of the young player.

That he knew 'nothing' about Hobbs seems astonishing. In fairness to MacLaren - one of the most splendid of England batsmen but arguably the crassest, most insensitive and obstinate of England's captains - it should be added that, since 1905, in 10 innings against Lancashire in the County Championship, Hobbs had a highest score of 72 and no other more than 25. 'Shrimp' Leveson Gower, on the other hand, wielded no small influence on and in the cricket of his time, and took pride in his powers of persuasion:

I strongly urged his claim on the England captain Archie MacLaren. MacLaren, to my surprise, opposed the young batsman's inclusion and it was only after considerable discussion that he rather reluctantly gave his assent saying that I was in a position to know more about him than any other Selector.

Hobbs was indeed in. And, almost before he knew where he was, Hobbs was out - in the first innings anyway.

Only three-quarters of an hour's play was possible on the first day. Although the weather was warm, it was showery and there was little drying wind. Much poor light and threatening weather were in evidence. The press had scant sympathy: 'Modern players have carried the adjourning for light

20

to an absurd pitch and in the circumstances credit must be given to the crowd for behaving as well as it did.' That comment, albeit differently phrased, might well have been written in the 1980s. Australia, always struggling on a slow wicket, were dismissed on the second morning for 74, mainly by Blythe (6/44) but with important assistance from Hirst (4/28).

When England's reply began, MacLaren played a maiden over from Whitty. Hobbs then faced Macartney. Charlie Macartney is best remembered as a gloriously confident (he was nicknamed 'The Governor-General') batsman. He may have been small of stature but he was immensely strong, and great of heart. A striker, not a stroker of the ball, he would have espoused the philosophy of Brigadier Ritchie Hook, to whom 'biffing' the enemy was the centrepiece of strategy. In Tests Macartney scored 2131 runs (average 41), between 1907 and 1926, banging the ball to the boundary with a relish that communicated itself to the crowds. He was, in addition, a not inconsiderable slow left-arm bowler, especially at this stage of his Test career, and on this tour he took 64 wickets at 17 runs apiece. He usually moved in off a long run, showed excellent control and had the skill to slip in an unexpectedly faster delivery.

Perhaps it was the quicker ball. Perhaps it was the batsman's nerves. Whatever it was, Hobbs, to his mortification, was dismissed by Macartney's first ball: lbw. Press criticism, in such circumstances, is not usually renowned for its moderation: 'Hobbs has an evil habit, together with many other batsmen, of getting right in front of his wicket before he even moves his bat. It is a detestable habit which in this case met with the fate it thoroughly deserved.' But Hobbs was his own fiercest critic. In his book *My Life Story* which appeared some twenty-four years later, the intensity of his disappointment is still clear even through the ghosted words: 'Can you see me, walking away, crestfallen? ... The rest of the day was a misery, to be followed by a night of remorse and wretchedness.'

England took lunch at 17/3, made but a small recovery and were all out for 121 by a quarter to five. At the close of play Australia, on 67/2, were by no means out of the wood. On the third and final day, although there had been overnight rain, the weather stayed fine. The highly-strung Blythe (he was advised by his doctor to play no more Test cricket after this game as the strain was too much for him) was, once again, at his best, bowling his slow left-arm spinners with a high confident loop to a good length. He achieved an occasional break frequently enough to undermine the batsmen's confidence, bowled to a well-set field and finished with 5/58. Hirst (also 5/58) was once again his able partner. Australia could find no answer. England were left with plenty of time to get 105 for victory.

Charles Fry claimed the credit, in *Life Worth Living*, for a change in the batting order. He, like Hobbs, had failed calamitously in the first innings:

The wicket was reckoned to be difficult. Archie MacLaren was pessimistic about our chances ... I asked him to let Jack Hobbs and me go in first to bustle for our pairs of spectacles. After sucking his pencil, Archie agreed. The result was that we knocked off the runs without loss of wicket. Jack Hobbs scored 62 not out, and, as a spectator at the other crease, I have to say that his was as great an innings as I ever saw played by any batsman in any Test Match or any other match. It is the only innings I have ever seen when batting at the other end that I rank with some of the innings I saw Ranjitsinhji play when I was with him. Jack Hobbs on the difficult wicket took complete charge of the good Australian bowling, carted it to every point of the compass, and never made the shred of a mistake. His quickness with his bat and his skill in forcing the direction of his strokes made me feel like a fledgeling; and when it comes to it, I was not so dusty a driver in those days.

This is as generous a tribute as one fine sportsman can pay another. The press, and not for the first time, changed its tune. Hobbs 'played fine cricket, scoring all round the wicket and timing the ball beautifully'. Not the least remarkable feature of this match was its short duration. Despite the brevity of the first day's play, the contest was completed before three o'clock on the third.

In a delightful display that was quite faultless, Hobbs played with confidence. He redeemed his reputation in the most convincing manner. From the moment he cut Armstrong's fourth ball to the boundary, he was himself again. In twenty minutes he moved to 26 out of 31, such was his dominance. His 50 came out of 88 in eighty minutes. When only 16 runs were required, Macartney was temporarily exorcised by Hobbs to the tune of three boundaries in the same over. The coup de grâce was administered by Fry who struck another delivery for four before the jubilant crowd rushed across the ground.

There is a very human touch in Hobbs' autobiography. When he arrived home he expected his wife to be 'standing at the door to welcome me as a hero returning from the battle-field'. She was out shopping, quite unaware of his achievement. There is almost a mournful note about Hobbs' comment: 'As far as she was concerned, I might just as well have not played.'

This was the high-point of England's fortunes in 1909 and, although Hobbs was to make two more centuries at Bournemouth (162 v Hampshire) and at Bristol (133 v Gloucestershire), he also had some quieter patches of ordinary form. Indeed, between those two centuries, he played seventeen innings, only two of which passed 30.

The match against Nottinghamshire, which immediately followed the first Test, must in particular have come as something of an anti-climax. He played too soon at a slower ball to be caught and bowled by 'Topsy' Wass. This was on 1 June. Hobbs may also have experienced some small personal disappointment in not reaching 1000 runs by the end of May, a feat achieved, up to this time, by only W G Grace (1895) and Tom Hayward (1900). This season's effort of 919 runs was the closest Hobbs was to come to that particular target.

Wass picked up Hobbs' wicket again in the second innings. One reporter admonished the batsman for showing bad judgement in making a rash hit which resulted in him being caught at extra-cover. However, in his 61 in the next match against Worcestershire Hobbs became, comfortably, the first batsman to score 1000 runs that season.

In the second Test, at Lord's, Noble put England in on a slow wicket which could not be described as really difficult. Throughout the day, the sodden state of the ground caused some slow scoring. Hobbs collected a lively 19 out of 23 with some attractive shots before Laver moved one away to have him caught at the wicket. Good batting by John King, Johnny Tyldesley and Dick Lilley was mainly responsible for ensuring the respectability of 269. The ominous press comment about the team's selection, not written with the benefit of hindsight, proved to be only too accurate on the second day: 'We are always unwilling to criticise the Selection Committee but it must be said that it does seem rather rash to play a Test match with only three bowlers.'

Despite the best efforts of the Sussex medium-pacer, Albert Relf (5/85), the Australians secured a lead of 81, thanks, in the main, to Vernon Ransford's fine 143*. England had to go into bat again on the second evening in uncertain light. There was an appeal against it which met with no success. Whether it was the darkening sky or Armstrong's skill or a combination of the two may only be surmised, but on 9 Hobbs drove the ball back firmly to the bowler for Armstrong to take a good low catch in his right hand. Stumps were then drawn for the day: England 16/1. An easy wicket and fine weather in the morning did not inspire the home team over whose undistinguished batting a veil had best be drawn. Armstrong achieved the best figures (6/35) of his remarkable 50-Test career. Australia secured an easy nine-wicket victory on what was described by *The Times*, with an uncharacteristic lack of restraint, as 'one of the blackest pages in the chronicles on this country's cricket'. Between the second and third Tests, although Hobbs reached double figures in each of seven innings, in none of them was he able to progress beyond 41. His ordinary performances against Yorkshire continued: 22 and 14. He had to wait until 1914 before he was to take his first hundred off that formidable team.

Five changes for the second Test had not brought success to England. Six more were made for the third game of the series. The result was the same. The bowlers, especially Rhodes (6/38), did their job well enough in putting Australia out for 188 on an easy wicket. When England batted there occurred the only controversial exchange in Jack Hobbs' Test career.

With the total 31/1, Hobbs hit the ball hard to square leg and, as he started to run, slipped, knocking off the bails. Had he stayed where he was, it is just possible that there would have been no trouble. As he himself wrote:

Thinking that I was out, I was starting for the pavilion when it occurred to me that I had finished the stroke before my foot dislodged the bails. So I appealed and the umpire gave me 'Not Out'. Then the row began. The Australians were very cross and gathered together on the field. A big argument was carried on, Warwick Armstrong having the most to say, and he was, in my opinion, unduly argumentative.

Hobbs says he was upset and two balls later he was bowled by Macartney. The press was uncertain as to what actually happened:

(He) appeared either to have hit his wicket or to have trodden on it. What really happened it was impossible for a spectator to say ... Two balls later he seemed to make little or no attempt to stop a ball from Mr Macartney and was bowled. Hobbs appeared to think he was out on the first occasion for he started to walk away.

The Rev. R S Holmes, an enthusiastic and informed historian of the first-class game, wrote to *Cricket*:

As I watched him through a powerful glass from the Press Box he appeared to me to let himself be bowled; he evidently thought he ought to have been given out the previous ball. I wondered whether for the moment he had lost his nerve or was his action dictated by a magnanimous refusal to take advantage of what was in his judgement a wrong decision?

This sporting interpretation is at variance with Hobbs' account but it was a view shared by the Australian captain Monty Noble for whom, incidentally, Hobbs had a high regard. Writing some seventeen years later in *The Game's The Thing*, Noble had no doubt about Hobbs' attitude:

My impression of the incident at the time was and still is that, believing himself to be legally out, he deliberately allowed himself to be bowled. It is a very difficult thing to allow yourself without betraying the fact to the bowler or someone fielding near the wicket. It was a match of small scores and the loss of a player of Hobbs' ability probably had a determining influence on the success of Australia. Yet that was cricket in excelsis.

It is not unreasonable to suppose that Hobbs *was* upset that anyone should think he would try to steal an unfair advantage. The constant record provided by opponents as well as colleagues is that sharp practice was not, in any sense his game. R E S Wyatt wrote, in a letter to the author, 'Jack Hobbs was a gentleman in every sense of the word.' Put at its lowest moral level he was too fine a player to have had any need to cheat. On a higher plane, however, to have done so would have been to go against his principles and his faith. Warwick Armstrong had many qualities as a man and as a player (courage and determination were not the least of them) but he was indisputably a 'hard man', in the modern sense of that phrase. He was not the easiest person to deal with, nor was he renowned for his tact and sensitivity. It does not seem too fanciful to imagine him browbeating the relatively inexperienced Test player - as Hobbs was, by comparison with the Australian at this stage in their careers - and putting him under intense pressure. Armstrong sometimes appeared a cantankerous, curmudgeonly cricketer and he was certainly no soft touch on the field. He was, however, a mightily effective all-rounder and a most successful Test captain in later years. He was to prove a tough, tenacious, thoughtful leader who marshalled well his own talents and those of others. A man who grew to huge dimensions, he bowled leg-spin with a deft control; he could also bat with a durable consistency. It is no coincidence that, of the eight series against England in which Armstrong appeared, Australia won six.

This incident is important because it shows the intensity of feeling that could be part of an international contest even in the Golden Age. More importantly, however, it gives an insight into how Hobbs believed the game should be played.

Despite fine resistance from the two Lancastrians, Johnny Tyldesley and Jack Sharp, who both passed the half-century mark, England were all out for 182 with Macartney getting the best return of his Test career (7/58). In response, Barnes, whose temperament and skills never allowed him to be long in the shade, kept England in the game with six wickets for 63. Australia, dismissed for 207, set England to chase 214 for victory. Before Hobbs missed a straight ball from Cotter he made 30. He was said to have played 'fairly well'. At this distance in time, this seems rather grudging praise when the whole side was out for 87, unable to cope with Cotter (5/38) or, once more, Macartney (4/27).

At this point in the season, Hobbs with 1450 runs stood easily at the head of the first-class averages (50) and might have allowed himself some optimism about how the rest of the season might progress. It is as well that he was too wise a cricketer to count any chickens for, in his very next match, against Lancashire at Manchester, while trying to take a catch in the deep from Walter Brearley, he damaged his hand so badly that he was out of the game until the beginning of August. 24 innings remained in his season and although there were four 50s among them, only one century was made. That, a score of 113 off the Gloucestershire attack at Bristol, has a certain curiosity value.

Hobbs was always regarded, quite rightly, as one of the finest runners between wickets, especially in Tests with the two remarkable Yorkshiremen, Wilfred Rhodes and Herbert Sutcliffe. Something in the West Country air, it seems, must have disturbed Hobbs' equilibrium on this occasion, for, first of all, he ran out his old friend, Tom Hayward, calling him for an impossible run. As if that were not enough, he then called his captain, Morice Bird, for a short single and sent him back too late. It was as well that he held the side together in the first innings and led the chase to an eight-wicket victory in the second with 59. This was the match in which some of the home supporters, aggrieved by the number of lbw decisions going against their side, gave voice to their feelings. During the last part of the Gloucestershire first innings every delivery was greeted with a great shout of "How's that?".

The Test series, it must be acknowledged, was a failure for Hobbs. He averaged 26. It was to be his only failure.

In South Africa in 1909-10, however, he was to move up a class as a Test batsman. But the particular interest of this tour was how South Africa's formidable quartet of googly bowlers was going to perform on their own wickets compared to their successful 1907 tour in England.

Bernard Bosanquet, of Middlesex and England, is generally credited with being the originator of the googly, the off-break bowled with a leg-break action, not least because his name is enshrined in Australia where the googly is called a 'bosie'. He had played with the South African R O (Reggie) Schwarz in the early years of the century for his county. Schwarz was an able student and acquired many of Bosanquet's skills. Slow in flight, Schwarz was deceptively quick off the wicket. He also achieved great break, mainly from the off. As he tended to break just one way, he should have been easy to play, but his pace negated any advantage the batsman might hope to seize by unhibited attack.

R E Foster's advice in the 1908 *Wisden*, interesting not least because of the criticisms that had been made of Hobbs' pad play, was categoric: 'Play him with your legs - old pavilion critics forgive, but we have to deal with bowling you never had to trouble about - don't hit him until the bad ball comes.' Schwarz had been top of the first-class averages in England in 1907: 137 wickets at 11.

Not so very far behind, with 119 wickets at 15, was Ernie Vogler, ' the finest bowler of a very good lot', in Foster's opinion. A bowler of many parts, he could swing the new ball, bowling a fast-medium off-break. With the older ball he adopted slow-medium deliveries, the stock one of which was the leg-break. His sparing use of the googly deceived batsmen because they were unable to distinguish any change of action. The combination of stamina, control, variety and intelligence made Vogler a formidable opponent.

In support were Gordon White and Aubrey Faulkner. The former was no mean Test batsman with 872 runs at an average of 30. As a bowler, however, in that context, he was unsuccessful with only 9 wickets in 17 appearances. His special skill lay in the delivery of well concealed top-spinners which had brought him a number of lbw decisions on the 1907 tour.

That same year had seen Faulkner make a major mark. A genuine all-rounder of the highest class, he was, in 1909-10, to experience the first of two great seasons in his career, the second being against Australia in 1910-11. Sharp powers of spin enabled him to break the ball both ways but, in the main, he brought the ball back from the off. His flight was puzzling while his yorker was, for that reason, a particularly effective delivery.

It was the unpredictable nature of googly bowling that affronted some contemporaries. Its cunning was regarded, not least by the batsmen who had to face it, as a form of deceit. Foster was firmly of the view that it would 'deteriorate batting...such bowling never allows the batsman to get really set because he can never make or go for his accustomed shots'. In September 1909, *The Morning Post* struck a lugubrious note when talking of the forthcoming tour in 1909/10:

The new googly bowling will be on its trial and we confess to feeling a heartfelt desire that it will fail...the pleasure of flogging the occasional full toss or long hop does not compensate for the ignominy of finding oneself entirely wrong in guessing what the ball will do when it pitches, even though the error of anticipation has not been fatal.

Is there an element of petulance here? The writer seems to be saying, 'I may not be dismissed - but I do dislike being made to look so *silly*.'

The English team could not be but aware of the prospect that confronted them. As events transpired, neither Schwarz (0 wickets) nor White (2) was to make the expected impact with the ball. On the other hand, the magnificent performances of Vogler, as a bowler, and Faulkner, with both bat and ball, taxed Hobbs and his colleagues to the limit. The team was: H D G Leveson Gower (Surrey), Captain; M C Bird (Surrey); F L Fane (Essex); G H Simpson-Hayward (Worcestershire); N C Tufnell (Cambridge University): E G Wynyard (Hampshire); and professionals C Blythe (Kent); C P Buckenham (Essex); D Denton (Yorkshire); J B Hobbs (Surrey); W Rhodes (Yorkshire); H Strudwick (Surrey); G J Thompson (Northamptonshire); and F Woolley (Kent).

F S Ashley-Cooper's analysis in *Cricket* was not very wide of the mark: "Whether the batting of the side will prove equal to all required of it, time alone can show...Hobbs is likely to prove one of the star batsmen of the side...It is to be regretted that a more representative team could not be got together". He had a point, which is amply demonstrated by the fact that there were nine changes in the side that represented England in the First Test at Johannesburg from that which had taken the field at The Oval against Australia. Only Rhodes and Woolley appeared in both games. Before the side departed, Leveson Gower, in an interview with Reuter's, explained: 'So many of our best amateurs who play all the summer through have to work through the winter months that we had to fall back upon professionals so as to get a team worthy of South African cricket.' The party was not sternly tested in the first month of the tour. A mixture of first-class games and fixtures against odds may not have been sufficiently taxing as a preparation for the Tests. The MCC was brought up with a jolt by the Transvaal in the match immediately preceding the first Test. A 308-run defeat was due in no small measure to the all-round qualities of Aubrey Faulker: 46 and 148*; 4/49 and 5/34.

Although not impressive in practice on matting, Hobbs had begun with a century in a minor match and followed it with another against Western Province, the Currie Cup holders. Indeed, he had batted well throughout and was to maintain his form. The first day of the first Test was England's most successful day of the match, in front of a crowd of 15,000. By its end, South Africa, having won the toss, had been dismissed for 208 (Faulkner 78; Simpson-Hayward, with his lobs, 6/48) and Hobbs had opened the bowling with Buckenham, but with no success. England were well placed. In just an hour and three-quarters, Hobbs (77*) and Rhodes (57*) had taken their opening stand to 147. 50 had come in just over half an hour and the hundred partnership in seventy-five minutes.

This was the beginning of a most successful Test partnership for Hobbs with the Yorkshire all rounder. Wilfred Rhodes was a remarkably durable cricketer. This tough, laconic and immensely talented player scored 39,802 runs (average 30) and secured 4187 wickets, more than anyone else, with his slow left-arm spin at a cost of around 16 runs each. His sixteen 'doubles' are eloquent testimony to his effectiveness and his consistency. His 2325 runs in Tests, also at an average of 30, show just how little he was affected by the big occasion while the 127 wickets he took in internationals bear witness not only to his penetration but also to his steadiness as they cost only 26 each. In a career which spanned the years 1898 to 1930 he developed his batting to such an extent that he grew from number eleven for Yorkshire to opener for England. Determined to the point of stubbornness, he never gave anything away, never mind his wicket. He may not have been the most glamorous figure to wear an England cap but no man fought more staunchly for his country.

Unfortunately neither he and Hobbs, nor the side as a whole, were able to build substantially on this excellent foundation. Rhodes (66) fell to Vogler early next day and Hobbs was dismissed by the same bowler when he was caught at the wicket to make the total 190/2. His innings of 89 included seven 4s. He had batted quite brilliantly for two hours and twenty minutes in a faultless display. No one else reached 30. The innings closed at 310 (Vogler 5/87; Faulker 5/120). England however were still in a useful position, with a lead of 102 and South Africa leading by only 22 at the close with three wickets down.

When the fifth wicket fell with their second innings total at 143, victory for the visitors must have seemed a foregone conclusion. The prodigious talents of Faulkner, however, were equal to the crisis. He had come in at 120/4 and was batting lower down the order than in the first innings, probably because he had bowled 33 overs. Staunchly supported by Snooke (47) and Commaille (19), he scored a splendid, chanceless 123 out of 216 in one hundred and seventy minutes, before he was ninth out with the score

332. The game had been transformed. England were set a target of 244 for victory. With the total 47, Hobbs was bowled by Vogler for 35. Vogler's powers of break and spin made him very difficult to deal with, so much so that his 7 wickets for 94 runs included the first five batsmen in the English order. Only Thompson (63) made more runs than Hobbs. Faulkner took the other three wickets for 30 runs, thus completing one of the great all-round feats in the history of the game. His performance and the high skills of Vogler were instrumental in giving South Africa an exciting victory by 19 runs.

Hobbs enjoyed further success with 163 in the first of two consecutive games against Natal. As he did not play in the second of these, Woolley opened the batting in his place but made little impression.

The start of the second Test at Durban was delayed by rain until 4pm. Normally the matting over a hard 'anthill' surface produced a fast wicket. South Africa were once more impervious to the wiles of Hobbs as opening bowler, but limped to 89/4 on a soft wicket by the close. On the second day, fine weather prevailed and the wicket had fully recovered, but neither batting side was able to take advantage of the improved conditions. Faulkner (47) and Campbell (48) were the main contributors to a total of 199. Simpson-Hayward with 4/42 and Thompson, who took the wickets of three early batsmen, did most damage.

England were given a splendid start by Hobbs and Rhodes, when they put on 94 for the first wicket in just under the hour. Their smart running between the wickets was favourably commented on - Hobbs in particular gave a delightful display, hitting freely all round the wicket. 50 came in 33 minutes. On this occasion, Hobbs, missed on 52, was unable to take advantage of his luck, for he was beaten and bowled by the fastest member of the South African attack, Jimmy Sinclair. His 53 included a 6, a 5 and six 4s. Vogler, having made no impression upon Hobbs, now came into his own and did much to reduce England to 148/6 at close of play.

There was further resistance by Thompson (38) but, after the excellent beginning to the innings, a sense of deflation must have been felt in the English camp that no lead was achieved. The weather was good, the wicket first rate. Vogler (5/83) was mainly responsible for England's disappointing 199. Such a tie on first innings is most unusual and has occurred only three times since.

South Africa juggled their batting order for the second innings with Faulkner moving up from 5 to 3. The move misfired and at 25/3 they were struggling. White then joined Nourse and they turned the match with 143 runs in 155 minutes. Nourse (69) was dismissed shortly before stumps were drawn at 171/4. White, missed on 36 and 96, eventually reached a fine 118.

England, set 348 to win, made a useful start with 48 runs in the partnership of Hobbs and Rhodes, but the rest of the principal batsmen, Fane, Denton and Woolley, failed as they had done in the first innings. Top scorer, Hobbs reached a chanceless 70 out of 106 in 75 minutes before he was caught at slip by Vogler off Faulkner. Thompson's dogged 46* in nearly three hours was not enough. Faulkner finished with 6/87 and South Africa with a 95-run victory.

A curiosity should be noted which suggests a flexibility that seems surprising in modern eyes. Rain fell just before 5pm on the fourth day causing play to be abandoned. It was reported, however, in *The Times* that 'it has been decided to continue the game tomorrow and, if necessary on Thursday'.

Playing in four of the five fixtures that preceded the third Test, Hobbs scored consistently (27 and 70, 40, 79, 33 and 55) and must have felt reasonably happy with his form. The third match of the series, like the first, was played in Johannesburg. Here there was no grass on the ground and the matting was laid on the red earth which was rolled and watered. The opening day was much interrupted by rain and thunderstorms; the crowd became impatient with the delays and 'when the teams came out they were hooted'. South Africa, having won the toss, batted solidly into the second afternoon to make 305, thanks largely to Faulkner (76), White (72), and Vogler (65) with his highest Test score. This was a much hotter day. Hobbs, most unusually, was affected by the sun. He did not field in the latter part of the innings and felt unable to open. Fane took his place, making a useful 39 but the star of the innings was Denton, atoning for his earlier meagre contributions. His brilliant 104, his only Test century, came in 100 minutes out of 161 scored. The runs could not have come at a better time.

On the third morning, with the score 201/5 Hobbs batted but, clearly still unwell, could manage only 11 before he was bowled by Faulkner. Woolley (58*) hit brightly to take England to a first innings lead of 17. Vogler and Faulkner finished with four wickets apiece. More rain prevented play for much of the afternoon which ended with South Africa 35/1. Although Snooke (52) and Faulkner (44) fought hard next day, Simpson-Hayward (5/69) did much to limit the total of 237 which meant 221 was required for victory. Thompson and Strudwick made 7/0 at the close of the fourth day.

On the following morning, there was a rapid tumble of wickets (16/1; 37/2; 42/3; 42/4) including those of Denton and Rhodes. Hobbs, batting at 5, struggled at first. When he began, the prospects for victory must have seemed negligible. In view of the state of the match, his own health and the quality of the bowling, what followed should surely be regarded as one of his best innings. His tenacity was admirable. As he himself wrote: 'Dashing play was out of the question; I set my teeth and decided to play carefully.' It might be supposed that 'carefully' was synonymous with 'slowly'. This was far from being the case. Fane (17) helped him add 50 for the fifth wicket but Woolley fell at once: 93/6. Bird (45) then had perhaps his finest if not his largest Test innings in a 95-run partnership. This lasted just 65 minutes, not the least remarkable detail of the match. When the three-wicket victory was won, Hobbs was still not out, having made 93 of the last 179 in 130 minutes, with ten 4s. The generosity of the crowd brought him a collection of £70. As they had also showed their practical appreciation to Denton (£88) and Vogler (£60) for his eight wickets in the match, it is possible to surmise their prosperity and enthusiasm. After a shaky start, Hobbs had found his best form after lunch. His was batting of flair and style, demonstrating his supremacy (although such a modest man would never have thought of it in such terms). This was a unique occasion in Hobbs' Test career as it was the only time he did not open in either innings.

The fourth Test at Newlands (where the matting was on turf) was notable not only because South Africa won the contest (and, with it, the series) but also because Hobbs had a match aggregate of 1. In his 61-Test career he was never again dismissed twice for single figures in a match. On a perfect wicket England won the toss but lost three wickets for 2 runs. Hobbs scored a single and was then caught by Faulkner off Vogler's second delivery. Rhodes, at the same total, and Denton, one run later, both fell to Snooke for ducks. From such disarray, a recovery to 203 all out (Woolley 69, Bird 57) was laudable. The varied South African attack shared the wickets.

Thompson, with four wickets, and Buckenham kept England in the hunt on the second day by restricting their opponents to a lead of 4 runs. Then Hobbs was well caught down the leg side by the wicket-keeper, Campbell. This was off the fast-medium Snooke's fourth ball before a run was on the board. Rhodes and Denton failed again: 17/3. Woolley (64) once more showed what was possible and with Fane (37) put on a hundred for the fourth wicket. Vogler was not to be thwarted, however. As the innings fell away to 178, he finished with 5/72.

Faulkner had picked up three wickets and three catches in England's second innings but he was by no means finished. Thompson, in particular, made South Africa fight hard all the way. Had Faulkner been snapped up from either of the chances he gave (on 10 and 16) the result might well have been different. With 49* he took his side to 175/6 on the third day when both weather and wicket were excellent. The loss of Buckenham with a strained thigh when the score was 55/2 hampered England's chances but the main responsibility for the defeat must lie with the failure of Hobbs, Rhodes and Denton. Their combined match aggregate was 16.

The first two made amends in the most positive manner in the final Test which followed immediately and, unusually, on the same ground. This provided the setting in which Hobbs first demonstrated that he was something rather more than a good Test batsman. As the series had already been decided, his masterly innings of 187 (his first Test century in his twelfth match) may not have been given the credit it deserves. After the embarrassments of the previous game, he had a point to prove. And prove it he did.

In delightful weather, England won the toss and made the best possible use of a perfect wicket to end the day on 406/7. Hobbs and Rhodes enjoyed the first of their great partnerships: 221 in less than two hours and forty minutes. This, by any standards, is a fast scoring rate. Rhodes, as was his custom, began cautiously but Hobbs scored at a good pace from the start. The 50 partnership was up in 35 minutes and Hobbs' own half-century (out of 80) was made at a run a minute. The century stand came in just under 70 minutes while the next 50 took a further half an hour. Lunch was taken with the score on 153: Hobbs 91*, Rhodes 47*. Neither batsman had given a chance. The Surrey batsman reached his century in two hours. Twenty minutes later they put up 200. Finally Rhodes (77) was bowled by Nourse. Their partnership was the highest first-wicket stand for England on a Test, beating that of Jackson and Hayward against Australia at The Oval in 1899. Hobbs and Rhodes were to pass it with their 323 at Melbourne in 1911-12.

Hobbs wrote warmly about the occasion in *The Cape Times* in which he recorded his comments on each day's play:

I must say I was none too comfortable at the commencement of my innings. In fact, I might have been out twice before I had scored ten. A hit to leg went dangerously near Zulch. Shortly after another went over the heads of the slips ...

Personally I was very pleased to be at one and when the record stand for first-wicket partnership in Test matches was beaten...It also gave Rhodes great pleasure to take part in establishing a new record. I must say he started in his best form. He was absolutely safe throughout, giving nothing away...As a first-wicket partner I just love to go in with Rhodes. His influence is great and he is such a splendid runner.

Hobbs developed this last point in *My Life Story*:

Nobody with whom I ever batted excelled him as a run-stealer. Even when I was about to play a ball, he would be three or four yards up the pitch, ready to run for anything I called for. Just a word or even nothing at all and off we ran. The secret of our success was confidence in each other. This practice of short, sharp singles was continued by the two of us in England and in the next tour of Australia.

Hobbs was eventually dismissed for 187, fifth out at 327 when he touched the stumps with his boot and dislodged a bail. For the only time in his 102 Test innings, he was out hit wicket. The bowler Norman Norton, playing in his only Test, must have been delighted with his four wickets for 47 runs, especially as they were those of Hobbs, Fane, Woolley and Bird. Hobbs had offered two chances but as the first of them came when he was on 146 they detract only very slightly from his achievement. He hit twenty-three 4s. The consistent Thompson contributed 51 to a final total of 417 early on the second morning. This was the one occasion in the series about which Vogler appeared to be mastered. He finished with 1/103.

Blythe was the chief destroyer of South Africa for 103 with 7/46. He performed the rare feat of twice dismissing batsmen with successive deliveries: Commaille and Snooke at the beginning of the innings to reduce South Africa to 4/2 and later, Bisset and Vogler. Zulch tenaciously carried his bat for 43*. Stiffer resistance was offered when the follow-on was enforced. Faulkner led the way with a valiant 99 while the captain, Snooke, defended durably for 47 and Schwarz hit 44. The last-named player had the distinction of being 'caught Bird bowled Hobbs' - Jack Hobbs' only Test wicket. 327 left England with a simple task to win by nine wickets.

Hobbs could contemplate his performance on the tour with quiet satisfaction. The figures tell the story. In all games: 1294 runs average 58. Second was Denton: 758 runs average 30. In the first-class matches the pattern was repeated: Hobbs 1194/62; Denton 689/34. Hobbs also dominated the Test averages: 539 runs at 67. Thompson (267/33) was second in these. Hobbs was in a class of his own. He returned to England modestly as always, but now with the stature of a great player.

4 Greatness Confirmed, 1910-12

The quality of his performance in South Africa had been such that great things were expected of Jack Hobbs in 1910. But, apart from his first season (1905), his last (1934) and one in which he suffered seriously from illness and injury (1921), there were two home summers in which he scored only three centuries: 1910 and 1912. Both followed strenuous, prolific tours overseas. Although his 1910 aggregate was 1982 runs, his average of 33 was the lowest of his career, other than that for 1905. He finished twenty-fourth in the first-class averages which, again, with the exceptions of 1905, 1921 and 1934, was the lowest position he ever occupied but it was a wet season and only the brilliant Lancastrian, Johnny Tyldesley, who headed the averages (2265 runs, average 46) scored more.

By contrast, 1911 was a dry summer. Hobbs' number of centuries (four), runs (2376) and average (41) all improved but he was rarely a dominant figure except perhaps during the Gentlemen v Players match at Lord's. 1911 was a year of Test Trials, in preparation for the selection of the team for Australia. Hobbs held a low opinion of this type of match and his view was shared by at least one reporter who, writing in *The Times* of the teams who played in the Lord's G v P, said: 'It may be assumed that the sides were not chosen from the point of view of a Test Trial match which would be a descent for a match which has such famous traditions.'

In the light of what was to happen in Australia, it is interesting to read the press comments on the leading bowlers who were playing in the Gentlemen v Players match at Lord's: Barnes was 'the most difficult seen at Lord's this year' while F R Foster's 'pace off the ground was so great that it is doubtful if any bowler in England can send the ball faster past the batsman'. The Lord's wicket had more bounce and life than the usual run of first-class grounds. The ball could be made to lift and fly. The Players were said to have a rooted dislike of the fast bowling of Foster and J W H T Douglas because of their first innings' failure - 201, in reply to 352. This seems a harsh assessment of a batting order beginning Hayward, Hobbs, Tyldesley, Hardinge, Tarrant, Rhodes, Hirst. Moreover it is doubtful if Fry shared this opinion for at 12.30 on the third day he set them a target of 423.

By lunch, forty-five minutes later, 95 was on the board for the loss of Hayward (35). Tyldesley (41) shared a partnership of 77 with Hobbs and Hardinge helped add another 41. 'The rest of the innings was indeed a case of Hobbs first and the rest nowhere.' On an awkward pitch which was both worn and lively, he played both the fast and the slow bowlers with equal ease. He scored all round the wicket, driving, cutting, pulling, to carry his bat for 154* out of 292. The innings was hailed as one of the greatest in the history of the contest. And Hobbs almost missed playing it altogether. After a mediocre performance in The Oval match between the two sides which finished two days earlier, one selector suggested that he should not play. Characteristically Hobbs made no fuss about this and was prepared to accede. Another change of the selectorial mind followed and he was retained.

This fixture was important both to the Players and to the public at this time, and it continued to be so throughout Hobbs' career and beyond. The best amateurs and professionals, who had first met in 1806 and last played each other in 1962, sometimes played two or three times a season but the main contest was always the match at Lord's. They were a high point of the season and had a prestige which, for some, was not matched even by that of a Test match. An invitation to take part was an indication of a man's standing in the game.

The touring party for Australia in 1911-12 apparently put together piecemeal in July and August, was as follows: P F Warner (Middlesex, Captain); S F Barnes (Staffordshire); J W H T Douglas (Essex); F R Foster (Warwickshire); G Gunn (Nottinghamshire); J W Hearne (Middlesex); J W Hitch (Surrey); J B Hobbs (Surrey); J Iremonger (Nottinghamshire); S Kinneir (Warwickshire); C P Mead (Hampshire); W Rhodes (Yorkshire); E J Smith (Warwickshire); H Strudwick Surrey); J Vine (Sussex); F E Woolley (Kent). This group was not viewed with overwhelming optimism by *Cricket*: 'This side is likely to prove sound rather than brilliant and should it not succeed in winning the rubber, it will not be for want of pluck.' And it seemed to be confirmed by the First Test which was played at Sydney.

Australia, winning the toss, took full advantage of the first day's perfect wicket to score 317/5. They were assisted somewhat by Douglas, captain in place of Warner who was ill as he was to be throughout the series. Failing to appreciate fully the temperament of Barnes, his most gifted bowler, Douglas did not marshal his attack as effectively as he might have done. The Australians wore black arm bands as a sign of respect for Reggie Duff who had just died, a young man - and destitute.

Armstrong was missed twice on his way to 60. Trumper, batting at no. 5, made a slow start, taking twenty-five minutes over five runs. At tea, with their opponents 198/4, England must have felt the game was not too badly balanced against them. Afterwards, Trumper, with great brilliance, took control to finish the day 95*.

Before a strong wind (and 35,000 people) on the second morning, Trumper completed his sixth Test hundred against England to establish a new record, although Hobbs believed he should have run him out at 97. Minnett's hard-hitting 90, his highest Test score, should not be forgotten on a day when the gale played havoc with players' caps and spectators' hats. The swirling clouds of dust troubled everyone.

Hobbs and Kinneir eventually opened, facing a total of 447. Theirs was an unusual combination. In view of Rhodes' later success and his performance in South Africa it appears surprising that he did not open. In fact none of the opening partnerships in the early part of the tour had struck gold. In the five first-class matches there seemed to be no settled policy: Hobbs/Rhodes; Hobbs/Kinneir; Hobbs/Rhodes; Hobbs/Vine; Rhodes/Kinneir. In six innings in these games, Hobbs had had a quiet start with a total of 200 runs. Rhodes had an average of 14, top score 34. Kinneir, on the other hand, averaged 28 and his highest score, 63, could not have come at a better time, in the match with 'An Australian XI' immediately preceding the First Test.

Dr H V Hordern nicknamed 'Ranji' because of his dusky complexion was a supremely gifted leg-break and googly bowler and clearly the danger man of the Australian attack. His skill was such that Hobbs was flummoxed by his first, second and third deliveries. The batsman nevertheless remained determined. Kinneir left at 45 and Gunn ten runs later. Hobbs had not quite come to terms with Horden's guile and thought his first twenty runs were made very slowly. On 39 Hordern deceived him yet again but he was missed by Cotter at silly mid-on. After Rhodes' departure (115/3) Hobbs took a sharp single with Mead. Hordern was tempted into a hasty shy at the wicket. The ball raced through the boundary bringing Hobbs five runs and his 50. He was said to have given 'an admirable display of resolute and restrained cricket'. At the close England, on 142/4 and with Hobbs still there, had some grounds for optimism.

This was dissipated at once the next day. Before a run had been scored Hobbs was out to a fine right-handed catch by Clem Hill at silly mid-on. This was off the fourth ball of the first over bowled by the left-arm fast-medium Bill Whitty. Thanks mainly to Hearne (76) and Foster (56) England reached 318. Australia's slow but sound response, with Kelleway (70) and Hill (65) in the van, ensured that 438 runs were needed to win. Although Foster (5/92) and Douglas (4/50) were the main wicket takers, Barnes' contribution was by no means a negligible one. He bowled for an hour and a half between lunch and tea, bareheaded, under a blazing sun on the fourth afternoon and took 1 wicket for only 23.

England's bright start flared through Hobbs who moved attractively to 22 before taking one too many risks with rising balls outside the off stump. Cutting at one he should have left alone, in the opinion of his tour captain, he was caught at the wicket by Carter off Cotter when the score was 29. Hobbs himself admitted that it was a stupid shot. A gritty fight led by Gunn (62) took the game into the sixth day but Hordern must have relished his first Test against England. He took a total of 12 wickets for 175 runs.

This was his finest match. He remained a strong influence throughout the series with 32 wickets in all at an average of 24. He himself was never really hammered but he lacked penetrating, economical support from his colleagues. Ten other bowlers were used by Australia in the five Tests. They managed between them 42 wickets - each of them which cost, on average, 45 runs. This is, of course, some indication of the English batting superiority after this uncertain start to the series. Hobbs was the mainspring of England's batting success and he devised a clear, logical, consistent method of dealing with leg-breaks and googlies:

When I was uncertain I played well forward to smother the break or played back and watched the pitch of the ball. Actually, when the ball has been new and bright sunlight has shone on it, a googly can be 'spotted' during its flight, but there is a risk, for you cannot possibly get into position quickly enough for a shot.

A much more reliable way to detect the delivery is to concentrate on the bowler's wrist action. A googly always comes from behind the wrist, never below it.

On 29 December, the day before the second Test began, Reuter's reported that the Australian selectors for the 1912 tour of England were to be Clem Hill, Franke Iredale and Percy McAlister. The Australian Cricket Board of Control wanted a secretary to accompany the team. Hill would be captain and Victor Trumper vice-captain. On the surface, nothing could be more simple than such an announcement. Unfortunately the conflict which followed, between the Board of Control and the players, not only shook Australian cricket to its foundations, but remained a running sore through the winter and cannot but have been a distraction to some of their players. Eventually it resulted in the refusal of six of their leading players to travel to England for the Triangular Tournament of 1912.

Those decisions, however, lay some way in the future. The immediate business was the continued defence of The Ashes; and the Australians were buoyant at the news that they had won the toss in the second Test.

Although the day was overcast and there had been some overnight rain, conditions were, in fact, excellent for batting. This is important, for what followed has been described as the finest piece of bowling in the history of The Ashes. Sydney Barnes was at the height of his powers and he now showed why he has been called the greatest bowler of all. His mastery of fast-medium leg-break and off-spin, with new ball or old, was complete. Length, flight, pace and the ability to vary all three were at his command.

Sydney Barnes was his own man. Never one to suffer fools gladly, especially those captains whom he considered made the wrong use of him, he was not an easy man to handle. Although he took only 719 first-class wickets, at an average of 17, he is always near the top of any short-list for the title, 'The Greatest Bowler Ever'. The reason? 189 of those wickets were in 27 Tests. Each cost just 16 runs and they were taken at a striking-rate of one every seven overs. This independent spirit bowled with complete control and inexorable purpose. Husbanding his resources intelligently, he played little first-class cricket in a long career, but made the most of his strength and stamina at exactly the right moment.

At one point Australia were 11 for 4 - Bardsley, Kelleway, Hill and Armstrong - all of whom Barnes had dismissed at a personal cost of 1 run. And Barnes was not feeling well that day! He had taken five wickets for six runs by shortly after lunch, but Hordern (49*) and Ransford (43) lifted Australia to a final total of 184.

During the remaining half an hour England made 38/1. That one wicket was Hobbs who succumbed for the second successive innings to the Carter/Cotter combination, this time for 6. The 31,000 holiday crowd of 1 January saw Jack Hearne, not yet twenty-one, go on to make a brilliant 114, his highest and best Test innings, with fine support from Rhodes (61). Hordern then destroyed the lower order batsmen so that from the security of 211/3 England subsided to 265 all out. The informal arrangements of the period can be inferred from the comment in *The Times*: 'It was then a quarter to six and it was decided to draw stumps for the day.'

Foster was the main instrument of Australia's downfall in the second innings when he took 6/91, and Hobbs had his best moment of the match thus far when, from cover-point, he ran out Bardsley by swiftly fielding the ball and throwing down the wicket. From 38/4 the home side was given ballast by Armstrong (90) but only Cotter of the others passed 40. His bright hitting was ended by a catch by Hobbs at point. In his account of the series Pelham Warner, who was never well enough to participate, wrote:

It was a great catch, for the sun was in the eyes of the fieldsman, and the ball went a great height and was spinning like a top. This is a catch of all others which a man is prone to make a mess of.

England needed 219 for victory on the fourth day. They had the advantage of fine weather and a wicket on which there was little sign of wear. Hobbs batted with confidence after being beaten and very nearly bowled in Cotter's first over. His early dismissal might well have tilted the match psychologically. This close shave (Macartney believed the ball touched the leg stump) must have lifted Hobbs' spirits and England moved smoothly to lunch at 52/0 (Rhodes 27*; Hobbs 20*). As they had reached this score in just 40 minutes, the crowd 'heartily cheered the batsmen on their return to the pavilion'.

The Yorkshireman departed shortly afterwards for 28 so, with the score 57/1, Gunn joined Hobbs. They comfortably negotiated the problems which the tight bowling and keen fielding presented. They took tea at 108/1 with Hobbs on 73* (his half century having come in 96 minutes with a cut for three off Armstrong), and Gunn 31*. The latter was in one of his slow and deliberate moods, taking nearly an hour to reach double figures. His talent was such that, had he been so disposed, he could have made fifty or more in the same time. Their running between wickets was as swift, well-judged and effective as that of Hobbs and Rhodes. More than once they benefited from overthrows. At 169 Gunn (43) was dismissed whereupon Hearne came in to help Hobbs complete the task. The Surrey opener had taken 3 hours and 4 minutes for his century which he reached with a single past point off Whitty. Forty-three minutes later he finished with 126*.

This fine achievement, his first century in nine Test matches against Australia, received much praise. In Warner's words, it was ' a truly magnificent and faultless innings. He may have played more brilliantly in the past but never more finely...his cutting was simply delightful, whether square or late, while he was also very strong in the off-drive and in playing to leg.' H S Altham focuses on what must be seen as a more important feature, when viewing the series overall: 'his mastery over Hordern was a great example and encouragement to his comrades.' All the greater, one feels, for his early uncertainty.

After a minor fixture at Geelong, the sides moved into the third Test at Adelaide where a record crowd of more than 96,000 saw the game over the four days. For the third time in a row Australia won the toss in beautiful weather and on a true pitch. They batted. To no avail. Foster's fast-medium left-arm, round-the-wicket deliveries were at their most venomous. His immaculate line and six fielders on the on side (four short-legs, a long-leg, and mid-on) inhibited the batsmen. As this was coupled with fine control, hostile pace off the pitch and a pronounced swerve he soon had the Australians in disarray. Kelleway played an early ball on to his leg and was limping afterwards. Ransford, who was batting at number four, took a blow on his left thumbnail, had to retire with the total on 17, and was unable to return until the fall of the ninth wicket at 123. Armstrong was also struck on the leg. Warner says: 'Never in first-class cricket has a bowler been seen who has hit the batsmen so frequently on the legs as Foster did on this tour.'

In the afternoon, when Australia were 88/6, Foster had taken 5/23. Their final score, 133, was not a formidable one. Hobbs (27*) and Rhodes (20*) took England briskly to 49/0 at the close.

12,000 people came to watch the second day's play. Again it was very hot and the pitch was in splendid order. Hobbs pulled Kelleway for a couple to bring up his own half-century out of 75. By the standards of the day, the batting was thought to be steady rather than dramatic or brilliant. The hundred partnership came in just over two hours before Rhodes pulled Armstrong for three to reach his fifty. At lunch: 138/0, Hobbs 81*; Rhodes 52*. Shortly after the interval Rhodes (59) was out lbw to Cotter. Gunn established himself quietly while Hobbs completed his hundred in three-and-a-quarter hours with an off-drive for four off Matthews. He waved his bat in happy response to the cheering of the crowd, an unusual sign of satisfaction from one who was normally undemonstrative in public. At 206 Gunn (29) was out, never having appeared assured against Hordern.

Hobbs was now on 112. Four runs later he gave a sharp chance to Hordern at slip off Cotter. Until this moment his innings had been without blemish but four more chances of varying difficulty were to follow as he tired in the heat. Tea saw England happily placed on 230/2 with Hobbs (153*) accompanied by Hearne (5*). They took the total to 260 before Hearne (12) departed. Hobbs finally fell,

c Hordern b Minnett 187

having struck sixteen boundaries in all, 'so very tired that I was not at all sorry to get out'. He had been 5 hours 34 minutes at the crease. His runs were made out of 323/4. The highest of his twelve centuries against Australia, it established the base for a big England score. Again Warner's assessment is worth noting: '...his batting was as delightful as it had been at Melbourne. Hobbs uses his feet perfectly and his judgement of the length of the bowling was masterly while he seems to have every stroke at his command.'

A curiosity occurred as a result of Woolley's batting. He drove Armstrong, the ball jumped and damaged Trumper's knee. Macartney, Australia's twelfth man, was already fielding for Ransford, so first Mead, and then Vine (who had the 'misfortune' to catch his own wicket-keeper), took the field on behalf of Trumper. The final English total of 501 owed much to Foster (71) in the later stages.

Australia was down but by no means out. Hill with 98 (his fifth Test score of between 95 and 99), and Bardsley (63) made their highest scores of the series while Carter (72) and Matthews (53) achieved the best of their Test careers. Not the least surprising feature of Carter's innings was that Hobbs misfielded a stroke when he was on 57, thereby missing an opportunity to run him out. Despite Barnes' unwearying skill (46.4 overs, 7 maidens, 105 runs, 5 wickets) a determined total of 476 was acquired.

Australia's innings finished shortly after 3pm on the fourth day and it was agreed that the tea interval should be dispensed with in order to finish the match. With 5 runs on the board, Hordern dismissed Hobbs lbw for 3. Rhodes (57*) and Gunn (45) did much to settle the matter and take England most of the way to a second successive Test victory for the first time since Melbourne in the 1903-04 series.

Hobbs relaxed with 74 against the not-too-taxing attack of the 'Fifteen of Ballarat' but was doubtless quite happy to be relieved, with Gunn, of the journey to Tasmania. He returned to the team against Victoria for a quiet 29 before the fourth Test began at Melbourne.

Recent heavy rain had made the pitch soft. Douglas could not have chosen a better moment to win the toss. Barnes (5/74) made the ball turn both ways and rise awkwardly while Foster (4/77) swung his deliveries effectively as well as making the ball jump nastily. Minnett (56) was the backbone of an Australian total of 191. In the remaining forty minutes' play,

Hobbs (30*) and Rhodes (23*) with more sharp running put on 54 and were in no trouble.

In front of 32,000, on the second day, their partnership prospered to 323 which remains a record for the first wicket for an Ashes Test. Everything was in their favour. Not only did they have a thorough understanding of each other, they also had the advantage of a fine day, a benign pitch and only a moderate set of bowlers to overcome. This was a series in which simply too much depended on one bowler, Hordern. If he failed, the Australians did not succeed. Their attack in general lacked sting and variety.

Hobbs batted with all his stylish authority while Rhodes, less eye-catching but professionally pragmatic, did all that could be required of him. He had a slice of luck on 27 when facing Hordern. Anticipating the stroke, Trumper jumped forward at square-leg and missed an easy catch.

Hobbs' innings was chanceless until he had passed his century. His fifty came in 74 minutes and by lunch he and Rhodes had progressed to 137: Hobbs 86*; Rhodes 48*. Thirteen minutes after Rhodes had reached his fifty (2 hours and 10 minutes), Hobbs completed his hundred by driving Hordern for a single. On 101 he offered a difficult stumping chance off Matthews. One reporter commented drily: 'the crowd appeared to be very indignant with Mr Carter.' As well they might be. The unfortunate wicket-keeper did make amends - but not until some time later. In general, however, Hobbs played with a fine touch. He brought up the two hundred partnership with two successive cuts to the boundary off Minnett before lifting a difficult chance to Bardsley at square-leg, off Kelleway, when on 126. Rhodes played a square cut which took him after 3 hours 40 minutes to his only Ashes' century. At tea the score as 249/0: Hobbs 138*; Rhodes 102*. On they went, until Hobbs cocked up the ball to square leg off Hordern. The crowd must have gasped with relief. Then Cotter dropped it. The crowd shuddered. No matter. Next ball, Carter redeemed his earlier blunder by catching Hobbs off Hordern. He had made his 178 in only 4 hours and 28 minutes, and 88 of those runs had come in boundaries.

Hobbs had made centuries now in three successive Tests; he was the first to achieve this feat. The stand of 323 far surpassed the previous record: the 185 of Tom Hayward and Stanley Jackson against Australia at The Oval in 1899. Herbert Strudwick had been watching Hobbs and Rhodes, and was unreserved in his enthusiasm: 'What I saw was a glorious display of all strokes, beautifully timed and placed, while Hobbs and Rhodes' running between the wickets was an education in itself.' A leading Australian newspaper, *The Argus*, had a rather different perspective:

They helped themselves to runs almost as they pleased; the weakness of the Australian attack was completely and mercilessly exposed. Some 31,795 paid £1,442 for the privilege of seeing their countrymen flogged about the field. Not for many a day has an Australian Eleven been so badly whipped. Those who consider cricket apart from country - possibly only a small minority - witnessed some very remarkable batting.

Hobbs by his achievements this tour has proved himself to be the greatest living batsman.

England now had Gunn to seize the moment with 75. Woolley contributed 56 and Foster 50 while Rhodes finished with 179 in the record total of 589 which beat Australia's 586 at Sydney in 1894/95.

Australia's resistance was, for once, limp. Douglas bowled especially well. So much so that, by the time the score was 117/7, his analysis read: 15-6-21-4. He finished with figures of 5/46 as Australia crumpled to 173 all out, leaving England the victors by an innings and 225 runs. It is hardly surprising that, on this last day, 'the crowd of about 10,000 persons were gloomy and for the most part silent'. The series was won. The Ashes were regained. Douglas himself described it as a happy contest in which there was 'no unpleasantness from first to last'.

Although Hobbs did little with the bat (38 and 14) in the final state match of the tour, he played a valuable part in a comfortable eight-wicket victory by taking four wickets for 25 runs.

The fifth Test, which lasted seven days, began in warm, muggy weather on an excellent wicket. After Rhodes' early departure, Hobbs was cautious while Gunn accorded proper respect to Hordern. Of the first 52 runs, made in an hour, Hobbs, out of touch, had only 20. When the score was 69, he was well caught by Ransford at deep mid-on off Hordern for 32. Woolley found his best form but half the side was out for 125 and a slow day's play ended at 204/6. Heavy overnight rain did not affect the wicket and England were able to compile 324 (Woolley 133*, Hordern 5/95). Australia then struggled to 133/5.

Rain prevented play on the third day. The following day, in bright warm weather all the English bowlers shared in the dismissal of Australia for 176. The wicket, soft on top but hard underneath, was treacherous. Hobbs, in particular, then played fine cricket. The 50 was up in 36 minutes and some members of the crowd became agitated, shouting to Hill, 'Haven't you any more bowlers?' The total was 76 and Hobbs' personal score 43 when he was marvellously caught at square-leg by Hazlitt, diving forward. With the exception of Gunn (61), the only player on either side to make two half-centuries in the match, the remaining batsmen laboured for runs.

On the next day, a score of 214 left Australia needing 363 to win. Minnett, who had the good fortune to be missed by Hobbs at cover-point when on 49, made a determined 61 but over the next two days (the sixth, like the third, was lost to rain) the rest of the side was defeated by the conditions and the Foster/Barnes combination. Each took four wickets. Hordern was brilliantly run out by a fast throw by cover-point which hit the wickets. This has been calculated as Hobbs' fifteenth run out in all matches in the tour.

The contemporary view of the series was reflected in one newspaper report:

Australia lost the rubber for the simple reason that they were inferior in both batting and bowling. They played at times as if they were dispirited; doubtless the strife between the players and the Board of Control contributed to this.

The figures support this assessment of the relative merits of the sides. In addition to Hobbs (662 Test runs, average 82), head and shoulders above the rest, four Englishmen averaged more than 40: Rhodes (57), Woolley (48), Vine (46), Gunn (42). The leading Australian, Armstrong, stood on 32. The bowling figures reflected a similar superiority. Foster(32 wickets at 21 each) and Barnes (34 at 22) were primarily supported by Douglas and Woolley whose wickets were not expensive either. They were all more economical than the second man in the Australian table: Minnett (5 wickets at 35 each).

Hobbs had performed exceptionally well after a not too convincing start to the tour. Perhaps the best description of his quality at this stage in his career is that of G H S (Harry) Trott, captain of Australia in 1896-98 who wrote these comments before the 1911-12 tour:

He is my ideal of what a perfect batsman should be, for he watches every ball carefully, his placing is perfection, and, being a firm believer in keeping every ball 'along the carpet' he rarely gives the fieldsman a chance of catching him. He has lovely strokes all round the wicket and can force the pace well when the ground is on the soft side. Being of an unassuming disposition, he is very popular with the crowd, and is really loved by his more intimate admirers.

5 Supremacy at Home, 1912

Four major factors militated against the success of that most imaginative idea, the Triangular Tournament of 1912 in which England, Australia and South Africa were each to play three Tests against the other two.

First, the weather was at its worst, with rain influencing or interrupting all but one of the nine Tests, the exception being the match between Australia and South Africa at Lord's. The two visiting teams, accustomed either to the consistency of matting or to hard, true surfaces, were very much at a disadvantage. Second, South Africa was in a period of transition after the splendid achievements of 1907 and 1909-10 when they had had strength in depth. They now had individuals of not inconsiderable ability such as Taylor, Nourse and Faulkner, but the team as a whole was weaker than it recently had been. They needed luck if they were to make the most of their talents, but they won only 13 of their 37 matches on this tour and they were defeated eight times.

Third, Australia, who also suffered eight defeats in their 38-match visit and managed only nine victories, were seriously weakened. The warfare between the players and the Australian Board of Control meant that Hill, Trumper, Armstrong, Carter, Cotter and Ransford among their leading cricketers were absent. Finally, England were at a peak of form and confidence after their tour of Australia. This is easy to forget while one is trying to be fair to opponents who were always, and for various reasons, struggling.

In the first match of the Tournament, South Africa was comfortably defeated by Australia before they came to met England at Lord's. The weather was so bad on the first morning that not only was play before lunch out of the question but the rainfall was such that the designated pitch had to be abandoned and a fresh wicket prepared.

Frank Mitchell, the South African captain, won the toss before a crowd of some 12,000. He must have agreed with the then current view: 'It is no easy thing to forecast how a Lord's wicket will dry', for just after three o'clock, South Africa began batting. By 4.30pm they were all out for 58 runs, of which 17 were extras. 'Dave' Nourse, the father of Dudley Nourse, was in the middle of a sequence of 45 consecutive Test appearances between 1902 and 1924. He alone reached double figures - 13. Foster (5/16) and Barnes (5/25) swept all before them. The latter particularly impressed *The Times* reporter:

A fine figure of a man whether in rest or action; a run up to the wicket lithe and 'springy' in which not a step is wasted; a beautiful action with the arm right over the head and then the ball is made to go away or come back; and there is always that inexorable length, the life off the pitch and the subtle changes of pace. It is the perfection of the bowler's art...

England had gained the ascendancy by the close of play with a score of 122/1. That wicket was Hobbs' who said, 'I played one on to my wicket in the first over, having hit a full toss past cover for 4. I tried to hit another; the ball swung a trifle and I got it on the edge of the bat.' Hobbs had, in fact, made a patchy start to the season, in which he had scored one century in fourteen innings before this game, although his 68 in an early Test Trial included a full complement of beautiful strokes.

E H D Sewell, in his book, *Triangular Cricket*, describes his dismissal vividly: 'Hobbs had the mortification to chop a swerving ball which pitched a yorker quite a foot off the wicket into his off-stump.'

England, however, were not unduly disturbed. Rhodes, at his most phlegmatic, was partnered by R H Spooner at his most stylish and attractive. The former was 36* when stumps were drawn while the Lancastrian had stroked his way to 67*. The wicket was easing and the bowling, in the main, unthreatening. Indeed, the overall performance of the visitors throughout the day was so disappointing that it prompted scathing comment from Hamish Stuart, writing in *Cricket*:

Great events of this kind do not tell their own story greatly, for the bare facts, though significant, fail to indicate how badly the South Africans batted, how wrong their methods were, how casual was their fielding and above all how poor was their bowling.

England's position was strengthened on the second day, when the pleasant weather attracted 13,000 people. Spooner moved gracefully to 119 his only Test century, and Woolley too batted in his most attractive style for 73. Lunch at 303/4 must have tasted sweet indeed. Four runs later, however, the departure of Woolley was the beginning of a cascade of wickets as the innings fell away crazily to 337 all out. The cause of the transformation was Sid Pegler who now bowled from the pavilion end for the first time. His medium-paced leg-breaks wreaked havoc. Seven runs came from his opening over before he took the last six wickets at a personal cost of nine runs and finished with 7/65. His delivery was high; his pace was varied; he had a quick break from leg. This tour, during which he took 189 wickets (average 15), was the high spot of his career. 29 of those wickets came in the Tournament and they cost him only 20 runs apiece. As *Wisden* put it: 'at one bound [he] sprang into the front rank.'

South Africa were soon in trouble in their second innings and it was left mainly to Llewellyn (60*) to carry them to 114/4 at the close, when bad light stopped play at 5.40pm. On the last day Hobbs bowled an over to enable

Barnes and Foster to change ends. When, later in the innings, Foster injured a hand taking a hard return from none other than Hobbs, the Surrey man bowled again, but without success. On the surface there was nothing significant about that but it was, in fact, part of a deep-laid plan by the captain, Fry, who was a theorist in the best (and worst) traditions of Archie MacLaren. Charles Fry always had a method in his madness:

When we had the situation in hand in this match, I tried to produce Jack Hobbs as a fast bowler. My experiment did not win the approval of the critics. Jack Hobbs was a batsman, therefore he could not possibly be a bowler. All the same, but for his innate modesty, I would have made one of him.

Had Fry's scheme borne fruit, one cannot but assume that the course of Hobbs' career and, indeed, that of English cricket, would have been much changed and for the worse. Of Hobbs' own views on the matter, there is his dry comment in *My Cricket Memories*: 'It is a puzzle to me why Mr Fry did not put Brearley on.' Clearly Hobbs had not been made privy to his captain's thinking. It was nevertheless reported that he bowled, now and then, a particularly good ball that came with the arm. Nevertheless, Hobbs was not unduly despondent about the failure of the manoeuvre.

Llewellyn's valiant resistance ended with his score on 75, and by 12.40 England's victory by an innings and 62 runs was secured. This came just in time, as it happened, for rain began to fall once more soon afterwards. Barnes (6/85) dominated his opponents as he was to do again both later in the summer and on the 1913-14 tour of South Africa.

Hobbs was to have the unusual distinction and pleasure of playing for four different teams which defeated the Australians that year. To each victory he made a significant contribution. At the beginning of September he appeared for the combined Surrey and Middlesex side which won by 10 wickets: Hobbs, 57 and 11. Later that month, C B Fry's XI had an eight-wicket success in which Hobbs made 25 and 42*. Much earlier, however, and a week after the Test defeat of South Africa, he was part of Surrey's 21-run triumph with 30 and a top score of 76 in the second innings. The fourth team was, of course, England at The Oval. Meanwhile, however, the Surrey fixture prepared him nicely for the first Test v Australia at Lords.

14,000 people braved the elements which, once again, toyed with the cricketers. England, having won the toss, chose to bat. After eleven balls Hobbs and Rhodes, with 5 runs each, were driven from the field by a heavy storm. They did not return until 2.15. They then moved fairly briskly on to 77 before a further stoppage at 3.10. In this period, Rhodes was very much in charge with 52 while Hobbs, unusually, trailed on 25. They both watched the tight, accurate bowling carefully. When the ball hung in the air, they loosened their grip on the bat and instead of going forward with all the arm muscles taut, getting under the ball and sending it up, they let it hit the bat

46

and drop down just in front of them before slipping through silently for another single. Their running showed an almost uncanny understanding. E H D Sewell was enthusiastic:

Such perfect unison in running between wickets I have never seen elsewhere. Neither called or made a sign. If one played the ball and thought a run possible he ran. His partner thought the same thing telepathically. Neither was ever in the least danger of being run out and their almost impudent run-getting had the instant effect of drawing the field in so that when a ball was forced many such strokes scored four which, but for the short runs, would have yielded only two and in some cases no run at all.

On their return to the crease at 4.30 the wicket was dead. Hobbs was quick to take advantage of this, and the partnership eventually realised 112 before Rhodes (59) was caught at the wicket off a kicking delivery from Kelleway. By now the pitch was livelier. Spooner appeared briefly before being replaced by Fry. Hobbs continued boldly, reaching his century just after six o'clock with a lucky single off Macartney, after 2 hours 42 minutes at the wicket. This was his first Test hundred in England (and he was not to make another against Australia here until 1926). His final score of 107, which contained 15 boundaries, was made out of 197/3. The plain-speaking unsentimental assessment of a tough fellow professional, E J 'Tiger' Smith, England's wicket-keeper in this match, would have pleased him:

Jack Hobbs got a fine century in this match on a tricky, rain-soaked wicket. That's why Jack's always been the tops in my book, he could get runs on any wicket at any time. Considering he suffered badly from migraines throughout his life, his career was magnificent. Many a time Jack would turn to me at the crease and ask if I had any pills for a headache but he never let people know how much he suffered.

This was a splendid innings on a largely unsympathetic wicket: there were several interruptions; the Australian attack conceded just this one century in six Tests in 1912. It came in for much praise. *Wisden* thought that only very rarely had he played finer cricket on a difficult wicket, while *Cricket* was even more laudatory:

His innings of 107 must be ranked with the historic efforts in Tests for the pitch, without being exceptionally difficult was never easy. It was ever a pitch on which nothing could be taken for granted; the ball was always turning and its pace and rise from the pitch varied. It was the sort of wicket on which daring and resolute methods, getting to the pitch of the ball and so forth, paid if conjoined with reasonable watchfulness but on which scraping was bound to be fatal.

'Scraping' is almost the last word one would use to describe the batting of Hobbs, although others may have been prone to it, as Fry makes apparent when commenting on the delivery from Emery which dismissed Hobbs:

One of the few unplayable balls I have seen; it was a perfect length, on the leg stump, came fast off the pitch and hit the off stump low down. Jack Hobbs being a batsman played back and was late; a lesser player would have scraped forward and might have snicked it.

As Fry was standing at the non-striker's end, his assessment must be accorded respect. Others less charitably suggested Hobbs had simply mistaken a leg-break for a googly. Be that as it may, Emery has no great record as a Test bowler (5 wickets at 49) and must have been delighted. One reporter was caustic about him: 'There is no lack of variety in Mr Emery's bowling - he bowls long hops and full pitches...' After Fry was run out for 42, England lost Warner quickly, also to Emery, but ended the day well placed at 211/4 thanks, in the main, to their openers.

Little progress was possible on the second day. The weather was foul for cricket - and not much good for anything else: chilly, windy, rainy. In under half an hour 30 runs were added. 3,000 endured patiently down the afternoon before play was abandoned at 5.45pm.

Fry declared at 310/7 on the third morning. The wicket was easy but he took the step in the hopeful belief that it would become difficult under the sun. Sadly the sun was never strong enough. 15,000 people, including, in the afternoon, the Prince of Wales, did get some entertainment, however, for Macartney's style and power did much to brighten the day. He had already become the first batsman in the country to make 1000 runs in the season. 'No player in the world has a prettier cut' was the view of one critic but all round the wicket he demonstrated his authority. He was unluckily out for 99 to make Australia 173/2: this must have been a bad decision, for Fry, unequivocal as ever, says 'if the ball touched his bat, it was the most delicate touch a batsman ever perpetrated. I would not have given him out from short slip.' The gritty obduracy of Charlie Kelleway, the opener, should not be forgotten. 4 hours 35 minutes at the crease produced 61 out of 233 and although his blocking aroused the wits in the crowd he remained imperturbable. At the end of the day the match was drawn with Australia standing at 282/7.

In their second meeting with South Africa, at Leeds, England's batsmen lacked conviction for the most part. On a rain-affected wicket, it was not an unmixed blessing to win the toss. Fry elected to bat. Although the wicket was fairly slow, the ball turned and sometimes lifted. The top batsmen in the order were bemused. Rhodes soon departed (20/1) and Hobbs was missed at square leg off Nourse before being well caught by the wicket-keeper, Ward, standing up to the same bowler. He had made 27; the total was 44. Neither Spooner nor Fry lasted. From 68/4 it was a 90-minute partnership of 111 by Woolley (57) and Hearne (45) that gave some substance to the total, 242. Theirs was the most profitable stand of the match and they turned not only the course of the innings but also that of the game.

When South Africa went in Barnes was once again on top, finishing with 6/52. When the visitors were reduced to 80/7, embarrassment threatened to turn into humiliation. Snooke (23) and Pegler, 33* at the close, did their best to redeem the situation but, next morning, the overnight 141/8 quickly became 147 all out.

It was an easy wicket throughout the second day but England did not take full advantage of it. Hobbs' quality was well demonstrated, not least by the speed of his scoring while most of his colleagues languished. He swiftly struck 35 of the 46-run opening partnership with Rhodes (who became Pegler's 100th victim of the summer) and 20 of the next 32 added with Spooner. Hobbs then mis-hit a leg-break from Faulkner to give a simple catch to Nourse at mid-off 78/2. His 55 was made in just over an hour in which he had successfully gone for the bowling. Spooner (82) shepherded the rest of the side to respectability and safety before being dismissed at 207/8. England finally set South Africa 334 to win. Had they reached this target, theirs would indeed have been a remarkable achievement as they had passed 300 in only two previous innings on their tour - and this was their nineteenth match.

They never looked like doing so, however. The opener Tancred fought hard for 39 but seven wickets were down for 105. Although Pegler (32) again resisted and Carter (31) struck out boldly, the final total of 159 was arrived at after only forty minutes on the third morning. Barnes' match figures? 10/115.

Australia next crushed South Africa by ten wickets at Lord's before moving to Old Trafford to meet England. There was a change in South Africa's captaincy at this time from Mitchell to Tancred because of the former's poor scoring. The weather at Manchester encouraged no-one. Play did not begin until 2.50pm. The wicket, very soft and wet, was not especially tricky early on but the ball moved a little and needed careful watching, not least because of the high wind which helped the swerve of Whitty and Hazlitt. Had Australia held their chances, England, despite winning the toss, would have been in even more difficulty. The ball did not run easily across the slow outfield.

Before Rhodes had scored he cut the ball uppishly to Hazlitt at point. The catch went down. Whitty was the unlucky bowler. Despite the frailty of his partners, the Yorkshireman remained soundness itself and plodded on patiently to make 92* at the close out of 185/6. Hobbs departed at 37/1 with 19. According to *Cricket*:

Hobbs who threw his new game down the gale and was his old steady self, keeping his brilliance in reserve behind his soundness, seemed certain to play a great innings when he fell to a ball from Whitty that would always have claimed a wicket. It seemed to me to swing in on the leg stump and then to break the reverse way.

What does this reference to a 'new game' signify? For much of the period immediately preceding the Test Hobbs had batted with an exuberant élan that did not meet with universal approval. It was a 'new game' of zestful attack to which he was giving full rein. In three successive matches, he had featured with no little brilliance. His 54 in the second innings for the Players at The Oval was dazzling, with his half-century struck out of 55 in only 21 minutes. Against Lancashire, a strong bowling side which finished fourth in the Championship, three places above Surrey, he stroked 111 out of 135 in 90 minutes. The merit of this innings is heightened when it is noted that Surrey made only 213 in all. His 94 at Lord's against the Gentlemen was thought to be both 'splendid' and 'reckless'. It took him 105 minutes and contained two 6s and nine 4s. He played 'a most dashing game taking risks innumerable'. It was this innings in particular which prompted the expression of concern about his flamboyance in *Cricket*:

When he cares to run risks and to give full play to his wonderfully accurate and wonderfully quick judgement of length - this is one of the chief secrets of success in batting, because such judgement eliminates the blind spot for the batsman who has such judgement - and his stroke-making ability, he can get runs with an ease that makes good bowling look simple and by methods that are apt, by their demoralising effect upon the bowler to convert good bowling into its opposite. Whether Hobbs' batting will benefit in the end by this new game, or rather by the habitual adoption of daring, forcing methods, is a question apart. Hobbs' new game tends towards recklessness; while it exhilarates the spectator, it is apt to intoxicate the batsman...

Hobbs' own quiet, matter-of-fact comment is revealing: 'I started about this time to liven up my batting. I had mentioned this fact in print so I felt duty bound to live up to it.'

In this Test it appears that he was fairly and squarely beaten by an unusually good delivery, having just struck the same bowler for two lovely boundaries. It was, nevertheless, his own fault, says Sewell. He was 'properly punished for his slavery to back play'. It is a hectoring, not to say contemptuous, comment and unworthy of both subject and writer.

Spooner made 1. Fry fumbled for 19. Hearne was put down by Whitty at mid-on before being bowled by Hazlitt. Although he made only 9 he helped add 57 for the 4th wicket, thereby raising England's morale, but neither Woolley nor Foster added substantially to the total. When play began at 5.00pm on Tuesday on the mud flat that passed for a pitch England faded rapidly after Rhodes played on to his second ball without adding to his 92. The side's total: 203. In the remaining half hour Australia reached 14/0. Wednesday was completely washed away and the match abandoned.

The third contest between England and South Africa began on a grey, cold cheerless day. The South Africans may have approached the fixture with some optimism as they had passed 300 and taken a first-innings lead in their final encounter with Australia which was a draw. Although South

Africa at The Oval must have been quite pleased to have dismissed England for 176 by 5.40pm, the time when bad light ended play, their batsmen must have been demoralised by their own dismissal previously for 95. The wicket was always giving the bowlers help and remained difficult throughout. The unseasonal autumnal nip in the air brightened no spirits.

Herbie Taylor showed his class while making 23, a small sign of greater things to come, but only Snooke, who banged away cheerfully to an identical score, managed to join him in reaching double figures. Barnes 5/28 was ably assisted by Woolley (5/41) who brought a pronounced turn to his left-arm spinners although they came slowly off the pitch. In two hours and a quarter the innings was over.

Most of the English batsmen did better. The failures of Rhodes (0), Spooner (26), Fry (9), Hayes (4), Woolley (13), and Hearne (20) throw Hobbs' fine performance into sharp relief. His 68 was the top score of the match (no-one else made more than 42) and with those runs he gave England supremacy, for without them, the home side would have been in difficulty, however well their bowlers bowled. He was the sixth out at 127 having hit eight 4s in 110 minutes. These figures are but the bare bones of an exceptional innings.

Throughout his innings Hobbs watched each delivery with the greatest concentration and, when he went out to drive, he was right to the pitch of the ball, hitting hard and cleanly. The unanimous view was that this was batting of the highest class. Hamish Stuart wrote in *Cricket*: 'One has seen Hobbs play so many fine innings that one hesitates about describing the last as the best, for there is always the special tendency to place the last first in this special sense, just as a gale newly weathered is the fiercest that ever blew.' There was no escaping the greatness of the display for Hobbs, yet again, played with comfort bowling over which other fine players had laboured and against which they often appeared inept. His defence was sound but he was always ready with a scoring stroke. His captain was appreciative: 'We owed our runs chiefly to Jack Hobbs whose skill in dealing with difficult bowling by Pegler and Faulkner was a lesson in technique.' Quick to judge and swift to act on his judgement he pulled and drove gloriously. His on-driving was remarkably fine as is shown by his three strokes to the boundary in one over off Faulkner (7/84), the pick of the South African bowlers. Sewell, this time was complimentary:

I have never seen Hobbs play a better innings, the conditions in no other innings I have seen of his having been so against run getting. Yet he made his runs as surely, as safely and as quickly as though he was batting on a true pitch against novices.

The Times said simply: 'It was the innings of a great master.' Perhaps this is the earliest use of this accolade. 'The Master' was the honorary title, of course, later bestowed on him by his affectionate admirers. It was appropriate perhaps too that he should finally fall to Faulkner (a good, low caught-and- bowled), who returned the best figures of his Test career.

There was no time for South Africa to bat again because of the bad light. This helped them not at all. More rain overnight dampened the wicket sufficiently to make it even more receptive to Barnes. His accuracy of the first day had worn an oval 'spot' about two feet by one foot, on a good length. He now exploited it to the full. Nourse (42) fought hard with typical courage but a total of 93 left England with only 13 to make. Hobbs (9*) took as his opening partner Hearne (5*) for the only time in Tests and they knocked off the runs without ceremony. The game occupied only two-and-a-half hours on the second day as Barnes had destroyed the opposition before lunch.

The second successive Test at The Oval was to be the final meeting of England and Australia before the Great War. It was decided that the winners would be the champions of the Tournament. On reflection, this seems rather rough justice, for England had already won three victories against South Africa while Australia's score was two. Some authorities either assert or imply that, from the outset, it had been agreed that this match was to be played to a finish but Sewell states that there was a meeting of the Board of Control on the second afternoon which, 'made no definite arrangement as to whether there would be another Test match in September in the event of the game being left unfinished'. On the first day *The Times* reported: 'The match which begins today at The Oval has been allotted six days and surely in this time there should be a finish. But the Board of Control will consider a proposition for another match should the game be drawn on Saturday.'

Heavy rain had fallen during the weekend before. Fry, according to his own account, was reluctant to make a start on time, and says play did not commence until late in the afternoon. His memory seems to have betrayed him as, on winning the toss, England batted only half-an-hour late, at noon. There were in all 4 3/4 hours' play during which time England scored 233/8 which Hobbs thought 'a jolly good performance'.

Not all commentators agreed about the difficulty of the pitch, however. Sewell here is in a minority, describing it as 'dead and easy'. On the other hand Fry, who, admittedly, may not be the most objective of judges, is at one with *Cricket*, *The Times* and *Wisden* in believing that batting was no simple matter. Easy or difficult? Only Hobbs and Rhodes achieved a hundred partnership on it - and that partnership was chanceless. It was their second century stand of the Test summer following their 112 against the Australians at Lord's. They were together for 110 minutes. Hobbs was in his element. Driving with certainty and playing on the leg side with composure, he was never afraid to loft the ball. He may have hit only four boundaries but he never made a really false stroke and this low number of 4s was due mainly, on such a large ground, to the slow outfield. There were seven 3s in his score. His understanding with Rhodes was as sound as ever; no run was wasted, no bad run made. The scoring was not fast. At lunch they had put on 65; Hobbs 42*; Rhodes 19*. With the total 107, Hobbs was caught at the wicket by Carkeek off Macartney for 66.

A slump to 144/5 meant that the advantage was lost, for after lunch the wicket presented more problems. Woolley had entered the fray, however, at 127/3 and, after a slow start, began to play his natural, beautiful game. His late-cutting was a particular delight to the spectators. Some splendid stylish hitting brought him eleven boundaries before he was lbw on the last ball of the day; 62 was as valuable as a century or more would have been in easier conditions. Steady bowling gave little away while the fielding was excellent. A crowd of some 15,000 had witnessed a tense struggle.

On the second day only ninety minutes' play, spread over three periods, was possible. England were all out for 245 and Australia, batting in bad light, lost two good wickets, Gregory, their captain, and Macartney, for 19 runs.

One description of the weather on the third day had a heavy irony about it: 'in point of temperature and light [it] would have done little credit to an average November.' Kelleway (43) and Bardsley (30) tenaciously but by no means slowly lifted their partnership to 71 in 75 minutes, and took the total to 90 before the third wicket fell. The rest of the side collapsed against Woolley (5/29) and Barnes (5/30) as the pitch gave them increasing assistance. Even so, England's lead of 134 in the prevailing conditions was by no means a guarantee of safety. This was immediately evident as they were soon 7/1 (Rhodes), and next ball, 7/2 (Spooner). The bowlers were in the ascendant and it may be argued that the weather foiled them. From about 2.30 and for an hour and a half, no play was possible. As a consequence of the rain, the wicket lost its spite.

Hobbs now reached 2000 runs in Tests. Scoring was restrained with, in one period of eight overs, only three runs accruing. Hobbs, however, did drive Whitty for six into the stand on the left of the pavilion. He pulled a muscle in his right leg but this did not greatly hinder his strokeplay, although he ran with a limp. The catch which dismissed him was an act of self-preservation by Matthews at point. Indeed, the fielder may still have been hopping in agony as not long before Hobbs had cut the ball hard, and such was the ferocity of the shot, had nearly splintered Matthews' shin: 51/3; Hobbs 32. Whitty was the grateful bowler. 13 runs later, not long after Woolley's departure, bad light brought yet another premature end: Fry 17*; Hearne 2*.

The wicket remained difficult. The batsmen continued to struggle. The start was once more delayed. These three sentences somehow seem to sum up the summer of 1912. There was, praise be, no further rain after play began at 11.45. Fry (79) played his longest and largest innings of the Tournament before being sixth out at 170. Hazlitt who, with his medium-paced, swerving off-breaks, came on for Whitty at 167/5, took the last five wickets for 1 run in 28 balls, to finish with his best Test figures, 7/25.

Australia needed 310. They fell short by 245 runs. Macartney scored 30. Over the rest it is best to draw a veil. Woolley (5/20) once again, this time supported by the left-arm fast-medium pace of Dean of Lancashire (with an analysis of 4/19 in his only Test). The other wicket fell in a controversial manner. Bardsley, ambling down the wicket, was run out for a duck by Hobbs. He made a brilliant throw from deep point - where he was fielding because of his pulled muscle,- which hit the stumps at the far end. The decision of the umpire, J Moss, caused all manner of a brouhaha. Bardsley departed unwillingly and, in the words of Hobbs, 'looked at the umpire with pained surprise'. The Australians were angry. Famous cricketers in the pavilion (where better placed?) were firmly of the view that an error had been made. Two of them, Ranji and Warner, whom ought to have had more sense than to criticise the verdict, went to the Australians' dressing room to commiserate.

So England were the Triangular Tournament champions. As far as 1912 was concerned for Hobbs himself, the final word should perhaps be left with his Test captain that year, C B Fry, in a mixture of high praise and drollery from his autobiography, *Life Worth Living*:

This was the only season in which I saw much of the batsmanship of Jack Hobbs. His grand career was spread over the years rather after my time. When one remembers the War cut out four of the seasons of his prime, his record in big cricket is the more admirable. But there have been other great run-getters who did not rival Jack Hobbs in polish and finish and mastery. He sailed through sunshine and storm on a perfectly even keel with an alert pair of aristocratic hands on the helm of the game. His quiet gentility disguises a thoroughly resolute and pugnacious subsoil of temperament. Jack Hobbs is an able fellow who can make a first-rate speech and he has drooping eyelashes which would be invaluable in Hollywood. He deserves his iron gates'.

These were the gates at The Oval paid for by members' subscriptions and formally opened in 1934. This was an unusual honour and one that Hobbs always greatly appreciated.

6 Domination Abroad, 1913-14

1913 was the year in which Hobbs for the first time, finished second in the averages with 2605 runs at 50.09. Mead of Hampshire was top - with 50.51. In 1914 when Hobbs had an average of 58 (second to Hearne's 60); in 1920 with a figure of 58 again (Hendren had 61), and in 1922 with 62 (Hendren top once more with 66) he was also runner-up. Interestingly, in the three later years, Hobbs had more innings, more runs and fewer 'not-outs'. Had he been more concerned about the acquisition of runs and his average he would probably have headed the list more often than he did, which was in 1925, 1926 and 1929.

1913 was the year in which Tom Hayward, in June, made his 100th 100 against Lancashire. He followed 'The Great Cricketer', W G Grace, the first to reach that astonishing figure in 1895. The same West Country side, Somerset was to be the victim when Hayward himself was followed by Jack Hobbs when he scaled that particular summit in 1923.

1913 was a year in which Hobbs positively galloped in his run-making. Gloucestershire suffered especially. At The Oval in May there was a hundred before lunch on the first day. Ascendancy established, Surrey won by 260 runs. In the August return at Bristol there was another hundred, also before lunch on the opening day. Surrey's victory margin: 303 runs.

Statistically, perhaps the most important hundred came in the partnership of 313 with Hayward against Worcestershire. This had immediately preceded the second Gloucestershire game. In only 3 hours and 20 minutes they demoralised the opposing bowlers before Hayward (146) departed. Hobbs' 184, with twenty-six 4s, was his highest innings of the summer. By the time Hayward retired at the close of the 1914 season, they had put on a hundred for the first wicket on no fewer than 40 occasions.

After such a prolific season, Hobbs was set for another visit to South Africa and the special batting problems it presented. One of the best analyses of what matting means to those who play on it is given in a sympathetic biography of Frank Woolley by Ian Peebles who was a good enough bowler himself, of course, to tour South Africa with England in 1930-31:

The mat has always been a responsive surface to the bowler who has mastered his craft and manipulates the ball, rather than depending on the fact that a cricket ball was originally made with a pronounced seam. It was ideally suited to Barnes in this respect, and his pace was the final ingredient in the almost unplayable quality of his bowling in the series. The slow bowler suffers on the mat by its unvarying consistency in pace and bounce. Barnes could bowl at around quick medium, and bend the ball either way with very little indication of his intentions from his hand. The leg-break flashed off the harder matting pitches, only suffering from one defect, which was that it bounced, for the most part, higher than the stumps.

It is appropriate that Peebles mentions Barnes; for, if Hobbs was the premier batsman on the 1913-14 tour in terms of consistency average and aggregate in Tests and other matches, Barnes had no superior as a bowler. Nor was the rest of the party weak. Indeed it was the strongest side England had yet sent to South Africa.

There were four amateurs: J W H T Douglas (Essex, captain); M C Bird (Surrey); Hon. L H Tennyson (Hampshire); and D C Robinson (Gloucestershire) who was the reserve wicketkeeper. He was taken ill on arrival, and had to return home without playing. E J Smith (Warwickshire) took his place thus joining nine other professionals: Barnes, Hobbs, Hearne, Mead, Relf, Rhodes, Strudwick, Woolley and M W Booth (Yorkshire). All but Relf and Booth had toured Australia in 1911-12. Thirteen was certainly not an unlucky number but it placed great demands on fitness and form.

Despite Hobbs, South Africa had triumphed on the last tour in 1909-10. This time the boot was very firmly on the other foot. The South Africans' cricket was still in a period of transition, and they were outclassed. The lack of stability in the home side's position is indeed reflected in that only five of the team who came to England in 1912 appeared in the first Test of 1913-14 (Taylor, Nourse, Cox, Hartigan and Ward) and by their choosing 23 players altogether in the series.

The MCC suffered only one defeat on their twenty-two match visit. That was at the hands of Natal in the nineteenth fixture. Significantly, perhaps, Hobbs was not playing. The major architects of the province's success were C P Carter (slow left-arm) who, with 10 wickets in the match, bowled himself into the fourth Test, and the great batsman Herbie Taylor, with a match double of 91 and 100. He was a stylist of the highest quality and held his country's batting together in the Tests.

Peebles makes an important comparison of Taylor to Hobbs:

Of the sides engaged, and possibly in any cricketing country of the day, only Hobbs could match Taylor's mastery on the matting. In certain respects they were much alike. Both founded an impeccable defence, and a great array of strokes, on a fundamental, but rare quality of batsmanship. When they played forward, they played at the maximum range of front foot and top hand, and when they played back it was as close to the stumps as practical considerations would permit. It was not easy for a bowler to drop on a spot where he could not be smothered or be conveniently be seen and met from the pitch. When the ball bites and turns as is always the case on matting, it is this ability which marks the great difference between the expert and, so to speak, the fair-weather sailor.

A contemporary assessment could not have been more accurate. The one that did appear on Saturday 13 December, the day on which the first Test began in Durban was: 'The MCC side will surely enter the field full of confidence. They have done very well in their games up to the present and they are believed to be one of the strongest sides that have ever left England.' They had, indeed, done well, winning five of their eight matches. Hobbs had already made over six hundred runs. All was set fair.

By the end of the first day, England 94/2 (Hobbs 59*, Tennyson 6*) in reply to South Africa's total of 182 were well on their way. Of that score, the captain, Taylor, had made a magnificent 109 out of the 173 from the bat. The fielding was sharp throughout and Taylor could not score quickly. But he stayed - which is more than his partners could manage to do. It was a perfect pitch. The weather was fine when play began at noon. The bowling led by Barnes was simply too good. Nourse (19) helped to get his side to 62/3 by lunch time. No-one else was able to reach double figures until Baumgartner (16), batting at nine slashed twelve off one over from Rhodes. Taylor was finally out after 3 hours and 18 minutes having hit eleven 4s and a fine shot for 6 off Douglas which sailed out of the ground. Barnes took 5/57.

Hobbs and Rhodes began batting under an overcast sky in front of about 5000 people. Rhodes was away briskly, reaching 18 before being dismissed at 24/1 and Relf, out of touch, left at 40. Hobbs went on to his fifty after 75 minutes to enthusiastic cheering from the impartial crowd. Progress was steady although the light deteriorated and the cloud cover became heavy.

By the second day's close, England were in charge: 419/7 with Douglas on 108* and Booth 0*. It could have been very different however for, on the Sunday, Hobbs, Strudwick and Booth were involved in a motoring accident. Reuter's reported: 'It appears that the car was approaching the Umbito level crossing when in endeavouring to pass a trap, it ran into a bank, smashed an open gate, and turned completely over imprisoning all the occupants beneath. They were released with little difficulty and were found to have sustained only a few scratches. Their escape was miraculous.'

Hobbs gives a slightly different account:

I was thrown over the windscreen, Struddy fell over the side and Booth and the driver lay beneath the capsized car.

Struddy and I picked ourselves up, by good fortune little the worse for our spill and righted the car expecting to find our companions badly injured. But they had a miraculous escape, Booth escaping with a slight injury to his back.

Hobbs was not obviously disturbed when play resumed in a tropical heat and oppressive atmosphere. The hundred was soon up before Hobbs, on

67, was missed by Tapscott at fine-leg. South Africa did not help their cause by putting down at least seven catches during the England innings. Their own reporters calculated that a dozen were missed. The cumulative effect of this succession of lost opportunities on their morale is not difficult to guess. At 136 Hobbs was the third wicket to fall, for 82 (115 minutes; one 6; seven 4s) when he was bowled by the slow left-armer Baumgartner. Hobbs may have been softened up by the kicking medium-pace of Blanckenberg as he was hit twice on the body in the first over from that bowler. Tennyson (52) and Mead (41) made useful contributions while Bird, chancing his arm, hit ten 4s in his 62 and was dropped three times. Douglas was the mainstay, reaching his only Test century in 3 $\frac{1}{2}$ hours.

On the third day there was only fifty minutes' play. England finished with 450 - Douglas' 119 included fourteen boundaries in his four-and-a-quarter hour stay. The last three wickets slipped away in four balls. Smith acted as runner for Booth, who was suffering from a strain because of the accident.

South Africa were 18/0 when the fourth day's play began at the agreed earlier hour of 11 o'clock. By 2.30pm the match was over. The matting at Durban was laid over gravel which made for a fiery wicket. On this clear morning which was freshened by a pleasant breeze, Barnes was irresistible. This time he won the duel with Taylor when he had him lbw for 8. Nourse (46) top-scored before he too fell to Barnes. The last three wickets went down to successive balls, one to Rhodes, two to Relf. The total was 111; Barnes' figures, 5/48. With 150 Test wickets he had now comfortably passed the Australian, Hugh Trumble's record of 141.

In seasonal spirit, Hobbs struck a pre-Christmas 102 (in under two hours with fifteen 4s and a five) against Transvaal at Johannesburg before the second Test took place on the same ground. The Christmas Day delights of the hospitality of the Mayor of the city and a native war dance were swept away by the dismissal of South Africa by inexorable pressure from Barnes. Although the weather was unsettled 7,000 spectators were present on this Boxing Day. Thunderstorms and variable light caused three interruptions. Having won the toss the home team were soon deep in trouble at 24/3. Barnes had taken them all at a personal cost of nine runs. Taylor was less confident than usual, and having made 29 out of 63, was the fifth wicket to fall after 87 minutes at which point lunch was taken. Barnes: 5/22. The elements caused the longest break in the action, fifty minutes, from 3.05pm. Hartigan made his highest Test score of 51, saving his side from complete disaster before he was dismissed by Rhodes who thus became the first Englishman to complete the Test 'double' of 100 wickets and 1000 runs. Barnes' final figures were 26.5-9-56-8 in the total of 160.

There was a surprise for the spectators when England's openers appeared at 5.30pm. Having appealed successfully against the dark clouds the batsmen then departed. Hobbs says simply: 'Relf went in with Rhodes to open our innings, Mr Douglas having decided to keep me back for the following day.' Why the captain should consider such a precaution necessary, it is difficult to determine. It may have underlined Hobbs' value to the team, but by this time in his career he was well able to look after himself. The Sussex all-rounder, on the other hand, had not met with much batting success and Douglas perhaps saw this as a tactical opportunity for Relf to play himself into form.

Relf seized his chance on a gloriously fine second day during which an early crowd of 4000 doubled in size in the afternoon before increasing to more than 10,000 after tea. Lunch was taken at 122/0 with Rhodes on 53*. Relf did not add to his 63* after the interval but it was a unique Test experience for Hobbs to come to the wicket with the score 141/1. He was given an enthusiastic reception and was quickly off the mark. The score rose rapidly to 181 but then Hobbs stepped across his wicket to hit Newberry (who bowled fast with great enthusiasm), missed a full toss and was lbw for 23. One reporter admonished him because he was 'out through apparent carelessness'. Yet Hobbs was not a careless cricketer. He was merely mortal, and made mistakes. Fortunately for England he made fewer than most players.

Rhodes (152), a century in 3 $\frac{1}{2}$ hours, and Mead (102) whose hundred took ten minutes less, were the main instruments of England's 403 reached after lunch next day. As the visitors stood at one stage on 354 with seven wickets in hand, this was not as large a score as might have been anticipated. Blanckenberg, who finished with five wickets, had a fine spell on the third day, of 14-5-23-4 which helped to keep England's total within bounds.

Taylor (34), and Zulch (40) did much kicking away of Barnes' leg-breaks in a sound opening stand of 70 but the side had slipped to 177/4 by the close. Nourse (52*) and Hands (40*) remained to carry on the fight but while the former added only 4 runs, the latter did not improve his score at all. Barnes took all 6 wickets on the last day for 21 runs. A further 54 runs completed the innings. Barnes' analysis was 38.4-7-103-9. Seventeen wickets in a match speak for themselves. It is a number exceeded only by Laker's 19 at Old Trafford against Australia in 1956. Hobbs' view of Barnes' achievement was brief and to the point: 'He never bowled better in his life.'

Two days later the teams met once more in the same arena. On a fine morning, England won the toss on a hard, true surface. Hobbs and Rhodes tucked into the bowling with some relish, the latter even going so far as to dispatch the medium-paced, off-spin of Dixon for three boundaries in one over. Their partnership of exactly 100 took only 71 minutes, a remarkably quick time on the first morning of a Test. Hobbs was 58* when Rhodes departed for 35. He was dismissed by Taylor. This was clearly an inspiration of captaincy as he bowled but rarely. Lunch was taken at 112/1 and there seemed to be no obvious reason why England should not have gone on to another substantial score. The South African bowlers had other ideas. Cec Dixon, in his only Test, began the collapse, with a caught-and-bowled dismissal of Hearne on 158. Mead departed on 159. Hobbs himself was then smartly taken, low down by the wicket-keeper, Ward, off Dixon, to leave his side on 163/4. The off-spinner was destined to take only one more Test wicket but as it was that of Hobbs again, he may not have felt too dissatisfied. Hobbs' 92 had lasted 2 hours and 8 minutes. A chanceless innings, it was another fine example of his consistency at the highest level. Containing nine 4s, it was the highest score for either side in the match; this too underlines his class.

The rest of the innings was undistinguished. Taylor, finishing with 3/15, actually took his three wickets for only 4 runs. Rhodes (whom he was to capture again in the second innings), Woolley and Bird were not a bad bag for someone who took only twenty-two first-class wickets in his career, but 238 was really rather a feeble effort considering the favourable conditions and following such an excellent start. South Africa batted briefly at 5.10 under overcast skies and vivid flashes of lightning. Perhaps these were seen as portents of the morrow's events.

By the end of the second day England were 204 ahead with seven wickets in hand. The main reason for the home side's disappointing 151 was Hearne. He had missed a month of the tour with a severe bout of influenza. He now produced his best Test performance. Its quality is heightened when one realises that he first came on when the score was 40/1. One report said he was 'a bowler of moods but when he does find his length his leg-break bowled low through the air at a considerable pace is a most disconcerting ball'. Zulch (38) fought through the morning but when Hearne deceived him at 82/4. the rest were unable to build a major innings.

When England batted again, Rhodes was out for a duck. Hearne needed a rest after bowling nineteen overs, so Mead came in at no.3 and with Hobbs brought up the fifty in half an hour. Their partnership of 79 took less than an hour before Hobbs was caught by Nourse off Dixon for 41: England 83/2. Next day England moved comfortably to 308 thanks in the main to Mead (86) and Douglas (77), thus setting their opponents 396 for victory. This formidable task was approached with determination by Taylor and Zulch who, before the end of the day, put on 124.

They extended their stand to 153 on the last morning but Relf then bowled his most important spell of the series and had Taylor (70) caught at square leg by Tennyson. Hands did not last (162/2) and the third wicket, the crucial one of Zulch, went also to Relf, a hard, low, caught-and-bowled.

South Africa lunched at 167/3. Barnes then plucked the heart out of the middle order with a sharp spell of 5-4-5-3. When his lbw appeal against Ward (40) was turned down, Barnes, ever a fierce competitor, allowed his annoyance to show and he was roundly barracked. With Blanckenberg (59 - his highest Test innings) the wicket-keeper took the total from 217/7 to 298, giving South Africa some grounds for hope - but, despite their tenacious 6 hours and 27 minutes at the crease, they were finally forced to concede defeat by 94 runs. England had won the series.

There were seven fixtures for the tourists between the third and fourth Tests. Hobbs played in five of them. He was generally reported to be batting with great brilliance and some luck while collecting a further 410 runs at an average of 102.

The first day's play at Durban was much interrupted by rain. South Africa, having won the toss, struggled against fine bowling and a dead out-field to 162/8. This was something of a recovery as, at one point, they were 84 for 5 wickets, all to Barnes. When he tired after bowling 26 consecutive overs from the start for just 51 runs, the score was 112/5. Dan Taylor, the older brother of Herbie, in his first Test, hung on bravely for 36 while Philip Hands struck boldly(two 6s and four 4s) for 51. Barnes 7/56.

By the end of the second day, however, South Africa (170 and 32/1) was leading by 39 runs and had everything to play for. England's thin response yet again owed much to the openers. 92 was their partnership on this occasion, the first 50 coming at a run-a-minute. Hobbs was hitting more freely. This is reflected in their respective contributions to the lunch score of 65/0: Hobbs 47*; Rhodes 16*. They enjoyed some luck, Blanckenberg, for example, having had Hobbs dropped on 39 and Rhodes on 16. The bowler was finally rewarded when Hobbs mistimed a drive to mid-off where Nourse held on to the chance. Hobbs' 50 had come after an hour but he batted some 82 minutes in all, stroking five boundaries before his dismissal for 64. By tea the cream of England's batting had been disposed of - 137/6 - and after 3 $\frac{1}{2}$ hours' batting they were all out for 163. Their failure was Claude Carter's success. Always an effective slow left-arm bowler on matting, he secured his best Test return of 6/50.

Twenty-four hours later, South Africa had made 249/7. There may have been some slow scoring but the tactics were sound against varied bowling and keen fielding. After much overnight rain, the cloud-heavy conditions did not permit a start until 12.30. Lunch saw the Taylors in situ with the younger on 42* and his brother on 36*. Their 69-run partnership was followed by another of 97 between Herbie Taylor and Nourse. At tea, on 177/2, the batsmen were 93* and 32* respectively.

It was fitting that the captain's very fine defensive innings of 3 $\frac{1}{2}$ hours was ended after the interval by Barnes who had bowled so well. It was without addition to his score. Taylor had only four boundaries and as many as 60 singles but the value of his innings to his side cannot be over-estimated. Nourse finished with 45, a total equalled by Carter, who thus made his highest Test score to complete a fine personal performance in the match. South Africa finally declared at 305/9 on the fourth morning. Barnes with 7/88 finished with 49 wickets in the series at an average a fraction over 10. It was the end of an extraordinary sequence for him. In 1911-12 34 Test wickets at 22; in 1912, 39 wickets at 10.

England were set a target of 313. Victory was out of the question but defeat could not be ruled out. By lunch Hobbs and Rhodes had 25. By tea 127 was on the board: Hobbs 91* and Rhodes 34*. They had not been dilatory. After a quiet start, Hobbs in particular punished loose balls severely. Their 50 partnership took 65 minutes and 100 runs came up three-quarters of an hour later. Hobbs' personal 50 needed only 75 minutes. It was distinguished by fine hits to leg and rasping square cuts. When he finally played on for 97 (one 6 and seven 4s) England, at 133/1, were safe, even though four more wickets were lost for 154 before bad light and rain stopped play.

There is a sense in which, in retrospect anyway, the final Test at Port Elizabeth seems only to have emphasised the superiority of England. On an antheap covered with matting which made a hard wicket, South Africa could only manage 193 on the first day. They had won the toss and were doubtless relieved by the absence of Barnes. Officially he was 'confined to bed with chest trouble'. In truth there was a disagreement over terms with the South African authorities who were responsible for the finances of the tour. Barnes felt he had been let down. He declined to play. Now forty, he never appeared in another Test.

In addition to the Taylors, the Hands brothers played, the first time two pairs of brother appeared together in Tests. It was the younger Hands, Philip, a regular members of the side throughout the series, who batted with great spirit. Coming in at 83/3 he scored a chanceless 83 himself in one hour and three-quarters, with two 6s and ten 4s part of his robust display. Douglas, at his fastest and bowling to a good length, dismissed him and eliminated the lower order in an impressive spell of 5.4-2-14-4. There was an hour left when England batted. Hobbs played some lovely strokes but was missed at short-leg when on 22 before lifting a drive to Nourse, eleven runs later. This gave 'Bill' Lundie, a fast bowler appearing in his only Test, the first of his four international wickets. When stumps were drawn, England were 48/1.

They moved inexorably to 357/8 on the overcast second day. The brightest batting was seen in Woolley's 54 which included a 6 and five 4s, but Mead's chanceless 117 in 3 ³/₄ hours was indispensable and made for a substantial first innings lead.

When England finally finished on 411, South Africa fought back with Herbie Taylor driving hard (he struck ten 4s in his 87) and Zulch defending sternly for his 60. Their admirable 129-run partnership was not enough, however. Their successors laboured to 204/5 to take the contest into the hot final day when the wicket remained good, but they reached only 228.

Booth ended his tragically short international career with some fine fast-medium bowling. 4/49 were his figures. It is a sombre thought that, together with three of his opponents in this game, namely Reginald Hands, Lundie and Newberry, he was a casualty of the Great War.

Hobbs made the 11 runs necessary for a ten-wicket victory with Rhodes at the other end and England came to the end of one of their great periods. Between 1911-12 and 1913-14 they played 16 Tests, as follows:

		Played	Won	Lost	Drawn
v	Australia	8	5	1	2
v	South Africa	8	7	0	1

In these games Hobbs and Rhodes had 21 completed opening partnerships: six of them passed the 100-mark and another five averaged 40 or more. Together they averaged 90 in 1911-12, 42 in the Triangular Tournament, and 68 in South Africa. Their consistency formed the solid base for England's scores as they frequently blunted the sharp cutting edge of opposing attacks. Hobb, at his attacking peak, hit 662 at an average of 82 in the first of these three contests and, as in the other two series, he scored more runs at a better average than anyone in his team: 387 at 48 in 1912; 443 at 63 against South Africa.

Hobbs was always very conscious of what was expected of him. On the 1913-14 tour: 'The newspapers remarked that I was not playing with quite the abandon of the time previous; perhaps it would have been nearer the truth to say that I knew more about it. My value to my side was more apparent to me and I felt my duty and responsibility.'

This is not to imply that an awareness of his responsibilities ever made him a dull dog at the crease as the 1914 season was to show.

This last summer before the First World War does occupy a special place - afterwards, it is said, nothing was ever quite the same - and it saw Hobbs, aged 31, at his height. It was a prolific time for him personally.

He had never made more centuries (11), or more runs (2697), or at a higher average (58). Yet not the least remarkable feature of his career was that all these figures were to be improved upon after the war.

1914 was made memorable not only because Surrey won the Championship. Since Hobbs' arrival in 1905 they had always enjoyed a challenging or respectable position (4th, 3rd, 4th, 3rd, 5th, 2nd, 5th, 7th, 3rd) but the title had always eluded them.

That year of 1914 was given a particular flavour and zest by the spectacular nature of Hobbs' batting. Although he was to make thousands of beautiful runs in later years, he never made so many so fast as he did in this golden summer.

It was not in his nature to look for easy pickings and, curiously, he had never previously scored a hundred against Yorkshire. Now, at the end of May at Bradford, he put the full might of Hirst, Booth, Drake, Rhodes and Kilner to the sword. This was still the best attack in the country: sharp, hostile, varied, experienced and cunning. Hobbs' was arguably the finest performance of the year. The statistics - 100 out of 151 in 75 minutes - give some idea of his splendour but they do incomplete justice to his play. *Cricket* described the pitch thus: 'The wicket was of the type on which the man who potters about usually gets himself out: it was soft, but not difficult, though likely to develop vice as soon as the sun got fairly to work on it.' Hobbs did not waste time. He began by banging Booth for six and Drake for three 4s in an over. One report said succinctly: 'It did not matter who bowled; he hit everybody.' He dispatched Rhodes, of all people, for 6 on to the pavilion seats twice in one over. There were altogether five 6s and eleven 4s in his score. The over in which Hirst finally secured his dismissal was eventful. When he was 88, a dropped chance at long-on brought him two runs. A pulled 6 and a driven 4 took him to the century. He was then bowled by the last delivery.

In the second innings he was more restrained: 74 at a run a minute with only three 6s and seven 4s. One 6 struck the face of the clock in the football pavilion damaging one of the hands. Gerald Brodribb describes this vividly in *Hit for Six*:

The time was four o'clock and the minute hand struggled on for ten minutes and then fell with a flop to 4.30 and stayed like that until the clock was repaired after the war. The somewhat disgruntled bowler (Drake) who felt that he had seen enough of Hobbs said that it was a pity that the hands had not been knocked on to 6.30 as then 'we'd have been finished with this mucking about for t'day'.

Hobbs remembered the incident differently:

Instead of apologising for injuring the clock, I am sorry to say that I waved my bat exultingly. The smash had the effect of sending the clock back half an hour and somebody made the remark at the time that 'progressive cricket had put the clock back'.

Surrey won, as they did the return match in August: Hobbs' 202 should have successfully scotched any talk, if there was any, that he could not deal with the Tykes.

Hobbs highest score to date (215*) was made when batting at no.3 as Strudwick had been sent in as nightwatchman. That was at Leyton against Essex. One account records that he 'made his partners look like cart-horses against a specimen of real blood'. It was a chanceless effort in which, initially, the emphasis was on driving but he later made runs all round the wicket, forcing away good-length balls with great skill.

This score was exceeded for the benefit of a Bank Holiday crowd at the Oval on 3 August when he hit 226 out of 375 and a first day's total of 472/5. This was a precursor to what he naturally hoped would be a productive benefit match. Sadly, international affairs had taken a rapid turn for the worse. War was declared on 4 August. The military authorities required the use of the Oval. Surrey's next two home matches were transferred to Lord's. The match against Kent was for Hobbs' benefit. On the first day just £24

14s 6d was collected. This was a staggeringly disappointing figure. The Surrey Committee came to the rescue and the whole question was, eventually, happily resolved, with a second benefit after the war.

At the end of the month Surrey was able to return to its home ground where they beat Gloucestershire, Hobbs making 141, his final century of the year. Surrey abandoned their last two matches because of the war. As a result they were not declared Champions until the MCC Committee met on 9 November.

At this point Hobbs had made 25,517 runs in first-class cricket at an average of 42, with 65 hundreds. He stood on a pinnacle. J N Pentelow wrote of him in *Cricket* on 1 August 1914 under the heading: "The Surrey Super-batsman":

Great is John Hobbs...Batting is spoken of as defence, bowling as attack. But when John Hobbs fairly gets going he is apt to seem the attacker...One thing certain can be predicted of Hobbs - if he stays more than half an hour or so he will be found scoring fast. No bowler can tie him up for very long. He will either get runs or get out...Who could say nowadays what is the great feature of Hobbs' play? It is all features! Let him start to exploit one particular stroke, and find it made dangerous or difficult by a re-placing of the field and he will bring out in its stead not one other, but half-a-dozen others. He was a good batsman in 1905; a great batsman in the making. Now he is a great batsman made, though even yet he may not have reached his zenith - who can say?

The post-war period was to provide the answer.

7 Triumphs and Disappointments, 1919-21

The First World War saw Hobbs working initially in a munitions factory until he joined the Royal Flying Corps in 1916. In *My Life Story* he seems to think he had somehow 'let the side down' by not becoming more actively involved at an earlier date. As he says, not everyone in England appreciated in 1914 and 1915 just how long the conflict might last:

I was only one of the those numerous individuals who failed to realise in the early days of the war, how serious the position was and I did not join up for some time. In considering my financial outlook, I had to take into account my obligations to a wife, to four young children and to a widowed mother.

Although he played some Bradford League cricket, the four years, 1915, 1916, 1917 and 1918 were lost to the tragedy and carnage of war on a horrifying scale.

Hobbs did appear against the Australian Imperial Forces team three times in 1919 twice for Surrey, once for Mr C I Thornton's England XI at Scarborough. The visitors had a very useful side containing some fine players and they were only defeated four times in 28 first-class matches. Hobbs played confidently against them, notably with 205* in Surrey's first meeting with the tourists and a particularly fine 93 out of 141 in pursuit of 191 which brought a two-wicket victory to Thornton's XI. But there was one portent of things to come which needs to be noted. A certain J M Gregory took ten wickets in the latter match and press comments are revealing. The bowling was 'inclined to be short throughout. Short fast balls are often as dangerous as good-length bowling and the majority of Mr Gregory's victims were caught behind the wicket'. In the second innings, as Hobbs struck out for victory, Gregory unleashed himself after lunch on that last afternoon. Hobbs received two nasty blows to the body. His riposte was to drive two full-length balls to the boundary.

Jack Gregory was always to threaten the batsmen. Blessed with a strong frame and a height of 6ft 3$\frac{1}{2}$ins he was a terrifying figure at the end of his run when he launched himself into a huge leap before hurling the ball at bewildering pace. Never averse to dropping the ball short, he frightened out not a few English batsmen in his Test and touring career when they were technically overwhelmed by his speed. His zest for the game was also reflected in his equally fierce, attacking batsmanship and his brilliant slip fielding.

In the previous week, also at Scarborough, Hobbs had completed what was to remain a unique treble with 116 against the Gentlemen. He had already made 120* (at The Oval) and 113 (at Lord's) against them that season but it was about the innings in the north that one reporter enthused:

Hobbs as usual adopted the maxim that offence is the best defence. He attacked the bowling in whole-hearted fashion from the moment he went into bat and scored 116 in a little over two hours. He made many beautiful and some audacious strokes and gave two difficult chances.

The innings which probably gave him most pleasure, however, was in his revived benefit match against Kent on 18 and 19 August. The County Championship in 1919 consisted of two-day matches, an unpopular experiment which was not repeated. Over 18,000 spectators came to The Oval on the first day, however. Hobbs, batting in the first innings was dismissed as 'free and easy and careless' when he was out for 17. As he passed over 2000 runs for the season (the only batsman in the country to do so in 1919) in that innings, he must have batted quite seriously elsewhere! Surrey were eventually set to get 95 to win in 42 minutes on the second day when 12,000 people were present. Hobbs (47*) and J N Crawford (48*) flogged the Kent attack, not with slogging but with scientific hitting, for 96 in thirty-two minutes after taking all of twenty-one minutes over the first 50. To their great credit Kent bowled 12.1 overs during the assault. Hobbs struck the winning hit and was carried shoulder-high to the pavilion. It should also be noted that this marvellous display took place in drizzle and bad light. £1,671 was the sum which Hobbs received. Even when every allowance has been made for inflation since, this was by no means an excessive sum. Hobbs used it wisely to establish his sports' equipment business which gave him, and his family, to whom he was devoted, security. It was enough also to provide a financial independence from cricket.

He had clearly lost little of his dash during the years that had passed. He was thirty-six years old when the season began, and seemed anxious to make up for the loss of the last four summers.

1920 saw another high Hobbs' aggregate, 2827 (average 58) which he was to exceed only twice, in 1925 and 1926. There were another eleven centuries including a sequence of four in a row beginning with 110 v Sussex at The Oval which was, oddly, his first against that county. The next three were in away matches: 134 v. Leicestershire; a century before lunch; 101 v Warwickshire; and 112 at Sheffield which included a 6 and thirteen 4s. This was the top score of the match and, with his second innings of 70, helped set up a 204-run victory against Yorkshire, who did not suffer such indignities frequently or lightly. Sandham, not yet always opening with Hobbs (when the amateur Donald Knight was available, he was accorded that privilege) made 81 and 89 batting at no.4. The sequence of four centuries in a row had only been achieved previously by Hayward (1906), Fry (1911), and Wally Hardinge of Kent (1913).

This was an unusual season for two reasons. First in the bowling averages was J B Hobbs. Admittedly he only bowled 83 overs but he did take 17 wickets which only cost him 11 runs each. There were some good cricketers among them: five of the first six Warwickshire batsmen and, a fortnight later, four of the first six against Essex. One suspects that the victim who gave his most satisfaction was J W H T Douglas whom Hobbs regarded as difficult as any bowler in his career and who dismissed him twenty-five times over the years - more often than any other bowler.

In the match at Leicester which preceded the Warwickshire fixture, Hobbs captained Surrey when Percy Fender was called away on business on the second day. Richard Streeton, in his biography of the Surrey captain, provides a revealing slant on this question of leadership and Hobbs' attitude to it:

Strudwick according to Fender had a far keener tactical mind than Hobbs, the senior professional who positively disliked responsibilities other than his own! It may have been because he was so unassuming a man. He would give his view if it was sought but that was as far as it went. It got to the point when I had to leave the field for a meeting or something I would say to Jack 'All right if Struddy takes over?' and Jack would say, 'Yes, please' and everyone was happy.

Such reluctance was not in evidence, however, in the Leicestershire match, and Hobbs lead Surrey to an easy victory. If he was, in fact, so diffident one wonders why he accepted, on so many occasions, the captaincy of the Players. He led them in 25 of his 49 matches. From 1921 to 1932 he was in charge in at least one of the contests each year. His was not a bad record. There were six victories, three defeats and sixteen draws. Nor was his batting greatly undermined as there were eight centuries during this period.

Neville Cardus wrote an appreciation of Hobbs in May of this year which while praising his play also places him historically:

Hobbs is undoubtedly our leading batsman; moreover he is an out-and-out product of the modern game...Rarely does he lose his wicket through incorrect or, rather, inartistic play. He does of course deviate from the conventions; that is, because, like the artist he is, Hobbs cannot go on from day to day just scoring runs in the way that comes easiest to him... I have said that Hobbs in himself would provide an ample idea of the scope of modern batting technique. And I should say that the great batsman of today differs from the great batsman of yesterday in his fuller command over back play as an offensive factor, and his ability to combine it easefully with forward play...

With Hobbs when he is on a bad wicket, back play is made positively dramatic. He times the strokes so beautifully that you catch your breath as you see the ball on the very wicket. Then he gives you that wonderfully quick swing round, the right leg as

68

pivot, and you have seen the finest on-side shot of recent years!...Besides, given a fast wicket, Hobbs can play the conventional forward game with the best of them. How superbly adaptable is his style we can understand from his success in this country, in South Africa, in Australia, against all conceivable sorts of bowling.

The Australians had been keen to have a tour by the MCC in 1919-20 but this was thought by the authorities, and rightly, to be too soon after the war. Indeed, English cricket had not properly recovered even by the following winter, 1920-21 - there is a close parallel may be seen with the circumstances following the Second World War. The team was the strongest available but its weaknesses soon became apparent. There were three amateurs: J W H T Douglas (Essex, Capt); P G H Fender (Surrey); and E R Wilson (Yorkshire). The professionals included the experienced travellers Hearne, Hobbs, Rhodes, Strudwick and Woolley and seven newcomers: A Dolphin (Yorkshire); E H Hendren (Middlesex); J W Hitch (Surrey); H Howell (Warwickshire); J W H Makepeace and C H Parkin (both Lancashire); C A G Russell (Essex); and A Waddington (Yorkshire).

Their prospects were examined in *The Times* as early as 5 June 1920 and the danger was seen clearly. The evidence of Gregory's quality, first seen in this country in 1919, was not forgotten:

He certainly will be the first choice for Australia as a fast bowler and one of her strongest batsmen. He can bowl at a great pace for the first five or six overs, has all the advantages of youth and appears certain further to immortalise the name of Gregory in Australian cricket history...the MCC team will have no easy task.

Hobbs' stature was unquestioned. His performances in either 1911-12 or 1926 are often awarded the palm when the subject of his greatest series is considered. In both series he scored many runs at a high average - and England won. For more than one reason, however, there is a strong case to argue that 1920-21 saw his finest performance. The following points are worth considering.

1. In 1911-12 Hobbs had the formidable security of Rhodes at the other end but in 1920-21 Rhodes was no longer the force he had been as an opening partner; his top score was 73; his average 23. Their highest partnership in eight innings was 54. In 1926 Hobbs was to be with Sutcliffe.

2. The rest of the batsmen on the tour, although strong on paper and whose 1920 form justified their presence, lacked the tenacity and consistency required in timeless Tests. During Hobbs' career, while Tests in England were limited to three days, with one or two exceptions, all Tests in Australia were played, as they had been for the most part since the sides first met in 1876-77, to a finish.

3. The Australians' bowling attack in 1920-21 had much greater depth and quality than in either 1911-12 or 1926. In Gregory they had genuine, threatening pace of the highest class. He was to be joined by the developing

Ted McDonald from the third Test onwards. Although the latter did not take many wickets, he ruffled quite a few feathers with his speed. In Arthur Mailey there was, by way of contrast, an exuberant, extravagant spinner of charm, versatility and penetration. In 1911-12 Australia had only Hordern. In 1926 there were still some famous names in the side but they were, without exception, expensive.

The 1920-21 tourists made an inauspicious start. They were quarantined for a week because of typhoid on board ship. This setback cost the side some valuable practice time. It did not appear to have much effect, however, on their early form as they made short shrift of South Australia by an innings and 55 runs (Hobbs 48), and Victoria by an innings and 59 runs (Hobbs 131). They lost to the very strong New South Wales side by 6 wickets (Hobbs 112 and 5) and this offered some clues as to what might happen in the Tests, as Gregory took 9 wickets and Mailey 7. Hobbs did not play in the next game against Queensland, the weakest of the states, which brought another easy victory. The comfortable draw with an Australian XI (Hobbs 26) and two minor fixtures then followed.

A Special Correspondent reported in *The Times* on 12 December, five days before the first Test:

In bowling the Australians have what may easily prove to be the winning factor for Mr Gregory has established that reputation for pace which so often cramps the true form - even of the first-class batsmen. Mr Mailey, the googly bowler, is declared by an Australian judge to be a better bowler than Dr Hordern.

The home team won the toss on a fine, cool morning in Sydney where the hard wicket was in excellent order. England's bowlers had one of their best days of the winter. Indeed, Australia's total of 267 arrived at on the second morning, was to be the lowest of the series. There were no dramatic bowling figures but Hearne with three wickets and Woolley with two made important breakthroughs. It would have been a greater success had the obdurate Collins (70, top score) not been put down on 16 and 43. Both chances eluded the unfortunate Waddington playing in his first Test. Missed chances were to be a miserably regular feature of England's performance in the 1920-21 series, but with 249/8 the score at the end of the first day, Australia knew that the honours lay with the visitors.

When Hobbs, in the covers ran out Ryder with a 'bad return' (according to one reporter) off the first ball next day and then caught Oldfield 'after a fumble' (the same somewhat jaundiced writer) England had made the best possible start. The crowd, which had risen to 23,000 on the opening day, now reached 40,000. Fine weather and a perfect wicket presented ideal conditions. Sadly, the batting did not rise to the occasion.

Russell, who had opened regularly with Hobbs for most of the tour thus far, and with some success, played on to Kelleway's first ball of the innings.

70

Hobbs (32*) and Hearne (14*) took the score to 47/1 at lunch. Hearne went immediately afterwards and Hobbs fell for 49 to make England 70/3. He was bowled round his legs by Gregory. Percy Fender described this uncharacteristic dismissal in *Defending the Ashes*:

Hobbs said afterwards that it seemed to him a plain straight ball and he was obviously surprised to find himself bowled. He seemed to think that somehow just for that ball he must have taken a wrong guard. If so, it seems an extraordinary error, especially as Hobbs had been batting for over an hour, during which time he had hit four 4s.

Hendren and Woolley (52), who played most felicitously, then added 74. The innings, however, fell away from 144/3 to 190 all out. This was a great disappointment and, it can be argued, one from which England never recovered, psychologically, in the series.

On the third day, Australia reached 332/5. In the muggy weather the limitations of England's bowling were exposed and their fielding suffered. Hobbs missed a chance of running out Collins (104) on 52. Strudwick marred an otherwise excellent display by fumbling a simple stumping opportunity when Macartney (69) left his ground having made 18. With Australia 222/1 (Bardsley had been dismissed for a mere 57), Douglas 'had a consultation with Hobbs' and soon went on to take the wickets of both Collins and Macartney.

Armstrong, however, dominated proceedings on the next day. As both captain and batsman, he was to cast a huge, not to say overwhelming, shadow across England's fortunes for two successive series. His massive 158 was an innings of weight, power and authority, in every sense. It removed the game far beyond England's reach as Australia totalled 581. England, needing a little matter of 659 to win, limped to 47/1. Russell was sunk, almost without trace, by Gregory's first ball. Hobbs gave two chances before he had made 13 but on 18*, with Hearne 23*, lived to fight.

They had a partnership of exactly 100 before Hobbs was lbw to Armstrong for 59 (with a 6 and two 4s) after two hours at the crease. One report said, 'he seemed to find Mr Mailey's bowling easy.' Mailey was to take his wicket nine times in Tests, more than any other bowler apart from Grimmett who also conspired his downfall on nine occasions.

Arthur Mailey always approached cricket with humour and in a spirit of friendship which gave a welcome perspective to the sternly contested Test Matches. But he was no fool on the field. His leg-breaks and googlies were good enough to bring him 99 wickets in internationals. He enjoyed himself and it is not difficult to believe that he gave pleasure to his opponents because of his enthusiasm for the art of bowling.

England were now 105/2. Hearne (57), Hendren (56) and Rhodes (45) did their best but it was nowhere near good enough. A total of 281 meant a crushing defeat by 377 runs.

It was said at this time, 'Hobbs is in a difficult position. He has to live up to such a tremendous reputation. Unless he gets a hundred, people think that he is out of form.' He was, however, to give more substantial evidence of his special quality in the second match.

At Melbourne, it was very hot on the first morning, 31 December 1920, and 36,000 spectators were attracted to the match. When Australia won the toss, which enabled them to bat on another perfect wicket, England would not have been human had their spirits not sagged. Howell on his debut bowled with fire and zest but had little luck, as when Rhodes put down Collins (64) off the fourth ball of the innings. At lunch, 85/0 looked ominous but England hauled themselves back into the game so that by tea Australia had slipped to 199/4. A close of play score of 282/6 (Bardsley 51, Taylor 68) did not place them in an invincible position but Pellew, batting at no.7, had been dropped by Hendren off Douglas when on 3.

On a still perfect wicket on the second day, Pellew amassed 116. The heat was intense while Gregory, no.9 in the order, collected a sparkling 100 with twelve 4s in 2 hours and 17 minutes. Both batsmen were playing in only their second Test and they put on 173 together, in just over two hours taking the score from 282/7. The Australians must have been well satisfied with a final total of 499, after Douglas had tried twenty-eight bowling changes. Hearne was not able to take any further part in the match after the first day and did not bat in either innings. Lumbago incapacitated him for the rest of the tour - a savage blow to English hopes.

In *Playing for England* Hobbs summarised the situation bluntly and listed the dismal catalogue of handicaps during the tour:

The plain truth was that Australia had a magnificent side, vastly superior to ours which was not helped at all by the illness or injury of 'Abe' Waddington, Harry Makepeace, Howell, Hitch, Parkin, Russell and myself - not to mention Jack Hearne.

The contrast between the teams was already apparent despite the early successes against the State sides. On 2 January, it was reported in Melbourne: 'Cricketers who have played in previous Test Matches do not think that Colonel Douglas's team ranges alongside its predecessors as a cricket combination.'

By the end of the second day England were 93/2: Hobbs: 53*; Hendren 29*. Rhodes had been bowled off his pads (20/1) and on 32 Makepeace was lbw. Hobbs played a sound, defensive game, taking an unusually long time, 110 minutes, over his fifty which came in the last over of the day. Patsy Hendren was solid if unaggressive, adapting his naturally ebullient, attacking spirit to the needs of the side. Having had the better part of two days in the field, it would not be surprising if they were a little tired. Some of the crowd may not have grasped this point and were less than appreciative of what they regarded as dilatory progress. England were by no means out of the wood. There were nevertheless some small grounds for hope after the Sunday's rest.

The elements then altered the picture. Heavy rain fell over the weekend. On its own that would have presented problems. When it was followed by a hot sun it produced a 'sticky wicket'. This is an expression which, since wickets are now usually covered when there is no play, is fast becoming forgotten in its true sense. The hot sun on the moisture produces a batting horror where the behaviour of the ball, after it has pitched, cannot be predicted. Selecting strokes becomes a lottery. Fender's description of what happened on this occasion after a late start at 12.20, needs no comment or embellishment:

The ball was jumping about from the first over bowled, some being simply short balls which bumped clean over the batsman's head or good length ones which went over the wicketkeeper's head, or nearly so, while a half volley was as difficult as anything to hit, because it got up absolutely perpendicularly. Slow bowling and medium bowling were possible to negotiate but, strange as it may seem to English cricketers, the faster the bowler, the more difficulty there was. Gregory, for instance, was hitting the batsman everywhere, from knuckle to neck - at least that was if they remained there to take it.

In these conditions, the stand between Hobbs and Hendren which added another 81 runs was remarkable, especially as they put on those runs in under an hour. Their partnership in all was worth 142 in 143 minutes. They rose above the nastiness of the conditions, never missing an opportunity to score. The contrast between their two styles was great and must have unsettled the bowlers. Hobbs's emphasis lay on driving, especially straight, while Hendren favoured the vigorous cross-bat shots, the pull and the cut. Hobbs' excellent judgement in calling his partner for quick runs was once again commented upon. When Hendren at last mistimed a ferocious drive off Gregory to go down for a stalwart 67, Hobbs was 95*.

Hobbs had been in for 2 hours and 58 minutes when he pulled Collins to the boundary thus making his score 103. By lunch he had moved on to 110*. Astonishingly it had been a chanceless innings until he reached this total when he was missed at mid-off off Gregory. Russell had been removed by that bowler but 190/4 at the interval was a far better position than can have been hoped for when the batsmen began their task. Woolley, however, soon went (201/5) and seven runs later Hobbs mis-hit a delivery from Gregory to Ryder at deep point. After 3 $\frac{1}{2}$ hours at the crease he was on his way back to the pavilion for 122, the highest score in the match, having played, in *Wisden's* words: 'from the English point of view, the finest innings of the tour.' In his own dry, laconic understatement, Hobbs considered it 'one of my best centuries, considering the state of the wicket'. In all he had hit nine 4s and added 69 runs on that third morning in ninety-six minutes in this, his third century in Test innings at Melbourne. In the opinion of 'Bertie' Oldfield, the Australian wicket-keeper, the batsman had coped admirably with a fiery pitch: 'Cleverly evading rising deliveries Hobbs stayed until he had passed the century. He was sedate, skilful and correct throughout his masterly innings.' It was a magnificent display, but his dismissal was the beginning of the end of the game.

By the close of play, England, having succumbed to Gregory (7/69; these were to be his best Test figures) in their first innings of 251 were effectively a beaten side on 76/5. Hobbs had scored 20 of these before being bowled by Kelleway. The ball in the opinion of the batsman was 'a masterpiece. It was a last moment in-swinger and if he could send me nine similar balls in succession I believe he would do the hat-trick on me three times over.'

Fine weather produced a good wicket on the fourth day, but it was too late for England. Matters were brought fairly quickly to a conclusion. Apart from Woolley (15* overnight) who made an excellent 50, the rest had no real answer to the bowlers. A total of 157 meant defeat by an innings and 91 runs.

It could reasonably be argued that England had not enjoyed the rub of the green. This was an opinion shared by their opponents: 'In an interview Mr Armstrong said that England had all the worst of the luck throughout the match. They had never had a fair chance.'

For the beginning of the third Test at Adelaide 18,000 people were present on a cool and cloudy day. Australia took advantage of a perfect pitch to score 313/7. Their chances of making an acceptable score looked slim when England enjoyed some early success. With 32 runs on the board, Bardsley was smartly stumped by Strudwick off Douglas. This says much about batsmen's attitudes in this period. It simply would not happen nowadays, at such a juncture in the match. The dismissal also says something about Strudwick's speed and craftsmanship, standing up to a bowler of Douglas' pace. Godfrey Evans taking Alec Bedser is a post-Second World War equivalent. 13 runs later Kelleway fell to a fine slip catch by Fender who would have cause to remember this in the second innings. With the total 55 Taylor was run out. Australia lunched uneasily on 85/3 (Collins 47*, Armstrong 8*).

When Armstrong (11) was fourth out at 96, the tourists were on top but 'Lucky' Collins - it must surely have been in this series that he acquired the nickname - remained. On 53 he was missed by Rhodes at deep square leg and seven runs after by Hendren at third man. Poor Harry Howell was the bowler on both occasions. Tea: 174/4 (Collins 96*). Fortunately Pellew was run out by a brilliant pick up and throw from Hobbs when Collins cut the ball into the covers and, in the view of one correspondent, 'failed to respond to his partners call'. Collins himself was finally dismissed for 162 out of 285/7.

Australia's total of 354 was by no means insurmountable but, if England were to save the series, their challenge had to be substantial. Conditions were on the second day in their favour; fine weather and a perfect wicket. A crowd of 32,000 would have been pleased to see a more balanced contest; but Gregory was now joined for the first time by McDonald and they were both hostile: 'Mr Gregory occasionally sent down a bumping ball and some of Mr McDonald's deliveries also rose, Hobbs receiving a nasty knock on the leg.' With Rhodes he survived until lunch: 13/0. 12 runs later a self-inflicted wound brought about the Yorkshireman's dismissal. Hobbs played a ball from Gregory to silly mid-on; the batsmen began to run; McDonald raced in and threw down the wicket. Fender is quite clear where the responsibility lay: 'Rhodes made three mistakes. First, he did not start as soon as usual; secondly, he did not run straight, but swerved across the wicket as the ball was thrown and left the fielder a clear shot at the wicket; and thirdly, he did not run hard.'

Hobbs (18) had made only 2 runs more than his opening partner when he himself departed at 49/2. He played 'a hard drive and Mr Mailey (the bowler) jumped up to hold a brilliant one-handed catch'. He had batted for forty-eight minutes. Makepeace's 60 became the cement of the early part of the innings which ended the day on 233/4: (Woolley 73*, Russell 21*).

The third day was a good one for England despite the early loss of Woolley (79) who never really recovered from a sharp blow in the spine. He had turned his back on the ball to avoid being struck in the face. Russell (70* in the lunch score of 321/5) moved to a splendid 135, batting in all for 4 hours and 10 minutes. Douglas, with 60, had given staunch support and must have been well pleased with a lead of 93 when the innings ended on 447.

This had been the one occasion in the series when the second half of England's order had made a major contribution. For once in a while, statistics do tell a full story. After the fifth wicket was lost, 197 runs were added. In the five Tests taken as a whole England batted ten times. They added, on each occasion, after the loss of the fifth wicket: 45, 103, 50, 87, 197, 127, 14, 114, 79, 198. By way of contrast, Australia, in their seven innings, put on, from the same point, 94, 251, 279, 178, 254, 236, 105. This is a comment on the relative durability of the respective sides' middle and lower-order batting. It says much too for the different strengths of the attacks - as of course do the opening partnerships. England's sequence makes for dismal reading: 0 and 5; 20 and 36; 25 and 20; 18 and 32; 54 and 1. Australia, on the other hand, managed 40 and 123; 116; 32 and 34; 117 and 71; 16 and 91. No startling by any means but far superior to their opponents' efforts.

There were 75 minutes left when Australia batted for a second time. In removing Bardsley cheaply Howell made an important breakthrough but then came what was seen at the time as a set-back and, in retrospect, seems the turning-point of the match. Fender, a very fine slip fielder, put down a difficult chance offered by Kelleway (whom he had caught superbly in the first innings) before he had scored. Howell was again the unlucky bowler. Australia were, however, only 71/3 at the close.

By the end of the fourth day they were 364/5. The slowness of Kelleway (19* overnight) may be seen by his score at lunch, 61* out of 158/3 and at tea, only 75*) when the total was 242/3. From the start of that morning, Armstrong had thundered to 104 in under three hours. Kelleway finished with 121. The runs for this century (his only one in Tests), invaluable to his side, were accumulated in 3 minutes over 5 hours. The partnership of 194 undermined England. Pellew (101) came in to flog a flagging attack. He was dropped by Woolley when on 53. Into the fifth day went Pellew, his assault culminating in 16 off an over from the hard-working Howell. In all this heavy scoring, it is easy to lose sight of Gregory's dashing 78*. Australia set England 490 to win.

In the hour left for play Hobbs with 50* bravely led the fight to 66/1 with his half-century completed off the last ball of the day. The wicket remained good on the sixth morning which was so hot that all the Australians wore sun-hats. Again Hobbs demonstrated his ability, which was both physical and mental, to come to terms with a huge task, the size of which overwhelmed others. Centuries were the order of the day. He responded with a score of the necessary proportion but his colleagues were unable to match his endeavours. What is extraordinary is his speed of scoring in a crisis. He completed his hundred after only 131 minutes' batting. A second-wicket stand of 105 with Makepeace (30) at more than a run-a-minute was the centre-piece. Hobbs was 88* when the Lancastrian was removed by McDonald. It was a great century, chanceless, fast, stylish, dominating. Finally on 123 (having been 112* at lunch) he played on to Gregory to make England 183/3.

Hobbs had now made a total of six centuries, more than any Englishman in Anglo-Australian contests. MacLaren and F S Jackson had each scored 5. Only Trumper (six centuries) was his equal in this respect. Fender praised the achievement: 'Hobbs had played a magnificent innings giving no chance and never once seeming at fault. He cut and drove with great power and while scoring easily and freely off all bowlers alike, he seemed to have a special liking for Mailey.'

The remainder of England's innings needs little detail. Hendren's 51 and Russell's 59 were useful but no more, in the context of this game. The total of 370 may have been a record for a fourth innings in a Test but the margin of defeat was still 119 runs. Although Mailey's 10 wickets in the match cost him 302 runs, his purchase of them was not uneconomic in view of the wealth of his batsmen, and some peccant English fielders, had given him.

The match finished on 20 January 1921. The next day, P F Warner, Hobbs' old England captain, wrote appreciatively:

Hobbs is a wonderful batsman and I have no hesitation in describing him as the finest in the world. His displays in Test matches have been greater than those of any other cricketer - greater even that those of Jackson and Trumper. He has both flair and a wonderful personality. His courage is marvellous and he almost invariably rises to a great occasion.

At Melbourne, the setting for the fourth Test, England at last won the toss. This was a mixed blessing. The wicket there was made from Merri Creek soil, unlike that of Sydney and Adelaide which were of Bulli earth. Melbourne was harder, glossier and more metallic. Up to lunchtime on the first day it was usually very lively. Against the ferocious pace of Gregory and McDonald in that 90-minute period England lost two wickets in making 89. As events transpired the most significant of the changes in the two sides was the replacement of the injured Oldfield by Carter, now forty-two, who had first kept wicket for his country against England in 1907-08. He was to capture six victims, including the first three of the match, none more important than Hobbs. This was a startling effort when the score was 57/1. The batsman edged a good length ball from McDonald which kicked:

The ball was travelling downwards between Gregory at first slip and Carter but more to Gregory than the keeper. The downward flight of the ball the players afterwards said would almost certainly not have carried to Gregory, whose catch it should have been.

Hobbs had batted for 50 minutes for his 27 runs and had only hit one 4. In addition to Carter there were several players taking part who were not in the first flush of their cricketing youth. Rhodes was 43; Armstrong 41; Hobbs, Douglas and Bardsley were all 38. One year older than this last trio was Harry Makepeace who now enjoyed his finest Test match hour with 117, a brave and tenacious effort which lasted 4 hours and 20 minutes. Apart from a stubborn 50 from Douglas, the rest of the batting was able to provide little towards the total of 284.

After Australia were given another excellent start of 117 by Collins (59) and Bardsley (56) England's bowlers clawed their way back into the game to pull the opposition down to 153/5. It was an open contest once more, but Armstrong now joined Gregory. In 83 minutes they added 100, taking their side to 267/5 at the end of the day. 35,000 people must have found no little satisfaction in this bright stand.

In the final Australian score of 389, Armstrong hit 123, thus passing 2000 runs in Tests following his countrymen Sid Gregory, Clem Hill and Trumper. England's backs were to the wall again. Hobbs' early departure for 13 (lbw to Mailey's first ball) signalled the beginning of a remarkable piece of bowling. Several English batsmen, notably Rhodes (73), Douglas (60) Fender (59) and Hendren (54) could all withstand the leg-spinner's wiles for a time but none was able to mount a really solid challenge which would have set Australia a large target. Arthur Mailey wheeled his way to cricketing immortality with figures of 47-8-121-9 which took his number of wickets in the match to 13. It was the first time nine wickets in an innings had been taken by one bowler in Tests between England and Australia. It is interesting to note that the bowler himself in his autobiography *10 for 66 and All That* wrote about his bowling to Hobbs with enthusiasm:

As a batsman pure and simple I found Jack Hobbs one of the most interesting I had bowled against. I knew that after my first over to him that he was going to be a great source of annoyance as well as interest - I was never quite sure whether he could pick the 'wrong 'un' but I knew, as when bowling against Trumper, that Jack's great talent would not allow him to be fooled too often. My experience against him taught me a good deal about the finer science of slow bowling.

Australia's general supremacy was underlined by their loss of only two wickets in their pursuit of 211 for victory.

In Hobbs' career, the most significant moment of the remainder of the tour came after the tea interval in the match with New South Wales. Running to field a ball in the deep he tore a muscle in his right thigh. This was to have both short-and long-term repercussions. *Wisden* is quite clear about its attitude to Hobbs' appearance in the fifth Test at Sydney. He 'ought not to have played, his injured thigh still causing him a great deal of trouble'. It is characteristic of the man that he did not cry off when he would have been completely justified in doing so. Instead, he responded to the appeal of his captain, Douglas, who really ought to have known better. The series had been well and truly lost. Hobbs was in no proper condition to play. He had nothing to prove. He could well have argued that as a conscientious professional he had done his duty. Whatever his personal inclination, however, his over-riding concern would have been his sense of responsibility to the side. Hearne, Hitch, Howell and Russell could not be considered, as a result of injury or illness. Hobbs did not join the list.

It was also typical of Hobbs, when asked to open in the first innings that he did not demur. No.1 was his rightful position and he again brought to the business his customary application and style. He was heartily welcomed to the wicket by the crowd, a fact which should be remembered in the light of what was to happen on the second day. Although hampered by the injury which he exacerbated, he made 40 good runs, albeit with a limp, before being lbw to Gregory. There were no short singles in the opening stand of 54, ironically England's best start in all the Tests. Only Woolley's attacking flair with 53 produced more than Hobbs in a disappointing total of 204.

Macartney had missed three matches through illness. He now came back with a vengeance. A chanceless 170 in just over 4 hours was both his first Test century (it was to be the highest of his seven international hundreds) and the mainstay of Australia's 392. A brilliant partnership lasting 2 hours and 13 minutes with Gregory (93) demolished England's attack although Fender returned 5/90. Among his wickets was that of Macartney, eventually caught by Hobbs at mid-on. There, and at mid-off, because his mobility was limited, was where he fielded in this match, not in the covers.

The most extraordinary incident occurred during this innings. Such a description is warranted for Hobbs was a popular cricketer with the Australian public as well as with his opponents. It started, perhaps, as a small ill-mannered insensitive outburst. In Hobbs' words: 'I had started lame and as I hobbled to field a ball the batsmen stole a second run. A few spectators, ignorant of my injury, jeered at me, but Charlie Kelleway apologised at the end of the over for his forgetfulness.' There the matter might have ended had a stringent comment not been cabled back to England. The amateurs Fender and Wilson (the team's vice-captain) were defraying their not inconsiderable expenses by reporting for the press. Their words were in turn edited and sent straight back to Australia where they were not well received. *The Times* reported the reaction on 28 February:

The day's cricket was spoiled by regrettable demonstrations which were made against Mr Wilson and Mr Fender. Great indignation has been aroused here by the telegrams which Mr Wilson and Mr Fender have sent to England alleging that the crowds jeered at Hobbs owing to his slow movements in the field due to his recent injury and both Mr Wilson and Mr Fender were subjected to strong barracking.

In his survey of Australian crowds, *'Ave A Go Yer Mug*, Dr Richard Cashman describes the scene:

When Wilson came to bat in the second innings there was 'vigorous and sustained hooting' and cries of 'liar', 'squealer' and 'Wilson the squib'. The crowd set out to make Wilson as uncomfortable as possible and succeeded in unnerving him; after he was dismissed cheaply he returned to the pavilion looking 'profoundly aggrieved'...Fender was also hooted, abused and counted out by the Sydney crowd but he did not allow them to get under his skin: he went on to score a brisk 40.

This was a spirited response. Only Douglas with 68 made more.

Not surprisingly Hobbs had not opened in the second innings, Woolley accompanying Rhodes. The move was not a success. Hobbs came to the wicket at 29/3. This was on the dismissal of Wilson. The atmosphere was highly charged. He did not know quite what to expect but he need not have worried. A friendly word from Monty Noble, the old Australian captain, calmed him. When Hobbs walked out, he received a tumultuous reception, the crowd cheering him all the way to the wicket. He was greatly moved, nevertheless managed to hit his second ball for 4 and was away. His thigh gave him less trouble and he was able to use his footwork in freely scoring 34 before being caught by Taylor at long-off off Mailey. England were then 75/4.

Their total of 280 left Australia with 93 to win. Their nine-wicket triumph victory completed an historic sequence of five wins in a row. How did Hobbs' reputation stand in 1921 at the end of such a wretched time for England's cricketers? The then brand new magazine *The Cricketer*, edited by Pelham Warner was unequivocal:

John Berry Hobbs, by general consent the best batsman in the world today....has perfected his game and he now shines forth as a star of the first magnitude, in the same constellation as Grace or Ranji and Trumper. He possesses a keen eye and his free natural style has the mark of inborn genius...He has a peculiar shrug of the shoulders when fielding or batting but he is neat and crisp in all his movements and gives the impression of thoroughly enjoying every ball of a match...he deserves his popularity, for in spite of his many successes, he is not in the least spoilt.

1921, however, was not a season which afforded Hobbs many happy memories. After Surrey's usual trial match in which he had the experience of being dismissed by a lob bowler, Maloney, Hobbs travelled to Attleborough where he was to play for Mr L Robinson's XI against the Australians who had sailed back to England with the vanquished English team in order to make their own tour.

Gregory and McDonald, who were to be the scourges of the English summer with 270 wickets between them, held no terrors for Hobbs, in partnership with Jupp. On 5 May, after the early departure of Knight, he began to establish an ascendancy with a scintillating display, when disaster struck. He described how he was on 85 and they had taken the score to 125, although, as he put it: 'the fast bowling knocked us about a good deal.'

Then came a calamity. I was making a sharp run when the muscle in my thigh gave out again. It was the same muscle that I had injured in Australia and had never given a chance to heal. Mr Jupp declared that, as he passed between the wickets, he heard it snap.

Hobbs performance had been impressive and was reported as such in *The Times*:

It was a great misfortune that Hobbs had to retire when playing at his best - and one knows what that is...Of his innings one can only say that it was the innings of a great master. The wicket was none too easy but this was a difficulty that a great batsman soon overcame. His attacking of the bowling was his defence and the effect on his fellow-batsmen meant much.

Hobbs did not reappear on the first-class scene until the third week in June against Oxford University. Batting then at no.5, he made 2 and then 49 before running himself out. The next fixture, with Yorkshire at Leeds, promised to be a sterner contest. When he was dismissed for 1 he must have been bitterly disappointed. He knew England had need of him as they had already been defeated heavily in both the first and second Tests. He made excellent amends in the second innings with some glorious stroke-play.

With Sandham (22) he put on 65 in 45 minutes before racing on to score 101* out of the first 144 made. He carried his bat for 172* (with twenty 4s) in Surrey's 294.

This was the summer in which England's selectors cast so desperately about them that they called no fewer than thirty players to their colours. Their relief at Hobbs' return, and in such a manner, must have been great. They immediately enlisted him for the third Test at Leeds.

Hobbs' thigh may have mended but he was not a well man. In no little pain he managed to take the field on Saturday 2 July but after tea Durston took his place. Next day, an urgent operation to remove Hobbs' appendix was performed. He was greatly missed. On the last day of the Test, in which he could not bat in either innings and in which England suffered an eighth consecutive defeat, the press reported:

The influence of Hobbs as a batsman on English cricket cannot easily be realised. He can, at his best, make all the Australian bowling appear merely ordinary and once that impression is formed, those that follow him can take the bowling at a normal valuation.

Unfortunately he could give no further example in 1921, as he played no more cricket that summer.

8 Resurgence, 1922-25

1922 was a fine season for Hobbs. Averaging 62 he finished second to Hendren in the first-class averages. He scored 2552 runs and ten centuries. In only two of his previous eighteen season had he managed more. This year Surrey finished third in the Championship. *Wisden's* comment is revealing:

Hobbs inspired the whole side. As regards technical skill he was as great as ever but his illness in 1921 had left him rather weak, and he seldom played a long innings without showing distinct signs of fatigue. Several times he seemed anxious to get out as soon as he had passed the hundred.

If this seems to read oddly, as seven of his centuries that year were 126 runs or more, Hobbs himself agreed: 'My operation had a certain affect on me. After reaching about 70 I began to feel fagged, and I do not believe that I have ever quite got over it.'

He was naturally invited to tour South Africa with the MCC during the following winter but declined to go for business as well as health and family reasons.

1923, on the other hand, was a disappointing year in several ways. 2087 runs was not a poor total but an average of 37 put him seventeenth in the national figures. The county slipped one place, to a Championship position of fourth. For Hobbs, though, it was a memorable summer for one particular reason: his hundredth hundred. It came in an extraordinary match with Somerset at Taunton, and it was his first such score against that county.

Rain limited the first day's play to three overs. On the second twenty-one wickets fell. Surrey 91 (Hobbs 0) and 23/1 (Hobbs 19*); Somerset 140. On Tuesday 8 May Ducat and Sandham were both run out while batting with Hobbs and Fender nearly suffered the same fate. Nervous tension must have been part of the cause: and Surrey were struggling at 45/4. Hobbs' first 50 took two hours; his second just over half that time. When Fender declared Hobbs (116*) had batted 3 $\frac{1}{2}$ hours, hitting three 6s and eleven 4s. Only at 112 had he given a chance. Surrey won a remarkable victory by 10 runs although this was only made possible when play was extended beyond 6.30pm as both sides had a real chance of success.

In 1924, with his 203* against Nottinghamshire at Trent Bridge, Hobbs passed the number of centuries made by his old mentor, Tom Hayward, who had compiled 104 hundreds. It was also Hobbs' 74th for his county. Only W G Grace with 126 centuries now lay ahead of him. At forty-two Hobbs remained trim and fit, but was he fit enough to pass that milestone?

At the beginning of the Test series of 1924 against South Africa his record as was follows:

	Innings	Not Out	Highest Score	Runs	Average
v Australia	37	3	187	1825	53
v South Africa	22	3	187	1145	60

In many people's minds it was accepted that *The Cricketer* put it well:

Since Test matches were inaugurated England has possessed many good men to open the innings but never a better than Hobbs. In such games, his success has been commensurate with his skill; in other words outstanding.

The wicket had largely recovered from the rain that had fallen on the two days prior to the first Test at Birmingham. When South Africa won the toss, however, there were still several damp spots and Herbie Taylor, no doubt hoping his bowlers would be able to exploit these, put England in. As 398/7 was reached on the first day, his decision seems to have been a blunder, but P F Warner agreed with the South African captain. The wicket turned out to be slow and easy throughout the day. The South African bowling was not strong, however, and their fielding was undistinguished. The only problem for the batsmen, and this a minor one, was that the slow outfield required more runs to be actually run rather than hit to the boundary.

This was the occasion of Herbert Sutcliffe's Test debut and he could not have had a better partner than Jack Hobbs to help him establish himself at the highest level; even so only 8 runs were on the board when Hobbs tapped the ball gently past the bowler Parker; Sutcliffe went for the run. Commaille raced in at mid-on with Sutcliffe yards out of his ground. The fielder hurled in from a few yards away. He missed.

After that near-disaster the new Test pair (they had first opened together in representative cricket in 1922) swiftly established an understanding. R E S Wyatt, watching a Test for the first time, was much impressed. He wrote in *Three Straight Sticks*:

I thought their partnership showed an almost miraculous understanding and co-ordination; they judged their runs excellently.

Looking back on that game, I feel it is a pity that today the art of playing the ball for a short single has been nearly lost. I never saw a pair better at it than Hobbs and Sutcliffe. They would run almost as they hit the ball after playing it deliberately for a single. This made the field move in close to try and stop their singles, whereupon it became easier for them to crack the ball to the boundary.

It was a perfect partnership. There can have been no greater pair of opening batsmen in the history of cricket than these two.

To encapsulate the character, style and approach to cricket of Herbert Sutcliffe, 'composed' and 'imperturbable' are the words which immediately spring to mind. Any bowler hoping to make him fidget, fuss or flap eventually became frustrated or flustered by his own inability to make an impression. Sutcliffe was never a hot and bothered batsman. He drove his opponents to distraction by his refusal to be routed by speed, spin or bad conditions. Proud, dignified and tough, he sold his wicket as dearly as any English batsman in the history of the game. Always immaculately turned out he mastered the skills as he did the opposition. There was, at times, a productive inevitability about his presence at the crease where he fought bravely and well for the cause. That he was a man for the big occasion is reflected in his Test average of 60 being nine runs higher than that of his career as a whole during which he made 50,138 runs. Interestingly, in Ashes' matches he averaged 66. Of those who played frequently in these contests only Bradman, average 89, has a more prolific record.

On this occasion Hobbs and Sutcliffe put on 122 by lunch before they were split up when Sutcliffe (64) was yorked by the persevering Parker. Parker was a twenty-five year old Bradford League professional in only his second first-class game who had been called in to strengthen his country's bowling. Sutcliffe remembered the experience in *For England and Yorkshire*.

It was a source of strength for me to see Hobbs take his stance at the wicket. When I walked out with him I gained confidence and that confidence was increased by almost everything he did...The first Test proved to me the vast gulf between county cricket and Test cricket. Hobbs I noted was as easy and graceful as ever in everything he did but there was a grimness behind it all that told me more than anything else could do, of the seriousness of the business immediately in front of us.

Hobbs' departure was not long delayed. He went right across in front of his wickets, attempted to force a good length ball wide of mid-on and was lbw to the medium-pacer Blanckenberg for 76. Woolley batted brilliantly for 64, Hendren solidly for 74 but both went to Parker, the latter being caught by Nourse at fine leg. It was a well struck blow and the fielder had to retire with a split finger. Parker took five of the first six wickets to fall but had to go off eventually 'exhausted by his hard work and unaccustomed heat'. Things were not going South Africa's way.

Nor did they on the second day. When England finished on 438, the visitors responded with 30. All out. Arthur Gilligan, the new England captain (6.3-4-7-6) and Maurice Tate on his debut (6-1-12-4) destroyed them in 75 balls in 48 minutes. The Sussex pace men did the job not with bouncers but with controlled break-backs and a sharp nip off the pitch. In at 11.50, South Africa was following-on at 12.55.

Nothing was more admirable on their tour than the way the South Africans fought back in the second innings. That they were not a successful side is shown by the bleak statistics of the tour: played 38; won 8; lost 9; drawn 21. But in this match they had redeemed themselves by the time stumps were drawn on the second day. Susskind, who had perished to Tate's first ball in Test cricket now made a solid 51, following Commaille's valuable stonewalling 29. Catterall (52*) after a first innings' duck as an opener, batted at no.5 with great élan. In partnership with Blanckenberg (56*) he took his side swiftly from 161/4 to 274/4, to the close 75 minutes later.

On the final morning, Blanckenberg went at once to be followed shortly afterwards by Deane who, handicapped by a limp, injudiciously attempted a fourth run off a drive. Kilner, a debutant, flicked the ball back to Hobbs who threw magnificently to the wicket-keeper, George Wood, another Englishman in his first Test, and the batsman was out by yards. Catterall stormed on lifting Woolley on to the top of the pavilion to bring up the 300. On 92 he struck Tate for three fours in a row, the second of which brought him a well-deserved century.

The final score of 390 left England victors by the margin of an innings and 18 runs. Ominously, however, five slip catches had been put down but this was to a certain extent concealed by the splendour of Gilligan (11 wickets in the match) and Tate (8 wickets).

At Lord's on the first day of the second Test all was not decorous, despite the fine weather. There was a perfect wicket and determined South African resistance after an early collapse had reduced them 17/3. Gilligan came under criticism from some of the crowd: 'A few ignorant and egoistic members of it desired to discharge Mr Gilligan's functions from their seats in the ring but they soon discovered that the sense of the meeting was against them.' So ran one report. *The Cricketer* put the matter into perspective: 'It was, however, but a very small but rather noisy section who showed such bad taste'.

It was not as if Gilligan had not made a more than useful start to the proceedings. He had personally removed both openers by the time the score was 5. He was very accurate and very fast. Catterall, however, put down when on 5 by Wood and again on 31 by Woolley, batted attractively to equal his first Test 120. Sixth out at 212 he was the mainstay of his side's 273 as only Susskind (64) made more than 33. That 33 was made by Aubrey Faulkner, summoned out of retirement at the age of forty-two and after a two-year's absence from first-class cricket.

Unusually, Hobbs' fielding received unfavourable comment. Although he was not a man to offer excuses, he was fielding on an old wicket which meant that the ball deviated more than normal. Such irritations did not distract him or Sutcliffe when they came out to bat. They productively negotiated the last fifteen minutes to make the close of play score 28/0.

Twenty-four hours later, England had declared. 531/2 had been acquired in flawless style. It was batting precisely and gracefully executed. By lunch the total was 228/0. This was after 2 $^1/_2$ hours' batting. Hobbs delighted in the event: 'We both felt in tip-top mood; we took all the risks in our stride yet we never seemed to be in danger. How thoroughly we enjoyed our run-stealing that dove-grey midsummer morning.' There was the occasional blemish. Sutcliffe, on 31, was put down at long-leg by Deane off Blackenberg. It was the only chance he offered. With the score 109, Hobbs was nearly stumped off Faulkner but he made no other mistake. He and Sutcliffe worked superbly in tandem. Practically every single takeable was taken. As one report had it:

This implies much more than a perfect understanding between partners. It means that each of them is making his defensive strokes so certainly that he can start to run almost before he has struck the ball and that the man at the other end feels his intention in time to make calling unnecessary. Hobbs, of course, has reduced the stealing of short runs to a system and by now has acquired the capacity of taking all the drive out of his bat whenever it suits him to do so.

Hobbs and Sutcliffe played forward to stop the ball in defiance of the current maxim of 'when in doubt play back'. They did not, however, lose their hooking or their cutting. Sutcliffe was first to 50 but Hobbs had his hundred by one o'clock (he actually went from 12 to 114 in the morning session) and his partner joined him before the interval. Their stand reached 268, a total they were to exceed only once in their long association. Sutcliffe was the first to go. He appeared to play rather lazily at a simple ball from Parker and turned it into his stumps. The partnership was a Test record in England.

The South Africans were then put to the sword by Hobbs and Woolley who together dashed along for 90 minutes, added 142. Hobbs finally departed with the score 410 when he lofted a ball from Parker into the covers where Taylor thankfully took the easy catch. Hobbs had hit his highest Test score, 211, at this point, shortly after four o'clock and had batted only 4 hours and 40 minutes. It was a chanceless display: fifteen 4s, six 3s, twenty-four 2s and eighty-five singles. As *The Cricketer* said: 'There has never been a better judge of a single than the great Surrey and England batsman which goes to prove what an exceptionally quick brain he has.'

Hobbs was not a record-grubber by nature but towards the end of his career he did aspire to the peak of 200 centuries. Of his Birmingham achievement he wrote about equalling and not passing the Australian W L Murdoch's record for a Test in England set at The Oval in 1884: 'Had I been aware of my nearness to that record, I might have made a special effort for the required single but players do not ponder over these figures when they are at the wicket.'

Woolley (134*) accompanied by Hendren (50*) rubbed further salt into the South African's wounds with an additional 121 in under an hour. Gilligan then declared to give South Africa some uncomfortable moments before the close at 19/0.

They fought hard down the last day but the English bowlers gradually worked their way through the order. Dick Tyldesley, on his debut, having picked up 3/53 in the first innings, did fractionally better this time with his leg-spinners: 3/50. These were the important wickets of Commaille (37), Susskind (53) and Catterall (45) without whom the total of 240, reached shortly after tea, would have been a sorry one. Hobbs' contributions were the taking of a straightforward catch at cover to dispose of Blanckenberg off the bowling of Fender and the running out of Faulkner from the same position. The speed with which Hobbs ran to cut off of a hard hit to his left and return the ball to the wicket raised much applause. The victory was, again, by an innings and 18 runs.

The weather was so glorious at Leeds on the first day of the third Test that the crowd was treated to an unusual spectacle: Sutcliffe in a cap. Did this result in some momentary confusion? Opening with Hobbs, after England had won the toss, Sutcliffe had found himself involved in another muddle. Hobbs hit the last ball of the first over into the covers. Hobbs ran. Sutcliffe ran. Deane made a brilliant stop. Both batsmen were stranded in the middle of the wicket. The fielder (shades of Commaille in the first Test) may have seen a chance of glory. Swept on by the excitement of the opportunity he whipped the ball at the wicket instead of taking his time. Result? He missed. The ball raced through to the boundary. Five runs to Hobbs.

72 came in an hour: ' no single stroke can be recalled that was ill-conceived or came near to being ill-executed.' *(The Times)*. Hobbs (31) flung his bat at yet another leg-side delivery from Nourse who frequently had only one fielder on the off side and directed his attack accordingly. Hobbs' misfortune was that, although he struck the ball firmly, he hit it straight at Pegler fielding at fine-leg about thirty yards away.

Hearne and Woolley contributed little and Sutcliffe (83) was beautifully caught at short third man by Nupen to whom he slashed a long-hop from Blanckenberg. Hendren, enjoying a life at 25 and another at 37, made the most of his escapes and attacked vigorously for 132. He was especially skilful in moving swiftly to leg in order to be able to cut leg-breaks off his wicket. With Tate, Gilligan and Tyldesley each making useful scores of nearly 30, South Africa had only half-an-hour's batting in pursuit of 396.

It was long enough for two good wickets to be lost. Deane mishooked Tate to give the bowler a caught-and-bowled dismissal. Commaille had a rush of blood to his head, having driven the ball straight to Hobbs. He called. He ran. Ward declined. Commaille departed. Close of play: 15/2. Early on the second day, on a good wicket, they were 34/5. Taylor (59*), who did his side much service, erred in calling Nourse for a short run on the off-side. Nourse compounded the error in not backing up. The result was reported thus: 'Hobbs came to meet the ball with remarkable speed of thought and foot and threw down the wicket before Nourse could make good his ground.' Their total was 132. Tate took 6/42 in conditions which gave him no help at all.

Resistance, as in the first Test, was stronger when the South Africans followed-on. Almost everyone contributed. Taylor (56) played another captain's innings and Catterrall equalled his leader's score. They took their side into the third day but the total of 323 left England needing only 60.

Hobbs (7) shaped to hook Blanckenberg, mistimed the stroke and pulled the ball on to his wicket: England 17/1. Sutcliffe and Hearne completed the business to bring the their team to a nine-wicket victory.

England's premier batsman was not selected to play in the Fourth Test at Manchester, which, as it transpired, was rained off after two-and-three quarter hours' play on the first day. Hobbs had declined to go to Australia in the following winter because he did not want to leave his family or his business. He might not have wanted to be seen 'picking and choosing' after he had turned down the invitation to go to South Africa in 1922-23. Three reports in *The Times* explain the sequence of events. On 21 July, the Cricket Correspondent wrote:

I am very sorry Hobbs is not going to Australia, but as regards his own interests I think he is wise to stay at home. At 41 years of age he may well feel apprehensive of playing through a winter season on the top of his labours in England and beyond that he has no liking for long sea voyages...he may still be our best batsman when the Australians come here in 1926.

Fair enough. All well and good. Then came the bombshell two days later:

It is stated that Hobbs and Hearne have been left out of the team (for the fourth Test) for the reason that the former has definitely decided not to got to Australia and there is considerable doubt about Hearne.

The selectors had made the cold but logical decision that, with the series decided, it was best to play those likely to be travelling. Hobbs felt hurt: 'This was a bit hard on me, I thought, seeing that I had helped to win the rubber against South Africa.'

On 2 August there was news of a further development:

In reply to an inquiry yesterday as to whether he would be one of the team to be taken out to South Africa during the forthcoming winter by Mr S B Joel, Hobbs said that he had been approached but had not had sufficient time to consider the matter fully. He said that, if he want, he would take his wife with him and that he would play in all the matches. The sea voyage was much shorter and the tour less arduous than in Australia.

Hobbs had been asked by Lord Tennyson, captain of Joel's team, if he would go to South Africa. He was also invited to take his wife, her expenses being met not by the cricketer but by the sponsor. Lord Harris heard of the business and negotiated with Hobbs. The batsman's principles were, in a sense, under examination. In truth, he had nothing to reproach himself for. Throughout his career there was no question laid against his integrity and his account in *My Life Story* is worth repeating in some detail because of the light it sheds on the man as well on the situation. Lord Harris asked if the news were correct:

Yes, the privilege of going with my wife having been granted, I find it possible to go to South Africa, and that is why I cannot accept the invitation for Australia. The question was then put to me whether I would change over to the Australian team if my wife was permitted to go...

A new difficulty now arose. I said I could not go if it involved turning somebody out of the team. Lord Harris suggested that one of the players could be transferred to the team for South Africa. This didn't seem to me fair...Ultimately it was decided I should go to Australia as an extra member of the England team and that my wife should go.

All Mrs Hobbs' expenses were paid by her husband. He received no extra financial inducement to travel. *The Cricketer*, having been greatly disappointed by Hobbs' earlier decision, commented in its issue of 16 August:

The announcement that J B Hobbs has definitely decided to go to Australia has been heartily welcomed by every cricket enthusiast in England. No national side could be complete without the famous Surrey batsman and the moral effect of his presence will be tremendous. Hobbs is still the greatest batsman in the world, as well as one of the finest of cover points.

The story shows the importance of Hobbs the cricketer, the dignity and independent spirit of Hobbs the man, and the wisdom of the authorities in making a concession to a valuable and valued servant of the game.

He returned to England's team for the final Test at The Oval and immediately made an impact when South Africa, having won the toss, decided to bat. Early on, Commaille cut the ball to Woolley at backward point. The Kent player misfielded. Hobbs, swiftly backing up from cover point, picked up neatly and returned the ball to the bowler, Tate. The other opener, G Hearne, was halfway down the wicket: South Africa 7/1. At the same score Tate bowled Commaille.

It says much for the spirit of the visitors that after all their tribulations on the tour, they did not collapse; rather the reverse. Susskind (65) proved his durability once more while Catterall batted as attractively as he had done throughout the summer to reach a fine 95. Everyone made a few or more than a few to take the South Africans to 342.

Rain fell quite heavily over the weekend and on the second day the wicket was difficult, especially in the pre-lunch period. Sutcliffe went quickly but the stand of 67 between Hobbs (30) and Hearne (35) was of more value than the number of runs scored would suggest. Hobbs was hit on the body by more than one bowler. He batted for an hour and a quarter before cutting at a ball from Pegler which rose sharply. The catch was well taken by the wicket-keeper, Ward. Hendren's 142 was the backbone of England's 421/7 but Woolley (51), Tate (50) and Sandham (46) all made their mark. This total was reached on the third day (the over-night score having been 332/6) when only fifty minutes' play was possible before rain set in.

Seven of the 1920-21 side returned to Australia in 1924-25, namely Douglas, Hearne, Hendren, Hobbs, Howell, Strudwick, Woolley. The other ten were A E R Gilligan (captain); two other amateurs, both from Kent J F Bryan and A P F Chapman; and the professionals A P Freeman (Kent), R Kilner (Yorkshire); A Sandham (Surrey); H Sutcliffe (Yorkshire); M W Tate (Sussex); R K Tyldesley (Lancashire); and W W Whysall (Nottinghamshire).

There was tremendous interest shown by the Australian public who turned up in record number to watch the Tests. The MCC had a dozen matches before the first Test and lost only once, to Victoria, when neither Sutcliffe nor Tate was playing and Hearne, with an injured knee, could not bat in the second innings.

At Sydney, where the first Test was played, Australia won the toss and first use of a perfect wicket. They moved confidently by six o'clock to 282/3. A crowd of 33,000 enjoyed the escapes of their batsmen. Bardsley on 13 (missed by Hendren off Tate) only made 21 but Hendren's second miss off Tate, Collins (then on 42) was to prove much more expensive. A lunch score of 72/1 had increased by exactly 100 runs when tea was taken: Collins 79* and Ponsford 64*. The latter, on 85, was put down by Sutcliffe off Woolley before becoming only the third Australian to score a hundred in the first innings of his first Test, following Charlie Bannerman and Harry Graham. Even Hobbs bowled a couple of overs when Australia passed 200 with the second-wicket pair still ensconced. Ponsford made 110 (236/2) and Collins an invaluable 114 during which he protected his younger partner most successfully. He departed at 275/3.

Hearne (arguably the most injury-prone cricketer to play for England before Chris Old) hurt his finger when stopping a hard drive on the second day. Tate, who had bowled magnificently with no luck at all on the opening day, came into his own despite the discomfort of a big-toe nail which had been driven back into his foot by the whole-hearted commitment of his thumping delivery stride. Australia, having lunched at 364/4, were pulled back to 388/9. That this happened was mainly due to Tate who had a spell

J.B. Hobbs.

WILLS'S CIGARETTES.

J. B. HOBBS (SURREY).

SPRING

AUTUMN

THE GREAT SURREY PARTNERSHIPS

WILLS'S CIGARETTES.

T. HAYWARD (SURREY).

WILLS'S CIGARETTES

A. SANDHAM.

Hobbs and
Hayward

Hobbs and
Sandham

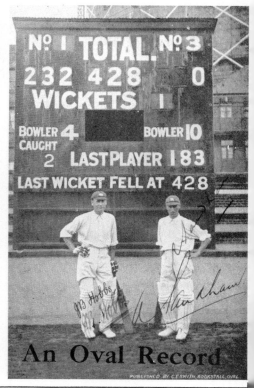

An Oval Record

PUBLISHED BY C.E.SMITH, BOOKSTALL, OVAL

THE GREAT TEST PARTNERSHIPS

Hobbs and
Rhodes

Hobbs and
Sutcliffe

THE TEAM THAT BROUGHT BACK
THE ASHES 1911-12

Back row (left to right): H Strudwick, S P Kinneir,
E J Smith, F E Woolley, J Iremonger, C P Mead,
J W Hearne, J W Hitch, J Vine

The battle against the odds: Hobbs and Sutcliffe chasing
600 at Melbourne 1924-25. Hobbs is facing

Hobbs equalling Grace's record: the 100th run of the
126th century at Taunton in 1925

The Oval team that won back The Ashes 1926

Back row (left to right): H Larwood, M W Tate,
G T S Stevens, G Geary, H Sutcliffe, E H Hendren

Front row: H Strudwick, J B Hobbs, A P F Chapman,
W Rhodes, F E Woolley

LORD'S 1926

Hobbs scoring the single which took him to his most
controversial Test century

MELBOURNE 1929

Hobbs steals a short single to bring up his last Test
century

A sharp chance well taken: Hobbs jumps to catch Fairfax (14), off Robins at Nottingham in 1930

The end of it all: Hobbs (9) bowled by Fairfax at The Oval in 1930.

of four wickets for 9 runs. From England's point of view there then came an infuriating last-wicket stand of 62 between Oldfield and Mailey which took Australia to 450. Tate's figures were 55-11-130-6.

Hobbs (42*) and Sutcliffe (28*) put on 72 in the last hour to give England some confidence for the third day when the weather was fine and the wicket good. They continued comfortably with Hobbs monopolising the strike. As one reporter saw it: 'The Surrey man appeared to concentrate upon the last ball of an over in making a scoring stroke.' Hobbs reached his 50 out of 89 when he cut Gregory to the boundary. It had taken him 79 minutes. Nothing disturbed the patience of Sutcliffe who arrived at his half-century after two hours. At lunch they were still together, having put on 151: Hobbs 93*, Sutcliffe 55*. After the interval all players appeared in black arm-bands as a sign of mourning for the Australian captain's sister and Bardsley led the side instead of Collins.

On 157 Sutcliffe (59) was caught at point. Hobbs was 95* at this point and soon, with a late cut for a single off Gregory, he reached 100. This was after 2 hours and fifty-one minutes. It was his seventh century in Tests between England and Australia and, therefore, beat Trumper's record of six. Monty Noble, the former Australian captain, wrote generously of this innings in his book of the tour, *Gilligan's Men*:

He was perhaps a little more cautious than usual, a little more scientific but his grace of style, his inimitable footwork, his beautiful playing, his clever hook strokes, his leg glancing and his stealing of singles by gently putting the ball to the off were all as fascinating as ever.

Hearne had already become Mailey's fiftieth Test wicket: 171/2. Woolley, troubled by an injured knee, did not linger: 172/3. The advantage gained by the fine opening stand was really lost, however, on 202. This was when Hobbs, who had uncharacteristically scratched about after passing the century, succumbed to Gregory's fourth delivery with the new ball. He was caught by Kelleway in the slips. He had batted for 3 hours and 39 minutes. The comments of one of his opponents, Jack Ryder, who was afterwards to captain his country, are worth recalling:

Hobbs played like the master he is; he never gave a chance. Most of his runs came from well placed singles...It is worthy of note that Gregory never hit him with one of his fliers. The same cannot be said of the others.

The rest of England's batting faded miserably with the notable exception of Hendren whose 74* did much to secure the eventual total of 298.

Australia, 61/1 overnight, moved to 258/5 on the fourth day which was cut short by a violent dust storm. A J Richardson (98), opening instead of Collins who was emotionally drained, was unlucky to miss a century. The captain appeared when the second wicket fell at 115 and must have been moved by the waves of sympathetic cheering that swept through the ground as the spectators remembered his bereavement. Undistracted by this, he remained not out at the end of the day. Woolley's injured knee prevented him from bowling but Tate continued valiantly.

When the sixth wicket was captured at 260, England must have felt they still had a chance. Taylor then entered the arena, a boil behind his knee having stopped him from batting at number four as in the first innings. On a rain-interrupted morning he scored very slowly, indeed until he was joined by the last man, Mailey, he had amassed 27 in 87 minutes. The score was then 325/9. With a bang and a flourish they put up a tenth-wicket record stand of 127 in only 79 minutes. The innings of Taylor was in two distinct phases: the first 50 in 2 hours; the second in 32 minutes. Mailey's 46* was his highest Test score - as was Taylor's 108. Tate's courage and skill brought him 5/98. Hobbs rarely commented on an umpire's decision but he felt most strongly that Taylor had enjoyed a slice of singularly good fortune:

When Mailey came in, an appeal was made against the other batsman, Taylor, for a catch at the wicket. It was such an obvious catch that we all began to walk away. But we had a surprise for the umpire said 'Not out'. Taylor knew well enough that the decision was a wrong one and he decided to give us a chance by slashing out. But everything came off for that brilliant slogger and he passed his hundred.

The umpire's error clearly rankled, years afterwards; but it is difficult to believe that Taylor was so consumed by guilt as to give England 'a chance'. Had he been so conscience-stricken, then he could have knocked his wickets down. The visitors were left to pursue 605 for victory.

Hobbs (13* overnight) and Sutcliffe (27*) began the sixth day, having struggled the previous evening for nearly an hour. They became the first opening pair to put on a hundred in each innings of a Test. Hobbs' 50 was followed two balls later by Sutcliffe's. They had batted for 105 minutes. The stand had collected 110 runs when Mailey deceived Hobbs with a fine demonstration of the slow bowler's art. 'Mailey tossed one high and pulled it back', Noble wrote. 'Hobbs jumped in to drive and finding it shorter than he anticipated, 'propped' in an endeavour to play it slowly along the ground. Not being quite over the ball he cocked it up and gave an easy chance to Hendry to silly point.' Hearne stayed but briefly: 127/2. Chapman (44) batted with great attacking flair, twice hitting Mailey down the ground and over the sight-screen for six before departing at 195. Hendren went quickly and, when rain fell at about 3.25pm, Sutcliffe, on 99, had to endure an unscheduled interval of some forty minutes. On the resumption he duly completed a hundred in his first Test against Australia. By the time he was out (263/5) he had batted 4 hours and 7 minutes for 115. A top-edged pull off Mailey flew over the wicket-keeper; Gregory, running round from slip had no problem with the catch. England slumped to 267/8 and all seemed over. By this time, however, Woolley was on 44, and suffering less trouble

92

from his knee. Accompanied by his Kent colleague 'Tich' Freeman, he took the game into the seventh day, a new record for a Test. Before they did so there was a curious breaking of the regulations. The sixth day's play was extended by fifteen minutes, obviously with the agreement of both captains, the intention being to finish the match that evening. Someone clearly forgot to tell the batsmen. The overnight 362/8 was lifted to 404 before Woolley, having square-cut Mailey to bring up only his second hundred against Australia, was caught in the slips for 123. He had batted only 146 minutes. The ninth wicket partnership of 128 was a record for England in Australia; but the total of 411 meant defeat by 193 runs. 189 of those came from Australia's two last-wicket stands. There was, nevertheless, a sense that England might be on the way back because of their fighting determination, best exemplified by the openers. Of the side's 709 aggregate, Hobbs and Sutcliffe between them scored 346. In the second Test they were to do even better.

At Melbourne on the opening day, nearly 50,000 (a Test record, as were the takings of over £5,300) saw Australia recover well from 47/3 to 300/4. The home team won the toss to take first innings on a good, hard wicket. It was a little lively initially but progressively became easier. With the score 47/1, Bardsley drove Gilligan. A J Richardson ran. Bardsley did not. A good return from Hobbs ('one of the best throws-in I ever saw' - Noble) to Gilligan did all that was necessary. In came Ponsford. Taylor joined him three minutes later when no additional run had been made. England were momentarily on top. The batsmen fought back. They took their side to lunch (60/3) and then to tea (193/3). On 208 Ponsford hit the ball hard to Hobbs in the covers. He called. He ran. Taylor (72) had no chance. Hobbs threw down his wicket. 'It was a piece of exquisite fielding' - Noble again.

Tate struck back next morning, bowling Ponsford (128) with his second ball. No other batsman had hitherto scored a century in each of his first two Tests. The bowlers had nothing to help them in either the intense heat or the quality of the wicket. One report stated: 'The surface was as hard as vulcanite and the bowlers were unable to get any turn.' Vic Richardson was then well supported by Kelleway (32) whose encouragement of the younger man in his second Test was of more value than the runs he himself scored. On 67, Richardson was missed off Tyldesley by Douglas who no doubt rued the moment, especially when the batsman took 21 off one of his later overs. At lunch Australia were 377/5. Richardson was run out for 138. Tea: 507/8. There was little respite for the fielding side. Hartkopf in his first such game made 88 and, yet again, there was little sign of weakness in the Australian tail. 600 was reached by the close. It was the largest total that had ever been made in a Test up to that time.

The challenge that faced Hobbs and Sutcliffe as they went out to bat on the third day was immense. The wicket was excellent but the bowlers were good and the fielding of the highest calibre. There were no easy runs. Their unique achievement was to bat through the whole day. At the close England 283/0 (Hobbs 154*, Sutcliffe 123*) were very much in the game. It was their third 100 partnership in a row. A crowd of 48,000 was engrossed throughout the day. Their batting was never stodgy. Their defence was sound but they wasted no chance to score. The fifty partnership came in 68 minutes and Hobbs' touch was so sure that he took three 4s in a row off Mailey. Lunch, 70/0: Hobbs 39*, Sutcliffe 28*. How did the character and attitude of the two men respond to the demands of the situation? Hobbs we know about, but his assessment of his partner is interesting:

Herbert is a great Test match player - one of the greatest that we have ever had. He has the temperament for a big occasion, if ever anyone had. We gave each other confidence; I had every trust in him for his successes far outnumbered his failures. He was a good judge of the game, and many a time we had a word together as to the line to adopt against particular bowlers...if he was beaten, he would go on playing his natural game, quite unruffled, just as if nothing untoward had happened. In that respect he was the counterpart of Wilfred Rhodes. Many players, when a bowler has been bowling his deadliest and they have been beaten a few times, are tempted to give it up, that was never the case with Wilfred or Herbert.

Hobbs came to his 50 with a late-cut off Hartkopf after 101 minutes at the crease. Twenty-one minutes later Sutcliffe joined him on that mark. Their personal scores were never very far apart. The 150 partnership, in just under three hours, saw Hobbs on 74 while his colleague had 70. At tea they had carried the total to 187/0 and their respective scores were 94 and 82. Hobbs' hundred was reached after 3 hours and 15 minutes. An extraordinary incident, which says much about control, composure and confidence, occurred. In the words of one observer: 'When the batsmen were running Hobbs' hundredth run, Sutcliffe stopped his partner for an instant between the wickets and congratulated him.' Just over half an hour later, Sutcliffe completed his second consecutive Test hundred against Australia. Noble was almost at a loss for words about the partnership:

It would be useless to try to describe that great day's play. It was flawless and when we say that, what greater tribute can we pay to ability, tenacity, resourcefulness and indomitable pluck? It was English cricket at its best. You have only to remember the total that glared in the face of these men as they went out to open the innings to realise the mental as well as the physical effort that was necessary.

Neither gave a chance. Neither looked like getting out. Neither was mentally or physically defeated. England were almost half-way to their target. For Sutcliffe it was an equally memorable occasion: 'There have been many fights since then, some of them on the most difficult of wickets but the recollection of those in no way dims the memory of that blazing hot day at Melbourne. The joy of our colleagues was sincere.'

Sunday's rest would have come most welcome to them. Preceded by a great performance, it was succeeded by a dismal one, however, Mailey's first ball was a full toss. Hobbs played it carefully. Mailey's second ball was a full toss, slightly different, perhaps, in both flight and pace. Hobbs missed it and was bowled. England, 283/1, never recovered from the shock. Woolley, Hearne, Hendren, Chapman, Douglas, and Tyldesley made 82 between them. Sutcliffe stood alone with 176 before being fifth out, bowled by Gregory with the new ball. 7 hours, 11 minutes and eighteen 4s give but a small indication of his strength and purpose.

Australia had a lead of 121 but were at once rocked back by the splendid Tate who removed Bardsley, A J Richardson and Ponsford at a personal cost of 5 runs. 27/3 at this point, they were saved by Taylor and Collins who held the fort adding 36 together before nightfall. Next day, when eight Australians were out for 168 including the durable Taylor (90), England were in with a chance but Oldfield (39) and Gregory (36*) added what was for Englishmen an infuriating 71 at a run a minute. They lifted their opponents' target to 372. Tate took 6/99.

Hobbs and Sutcliffe appeared to be in no difficulty when they faced an hour's batting before the close of the fifth day. On 36, however, Hobbs (22) put his leg in front of a straight ball from Mailey. Sutcliffe (12*) in partnership with the nightwatchman, Strudwick (15*), saw England to 54/1.

Next morning the wicket was said to be 'as hard as flint' and the cuts on the ball looked 'as if they had been made by a carpenter's plane'. Sutcliffe's supporters had a fright when he was put down in the slips off Mailey before he had added to his overnight score, but the batsman revealed no dent in his calm. Lunch: 121/2: Sutcliffe 46*, Hearne 23*. After the interval, Hearne did not last but Sutcliffe reached his 50 after 2 $\frac{3}{4}$ hours in all. Always keen to score, he took 14 off one over from Gregory. At tea there seemed to be no reason why England should not win. They were 200/3 (Sutcliffe 78*, Woolley 40*). Woolley, however, lost his splendid touch after the break and added only ten more. Sutcliffe hit Gregory for an all-run four, just before 5.30, to reach his third century in a row. All the Australians, led by their captain, personally congratulated him. The fairly swift eclipse of both Hendren and Tyldesley meant that a close of play score of 259/6 left England with less rosy prospects than had at one time seemed likely. Sutcliffe, however, was still there, 114*, having completed the unusual feat of batting throughout the day twice in the same Test. All things were possible or so he seemed to make them appear.

Finally, Mailey (5/92 in this innings) beat him when he had made 127 and the score was 280. Wickets 8, 9 and 10 were lost for the addition of 10 runs and so was the match, by 81 runs. Analysts afterwards said the winning of the toss had been crucial to Australia's success. Perhaps. But an examination of the respective sides' performances, after the fall of the seventh wicket in each innings, also tells a tale. Australia, from that point, managed 161 and 82. England, by contrast, could only collect 61 and 10.

The third Test at Adelaide provided one of the great close finishes and further evidence that England's cricket was on the mend, despite the vagaries of fortune. Collins won the toss, as was his custom, but England drew first blood, metaphorically, when Tate removed both the Australian captain and Taylor cheaply while Freeman disposed of Gregory - Australia 22/3. There was, however, a problem. The nail on Tate's big toe had dropped off. In great pain, Tate had to retire at lunch. A J Richardson (69) and Ponsford (31) saw their side to the interval. Gilligan then dismissed the latter but strained his left thigh or groin and was unable to complete his eighth over. He bowled no more in the match. Kilner picked up both Richardsons and Australia were on the ropes at 119/6 but with Tate, like his captain, incapacitated, there was no one able to press home the advantage. By tea there was the beginning of a recovery: 171/6. Andrews made 72 and by the close Ryder (72*) and Kelleway (8*) were in place at 275/7.

On the second day, Chapman, captaining in Gilligan's absence, found his limited resources stretched almost to breaking-point when Freeman damaged his right wrist when trying to catch Ryder on 145. Hobbs bowled three tidy overs and fielded as athletically to his own bowling as he did to everyone else's. 308/8 gave a little hope but then Oldfield (47) proved, if any further proof were still required, what a useful performer he was with the bat. On the fall of the ninth wicket at 419, there came an amusing moment: 'Mr Mailey was next in and was followed by a kitten, which, walking sedately and with its tail up, caused roars of laughter.' One suspects that England found it difficult to raise a smile when the last pair proceeded to add a further 73 with Ryder finishing on 201*. It was some small consolation that all accounts agree that England fielded very well indeed throughout the innings.

Whysall and Tate opened in the last hour. Whysall and Strudwick were dismissed. 18/2 was the cheerless score; it was doubled before stumps were drawn. Neither Chapman nor Tate lasted very long in the morning and at 67/4, Hobbs was joined by Sutcliffe. The wicket was perfect. The day was hot. A steadying of the ship was required; and achieved. Slowly. Hobbs took fifty minutes to reach double figures, Sutcliffe an hour for his first 8 runs. At lunch they were on 19* and 17* respectively: England, 103/4. In the afternoon only 71 runs were added for the loss of Sutcliffe (33) but Hobbs, according to one report, 'plodded along patiently'. A less plodding batsman it is difficult to imagine. Two hours however was the time it took him to reach his 50. Seven runs later he went in to tea (174/5) with Woolley (11*) his partner. The latter soon perished (180/6) but Hendren once more adapted his normally pugnacious technique to the demands of the situation. They were together that evening (270/6) with Hendren on 47* and Hobbs poised on that most difficult of 'overnight' scores, 99*.

Two minutes into the following morning he scored the single which took him to his third hundred of the series and his ninth against Australia. The partnership was only broken at 297, having provided 117 at a run a minute. It took a fine catch by Gregory low down in the slips to remove Hobbs for 119. The bowler again was Mailey. It had been another chanceless innings in which he hit only seven 4s in nearly five hours; 61 singles were part of his total. His stay at the wicket had lasted. Noble's view - that of an Australian, be it remembered - repays attention. He comments first on the care taken by the batsman:

His breezy way of walking out to the slow bowler and rendering his breaks innocuous and of playing back to the fast bowler, was lacking. He did not take any risks in forcing the ball to the on-side or cutting it behind the wicket but rather contented himself with playing 'safe' most of the time. Yet it was the correct game to play in the circumstances and one could only marvel at his infinite capacity for suppressing himself and playing wholly for his side when the occasion demanded it.

Kilner and Gilligan (the latter still unfit) were unable to offer Hendren much support but Freeman showed again that he was by no means negligible at the tail end of the order. They added 41 before Hendren was out to Gregory for 92.

Australia piled on the runs to reach 211/3 by the fourth evening, thus increasing their lead to 335 with 7 wickets in hands. The prospects for the rest of the game could have done little for England's morale with Ryder 86* and Ponsford 40* when the next morning's play began. It did not, however, begin on time. Heavy rain fell, which delayed the start for some 45 minutes. Australia, caught on a 'sticky wicket' could not cope. In the three-quarters of an hour before lunch they lost 5 wickets for 18 runs. Kilner (finishing with 4/51) and Woolley (4/77) did all that could have been asked of them. Australia were all out for 250.

Hobbs and Sutcliffe, restored to their rightful position, took England to tea at 50/0 with 25 apiece. Their batting, it was said:

afforded a fine contrast to that of the home side. These two are truly wonderful performances under such conditions for both are masters of the bat on bad wickets. When playing back they watch the ball right on to the bat; they are quick on their feet and they get down the pitch with alacrity to any thing that looks dangerous, thus preventing it breaking.

At 63, Hobbs tried to hit A J Richardson, who bowled medium- paced- off- breaks. Unfortunately, in pulling the ball, he lofted it hard to Collins just behind square on the leg side. It was a good catch and in the second over after tea it might have presaged disaster. Hobbs, acutely aware of his example and his responsibilities, was stricken with remorse: 'How bitterly disappointed I was! I feared the effect on the rest of the side. As it turned out, however, I had no need to be worried.'

On the sixth day, during which England's resistance lifted the score from 133/3 to 348/8 it seemed that everyone was a hero; Sutcliffe 59, Whysall 75, Chapman 58, were all prominent. Gilligan (29*) and Freeman (17*) had already put on 36 together when rain brought an early end to the excitement.

27 runs were needed on the seventh morning. *The Cricketer* may have been guilty of an overstatement when it asserted: 'The British Empire may be said to have held its breath while awaiting the result', but only a slight one! Amid mounting tension Gilligan finished with 31, Freeman 24, Strudwick 2 not out, and England 363. They were just eleven runs short of what would indeed have been a famous victory.

At lunch afterwards with Lord Forster, the Governor-General, the team was told, 'England was now restored to their former position in the cricket world.' If one match may be said to have enabled a side to turn the corner in its fortunes then the game at Melbourne was such a Test. That a temporary relapse followed is true, but the result gave England back confidence in her cricketers and the cricketers confidence in themselves; and it was fitting that Hobbs and Sutcliffe should lay the foundations.

Gilligan at last won the toss which immediately lifted the side's spirits. The wicket was in good condition but for the first session at Melbourne needed careful watching. As Hobbs wrote afterwards:

We have to work for [the runs] as the Melbourne wicket is always a wee bit treacherous for the first hour of the first day's play. The ball kicks unexpectedly and the explanation is that the wicket becomes sticky with the sun getting at it and causing it to 'sweat'.

Up until lunch it was usually two-paced and deceptive. For example, Australia were 47/3 early on in the second Test. There was one huge slice of good fortune when Sutcliffe, on 14, pulled Gregory high but directly to Ponsford at fine-leg. Down went the chance. On went Sutcliffe. The fifty partnership was up in an hour. At lunch, by which time the wicket's dangers had been quelled, they had put on 70 together: Hobbs 41*, Sutcliffe 27*. The wicket was now perfect: hard, true, consistent. Hobbs was, nevertheless, struck on the hip by Gregory but went to his 50 in 95 minutes. He was then dropped by the same bowler when he drove the ball hard back to him at catchable height. Cutting Mailey to the boundary, Hobbs brought up the 100 shortly afterwards. Sutcliffe's 50 came ten minutes later. They posted their fourth century opening stand of the series and seemed to be moving on inexorably to a huge partnership when a fine piece of cricket brought their partnership to a halt. Hobbs wrote later:

I tried hard to get a hundred in that match. Indeed, I think I have seldom tried harder. I felt free of my usual responsibility now that the fate of the tournament was settled. But some superb stumping on the leg-side by Bert Oldfield when I was 66 brought about my fall.

98

This was one of only two occasions when the fast-medium change bowler Jack Ryder, more renowned as a batsman, dismissed Hobbs. Although Ryder took only seventeen expensive wickets in his Test career, he was capable of moving the ball away from the bat to give Oldfield the chance to provide 'one of the cleverest bits of work I had seen for many years' (Noble). The score at that point was 126/1. By tea England were 62 runs richer: Sutcliffe 83* and Hearne 32*.

Immediately after the interval Sutcliffe escaped again when he was put down by Oldfield off Ryder. In the next extraordinary quarter of an hour he scored 32 while Hearne added a single. Sutcliffe's hundred, his fourth of the series, came in this purple patch. Hearne (44) left at 232/2 but there was, for once, no throwing away of a hard-won advantage before the close when England stood splendidly on 282/2.

Their batsmen happily occupied the whole of the next day to drive on to the heights of 548. Woolley (40), Hendren (65), Whysall (76) and Kilner (74) pressed home the position which Sutcliffe (143) in company with Hobbs had secured for them.

Tate struck early on the Monday morning, removing Collins and Ryder cheaply. This was just the start England wanted. And then Bardsley (old enough and experienced enough to know better) blundered. Noble's description cannot be bettered:

Up to this time Hobbs had been fielding quite indifferently - suggesting to me a deep-laid plot. He had failed to reach one or two that normally should have been easy for him to stop; then suddenly, he dashed in and picking up with one hand, threw the wicket down before Bardsley, who had made the call could get back. Truly, it was never safe to trifle with an astute and resourceful fieldsman.

Australia 64/3. They lost one more wicket before lunch when the score was 95. At 3.15 rain caused a loss of 20 minutes. There was a brief return but the ball was judged to be too slippery for the bowlers. Just before the tea interval some of the crowd jumped over the fence in order to make their own assessment of the wicket. Slight damage was caused to the pitch and one of the stumps was snaffled as a souvenir. Taylor (86) was the major contributor to the final 269, on the fourth day, with 68. When they followed-on, he again offered most resistance. Tate (5/75) was the main instrument of Australia's destruction. He bowled so fast that Strudwick had to stand back. Indeed, he took 4/21 on the fifth day when the cricket was all over by 1.30pm. England had deservedly won by an innings and 29 runs. And how the Englishmen relished the moment when the last wicket fell! It was their first victory against Australia since 1912 at The Oval. Hobbs and Hearne and Woolley had played in both matches but Bardsley was the only Australian to have done so.

Would that it were possible to report a further triumph at Sydney in the final meeting of the series. Unfortunately, for England, the less said about it the better. It was an astonishing contest not least because both Hobbs and Sutcliffe failed. Twice. So did their team-mates. Twice. This is revealed in totals of 167 and 146. They were unable to withstand the guile of a 33-year-old leg-break bowler, Clarrie Grimmett, who in his first Test secured 11 wickets for only 82 runs. Even so, the immense contribution of the opening pair throughout the other matches was not forgotten by their captain. In an interview A E R Gilligan said: 'No words of mine can convey accurately how splendidly they played or what they meant to the side.' As an opening partnership they had averaged 97.

The defeat at Sydney was a comprehensive one by 307 runs. It was one of only three Tests in Hobbs' career in which he failed to make an impact in either innings. He scored not at all in the first, when he was brilliantly caught by Oldfield moving swiftly to leg in anticipation of his glance off Gregory. In the second innings he was again a victim of the wicket-keeper's skill when he was stumped for 13 off Mailey.

At the end of the series two tributes were paid to him and show the esteem in which he was held. That from *The Cricketer* was to be expected:

Hobbs is the master bat of his time and his reputation had much to lose and little to gain by a further visit to Australia at the age of forty-two. That he enhanced his reputation - and no one will dispute it was certainly remarkable...In the field he still showed that extra quickness which forbids any liberty on the part of the batsman, as the latter often found to their cost. In a word he is indisputably our greatest living cricketer, a batsman pre-eminent in any age and unique in his own generation.

Fulsome words. Englishmen of the time would doubtless have concurred. But to hear them echoed by the distinguished former captain of Australia, M A Noble must have given Hobbs cause for quiet satisfaction:

We must judge J B Hobbs as we find him, a player of great ability and mighty achievements under all conditions, on all wickets and against players from anywhere and everywhere...In our day he has established himself as a batsman on a plane higher than that occupied by any of his contemporaries. What more can be said of anyone?

9 The High Peaks, 1925-26

1925 was one of Hobbs' best seasons and, although it contains no Test match, his talents continued to bloom with richness and consistency at an age when most cricketers would be thinking of retirement, if they had not already retired! 1925 also shows what a high place he occupied in public affection and admiration. Finally, it tells more of the character of the man through the manner in which he responded to his fame. In his autobiography he entitles the chapter 'My Big Year'.

At the beginning of the summer Hobbs, with 113 centuries to his credit, needed 13 more to equal W G Grace's record of 126. Oddly enough it was the equalling, not the beating, of the record which at the time captured the public imagination. In May, however, few people regarded this as possible during 1925. After all, Hobbs had never made more than 11 hundreds in any one year, although he had done that twice, in 1914 and 1920. In addition Hobbs had just returned from a strenuous overseas tour. This time, however, unlike in 1910 and 1912, let alone 1921. Hobbs had no problem in this respect: 'After my return from Australia, I was feeling remarkably fit. I was in phenomenal form and started scoring centuries right away.'

In the second Surrey match at The Oval (13/14 May), on the first day, he took full advantage of a perfect pitch and the moderate Gloucestershire attack to hit 104. It was an innings of two distinct phases: the first 50 took 85 minutes; the second required only 30 minutes. He dealt summarily with five balls of one over of the medium-pacer Percy Mills: off-drive (4); pull (4); straight-drive (4); straight-drive into the pavilion seats (6); pull (4). At lunch Hobbs had 102 out of 163.

In the next game, at home to Glamorgan (16/18/19 May), he became the first man to score a hundred against all the other counties. It was in the second innings that he gave a coruscating display to reach 109 in 130 minutes. A partnership with Alfred Jeacoke (140) produced a sparkling 216 at the rate of a hundred an hour. Hobbs hitting three 5s and eleven 4s was said to have explored almost every conceivable stroke.

Against Warwickshire at The Oval (20/21/22 May) Hobbs 120, and Sandham 180, put on 232 in two-and-a-half hours doing pretty much as they liked with the attack, which included three who had bowled or were to bowl for England, namely, Harry Howell, Freddie Calthorpe and R E S Wyatt. Again Hobbs made a careful start: he was at the wicket for 80 minutes before he hit a boundary. His first 50 runs took 90 minutes, his second 50 less than half that time, although he did give two difficult chances in the later phase, on 61 and 80. It is a tribute to his fitness that no fewer than 50 of his runs came in singles. *The Cricketer's* comment on the innings shows that even at this early stage of the season, expectations were already high:

The record of the immortal W G Grace is obviously in danger... Hobbs returned from Australia in fine health and condition and, with ordinary luck, a great season is in front of him. His batting was almost up to his own very high standard. Quiet for the first hour or so, he afterwards made many beautiful strokes, particularly on the off-side and the effortless grace which is so characteristic of his play was as conspicuous as ever.

Surrey then travelled to Leyton (23/25/26 May) where Essex were put to the sword by Hobbs (129) and Sandham (90) in an opening stand of 216. In this match Hobbs strained a muscle in his heel and did not bat in the second innings. This game was a draw, unlike the four previous ones which had been Surrey victories.

Kept out of the next fixture, against Sussex, by the heel injury, Hobbs returned to the side which went to Trent Bridge on 30 May-1/2 June. There even a partisan Bank Holiday crowd of 20,000 must have enjoyed Hobbs' 189. With Sandham (50) there was a brisk start of 100 in 105 minutes. Although he had seemed to develop a partiality for the Nottinghamshire bowling (in 1922 he made 151*; in 1923, 105; 1924, 203* and 105) this was not, early on, one of Hobbs' most dashing displays. He was careful until he had passed the hundred mark which took him 3 3/4 hours. The remaining 89 required just over an hour. The contrast was commented on by one cricket correspondent. His innings was a mixture of 'splendid defensive batting at the start and his equally splendid hitting later on'.

There was a quiet period, in two away games. The Hobbs/Sandham combination had two stands of more than 50 against Leicestershire and the victory was achieved, but Hobbs made only 19 and 42. At Old Trafford he scored 3 and 30. Lancashire were able to inflict on their visitors one of only two Championship defeats in the entire summer.

On June 13, 15, 16 Surrey returned to London, and to form, with a convincing victory over Essex. Hobbs hit 107 (not to mention 87 in the second innings) but he seemed uneasy at the start when the pace of George Louden swiftly removed both Sandham and Jeacocke. He scored 60 before lunch and 'as he gradually approached his hundred, the atmosphere all round the ground became electric'. This was not only because he was on the quest for his sixth century of the summer but also because he was in a race with Percy Holmes of Yorkshire to see who would be the first batsman in the country to make 1000 runs. When the match commenced Hobbs needed 104 and Holmes, playing against Nottinghamshire required just 14. The gods smiled on Hobbs, for whereas Yorkshire fielded in their game, Surrey batted. Hobbs, lingering on 99 for some little while before he took the necessary single, then hit a boundary to bring up the 1000. He had batted nearly 3½ hours and about half his runs came in singles. It was, nevertheless, a great achievement and the third time he had been the first to his target. The two previous instances had been in 1909 and 1920. Essex were duly defeated.

On 17/18/19 June Cambridge University were welcomed to The Oval. Although Fender, Sandham and Strudwick did not play, Surrey, led by Douglas Jardine, were by no means a weak side. Surrey batted first. Hobbs, looking for singles rather than 4s, took them as and where he pleased on his way to 104. Surrey's 344 was answered by Cambridge's 179. In the county side's second innings, Hobbs, without any trouble, reached 143* just before Jardine's declaration left the University to get 426 on the last day. Thanks to the brilliance of Dawson (125) and Duleepsinhji (98) in particular, the runs were made. Hobbs had reached a hundred of each innings of the same match for the second time. Public interest could not have been more intense, yet one somewhat jaundiced reported looked forward to a little respite. 'It will add to our comfort when we no longer have to count the number of his hundreds and it would not be a miracle if relief came towards the end of August.'

On went Hobbs. Somerset were the visitors on 20, 22, 23 June. Hobbs' 101 against them them, unlike his other recent efforts, was not chanceless. On 8 he was dropped by White, a 'simple' slip catch. 20 runs later, the wicket-keeper, Hill, put him down. The unlucky bowler on both occasions was the fast-medium Bridges. As the ground authorities had not been prepared for the huge crowds - estimates ranged from 15,000 to 20,000 - the arena had not been adequately roped. Many spectators encroached on the playing area despite the best efforts of a valiant solitary policeman.

Hobbs made his first 50 in eighty-five minutes. His 111 included seventeen 4s. Half an hour had been taken to move from 80 to 100. The Somerset side were below strength and Surrey had no difficulty in obtaining another win.

In Birmingham on 24-26 June Hobbs made his highest score of the season so far. Warwickshire fielded out to 215 from his bat. Again, he was put down in the slips on 8, this time by Croom. From that point on Hobbs played easily over 2¼ hours to his century. It was his fourth in a row. Indeed, apart from his 87 against Essex (when under instructions to go for quick runs) he would have achieved six in succession. After the hundred had been reached, he was the only player in the picture as far as the first innings was concerned. As *The Cricketer* said: 'Using the long handle with the greatest freedom, he simply hit all the bowling when and where he liked. The spectators shouted with delight. 'Fetch a Lewis gun!' yelled one of them.'

He made 101 out of 154, 153 of 235 and finally 215 of 311 before being dismissed after 3½ hours' batting. It was a remarkable rate of scoring but for a man of 42 who had already scored seven centuries it was little short of astonishing. And this was the batsman said to have lost his 'dash' after 1914! There were two 6s and twenty-six 4s in his total. In the second innings' successful run chase, Wyatt, who had been struck by Hobbs for 27 in two overs on the first day, had the pleasure of taking a caught-and-bowled chance when the batsman had reached 31. Thus was the great run-making sequence broken.

At Bradford Yorkshire beat Surrey in two days, 27 and 29 June, Hobbs made no more than 20 (of a Surrey total of 105) and 11 (Surrey 175). Emmett Robinson and George Macaulay were the bowlers concerned. There is no mention of an injury sustained in this match. Hobbs, as captain of the Players, may then have become involved in the selection of his side to play the Gentlemen. Whatever the reason, he did not go to Portsmouth for the Hampshire game which Surrey won.

At The Oval on 8, 9 and 10 July, the Gentlemen won an exciting match in the last over which suggests that Hobbs had timed his two declarations (403/8 and 252/7) rather well. His own fortunes did not improve significantly. He was out for 5 (bowled) and 51, run out when his partner, Ted Bowley, refused his call.

Surrey were pleased to gain a proper revenge against Lancashire in the return fixture. Hobbs, however, failed, going down to the pace of Ted MacDonald for 3 and the spin of Cec Parkin for 5. Coincidentally these were the two bowlers who had claimed his wicket at Manchester.

Hobbs was once more leading the Players on 15, 16, 17 July at Lord's. In reply to the Gentlemen's 309, Hobbs and Sutcliffe opened with a stand of 140. In the first half-hour of the second day's play, they added 21 to their overnight 9. In the next thirty-three minutes another 70 accrued. At first Sutcliffe scored the faster. It was observed: 'Later it so happened that Hobbs got two-thirds of the bowling and went away from him. For an hour we saw all the orthodox strokes precisely executed.' The ending of the partnership came about in a most unusual manner. Sutcliffe hit the ball into the covers and ran. Hobbs sent him back. Exit Sutcliffe for 50. As his innings developed Hobbs impishly indulged himself with some entertaining improvisations. G O Allen, who was fast, bowled a short ball to which the textbook response would have been a square cut. Hobbs pulled it to the boundary between mid-off and the bowler. Allen pitched the next ball well up. It was ideal for driving. Hobbs cut it late and fine for another 4. He batted for one hundred and seventy minutes and made his runs out of 236. The game was drawn. He had produced 'a masterpiece of the art of batting.'

The form of Hobbs and Sandham against Kent at Blackheath was such that 'the fast bowlers wanted 16 fieldsmen'. Chasing Kent's 281 they put on 199 scoring respectively 105 and 88, establishing a base on which it was possible to build a big innings' victory. Hobbs completed 2000 runs for the season and the 125th century of his career. Unusually he did not think he was out. When he chopped down on a ball from Woolley which finished in

Day's hand at slip, Hobbs did not walk but the umpire ruled him out, on appeal. This was 20 July.

This century left him one behind 'WG'. During the next six Surrey matches, the nation was willing him on to break WG's record. If this seems an absurd overstatement, Kenneth O. Morgan in *The Oxford Illustrated History of Britain* (published in 1984) shows the esteem in which Hobbs was held:

The sporting hero of the decade was Jack Hobbs, opening batsman for Surrey and England who in 1925 overtook the record number of centuries scored by the legendary W G Grace. Modest, unprotesting, a devoted church-goer and teetotaller, a model family man, Jack Hobbs was the prototype of the loyal artisan, dedicated to Crown and country. He was a professional 'player' content to be led by amateur, public-school 'gentlemen' (who entered The Oval playing area by a different gate). He always played a straight bat and always accepted the umpire's verdict, however disappointing or unfair, without complaint. Jack Hobbs' placid, kindly personality provided an acceptable touchstone for a society struggling to preserve a traditional order in the swirling tides of the post-war transformation.

But Hobbs now lost his touch - or perhaps he was a little tired?

I felt that every eye in England was focused on me and I began to get rather harassed. Surely there was plenty of time; it was bound to come sooner or later. The end of my career was not exactly in sight but no, the Press wanted it at once, and I was expected to get it every time that I went to the wicket...After such a phenomenal series of centuries, a reaction had set in, and the mental strain was beginning to tell...It seemed that the whole circus was following me around. The newspapers were working everybody into a fever heat.

Against Sussex (away) he was out for 1, victim of Maurice Tate, but the game was won. At home to Kent, in a draw, he scored 22. Travelling to Gloucester, he helped his side to an easy victory with 52 and 38. This did not go down very well with one disgruntled chronicler who felt the job should have been done then, 'so a very interesting piece of cricket history was not made at the Festival after all'. A game with Nottinghamshire came next at The Oval but like the two matches, also at home, which followed, it ended in a draw: Hobbs 54 and 1. Middlesex dismissed Hobbs for 49 although he was 4* in the second innings. Hobbs' score against Leicestershire was 31. All three matches were badly affected by rain and Surrey's inability to come out on top led them to losing their momentum in the race for the Championship.

Even at this stage of his career, after years of adulation, which had never turned his head, Hobbs was under intense pressure.

Came the meeting with Somerset on 15, 17, 18 August and it was felt that the short Taunton boundaries might give him some encouragement. On a beautiful day Somerset were put out for 167 leaving Surrey with 2 hours and 20 minutes' batting. 151/3 was their score at the close of play: Hobbs 91*, Jardine 0*. Hobbs had had to work for his runs. On 14 he was missed at the wicket off Bridges (again!); on 87 he was nearly run out. Donald Knight sacrificed himself when Hobbs uncharacteristically dithered over a call. He had approached the task of batting with some caution. There was a 4 in the first over he faced but not another for nearly an hour. He naturally overshadowed his colleagues. Each played second string to him and did it well. The sympathetic crowd watched in appreciative silence for much of the time: 'They appeared to feel that they themselves had a part in the accomplishment of one of the memorable innings of cricket history.'

R C Robertson-Glasgow, an enthusiastic and capable fast-medium bowler for Somerset as well as a distinguished cricket writer, has left an engrossing account of the event in his autobiography *46 Not Out*:

It should be said that, from start to finish of the match, everyone concerned went flat out to have Hobbs' wicket. There was no arranging. Such a cricketer did not invite the indignity of help...Old Man Record sat heavily upon him. The timing was often imperfect; each stroke to the length ball was a considered effort. He was batting as Arthur Mailey would say, from memory. He was saved by perfection of style.

On the second morning the queue stretched for nearly half a mile waiting for the chance to get in. Hobbs' superstition had compelled him to change his hotel room with Sandham because of his aversion to the number 9. As he had only nine runs to make his nervousness is understandable. Sunday had been quiet as he did his best to avoid the press by venturing outside only to go to church.

On that historic second morning he had moved to 94 when Robertson-Glasgow took up the attack again:

How I longed to unloose something supremely and eternally unplayable, an in-swinger, say, pitching on the leg stump and sending the middle flying. Never the time and the place and the 'snifter' all together! I bowled four running that were very straight and proper. He played back to each one and I chose to believe that he was nearly late to the fourth. Then, Lord bless me, I bowled a no-ball. Whack went she to the square leg boundary. From the sixth and last ball he scored a single: 99. Then with a single to leg off Bridges, he was there.

He had needed to face nine balls in five overs to complete his task. The innings lasted 2 hours and 50 minutes before he was out for 101. He scored off 61 of the 192 balls he received: eight 4s; two 3s; twelve 2s; thirty-nine singles. With this century he not only equalled WG's total but also the record of 13 centuries in one summer held by Fry, Hayward and Hendren.

In the words of *The Times* in a leading article:

Hobbs has gratified the pious wishes of his hundreds of thousands of admirers...during this trying period (of low scores), on the testimony of his county captain, he has always played primarily for his side and has never looked at the situation from a personal point of view... In the field and off it he is a great cricketer and sportsman in the highest sense of the words.

In a personal tribute, Warner, of *The Cricketer* wrote:

His cricket indeed needs no praise from me, but I would say that when he went with me to Australia in 1911/12 he was a delightful companion in every way - level-headed, easy to get on with, good-tempered and cheerful in success or failure...I place him very high indeed amongst those who have combined a straight bat with a modest mind.

Somerset's spirited 374 in their second innings' response to Surrey's 359 left the visitors with 183 to make for victory. By comparison with the enormous crowds present on days one and two, only a few were at the ground to witness the assault by Hobbs and Sandham (who generously held himself back in the scoring to give his partner the chance to make the necessary runs) which lasted 2 hours and 25 minutes. In an hour they had 73 (Hobbs 38, Sandham 30) and Hobbs' 50 came five minutes later. He needed 25 of the last 47. At 4.38pm the deed was done: a new record of 127 centuries in a career; a new record of 14 hundreds in one season. He had hit fourteen 4s and had batted with something approaching his old élan as Robertson-Glasgow makes clear:

Hobbs' second century in the match was a beauty. His cares dropped from him, as the poet has it, like the needles shaken from out the gusty pine. The same balls which in the first innings he had pushed severely to cover point he now cracked to the boundary with serene abandon.

He finished with 101* (made out of 174) and it was a chanceless display. In a speech afterwards Hobbs described himself as 'the happiest man on earth' with his only regret being that the centuries had not been made at The Oval. He later thought carefully about what his performance meant in relation to Grace's:

He had one outstanding natural advantage over me - his powerful physique. On the other hand, he had had to overcome technical difficulties in regard to wickets that did not exist in my case.

There was a detailed tribute by 'Ignotus' in *The Cricketer* which admitted how difficult it was to describe Hobbs' batting and do it justice:

Tom Hayward was admittedly his model. Hayward's batting was splendidly orthodox and this ensured Hobbs a magnificent method; to this was added a mastery over all the strokes of batsmanship combined with a perfect execution that few cricketers have even approached. Beyond this Hobbs is essentially an individualist, not merely content to exploit with superb skill all the known strokes but with a daring initiative intent on making every ball a scoring proposition. In this respect there is perhaps only one batsman with whom he can be compared - the late Victor Trumper.

The effect on the nation was even reported overseas, in places where cricket, if not unknown, had scarcely the same popularity. *The New York Times*:

Any American in London or elsewhere in England yesterday and today instantly realised that something had turned the country topsy-turvy. Barbers, bus conductors, financiers, shop keepers, policemen, stenographers tripping to and from work, dignified lawyers and vociferous street vendors - all had a topic in common which made them kin for the moment.

Tonight there are newspaper cartoons showing Jack Hobbs leaning on his cricket bat amid the dumb admiration of Julius Caesar, Mahomet and Napoleon and other lesser lights...Matters such as international politics and imminent coal strikes must wait their turn in line. Today is Hobbs' day. They are even naming babies after him all over Britain.

After the victory in Somerset, Hobbs may have experienced something of a reaction. His county sympathetically excused him from travelling on to Cardiff where the Glamorgan game was washed away for a draw. The last two county fixtures did see him at the wicket once more but 19 against Yorkshire at The Oval was followed by 15 and 5 at Lord's off the Middlesex attack. Surrey finished second in the Championship to Yorkshire. But if anyone thought that Hobbs was content to let the rest of the season slip away gently, this was far from being the case.

Scarborough was the setting for the third Gentlemen v Players' meeting of the year at the beginning of September. In response to the amateurs' 270, the professionals compiled 480/3, led in style by their captain. The Gentlemen's attack, consisting as it did, in the main, of Haig, Calthorpe, Douglas, Stevens and Jupp, was more than respectable. 12* overnight, Hobbs batted throughout the second day to 207*. It was a perfect wicket put to the best possible use. He played each ball on its merits and took few liberties with the bowling before he had reached 150. Afterwards he lofted Douglas for two superb 6s off successive balls and generally made merry. The cool north wind kept the batsmen fresh. It was noticed that he batted with his shirt sleeves down. His first hundred occupied nearly 3 hours but his second only 85 minutes. A partnership of 298 with Hendren (129) lasted two hours and fifty minutes before the Middlesex man's departure on the third morning. When Hobbs declared he was 266*, made in 5 hours and 5 minutes. It was the highest score of his career thus far and the biggest individual total ever in a Gentlemen v. Players Match. He made the runs without a mistake of any kind, carried his bat and was at the wicket on all three days. The match was drawn.

In the second game of the Scarborough Festival, playing for the MCC Australian XI he made 31, run out and, at last, a duck. It was his only one of the season and his first in England since 7 August 1923, in a game against Nottinghamshire. The bowler at Scarborough, be it noted, was the versatile George Macaulay, equally adept at swing or off-spin, who achieved the distinction of removing him no fewer than five times in 1925, something no-one else achieved. For Gilligan's XI against Tennyson's XI Hobbs hit 64 before signing off at The Oval for the Rest of England v. Yorkshire. He did so with 106 out of 187 scored in two-and-a-half hours, and 30. During this latter innings he reached 3000 runs in a season for the only time. As *Wisden* put it in 1926: 'A masterly batsman under all conditions, possessed of exceptional grace of style, remarkable in the variety of his strokes, ready to run any risk for his side and a superb field, [Hobbs] has been at once the wonder and delight of all cricketers of his generation.'

In 1926, professionals were co-opted on to the Selection Committee. One to come from the North and one from the South was the decision. What better choice could have been made than that of Wilfred Rhodes and Jack Hobbs? Their wealth of experience at home and abroad, their good cricketing brains, their soundness of judgement, were all factors contributing to their choice. The other selectors, appointed by the Board of Control, were Percy Perrin (Essex) and Arthur Gilligan of Sussex, the former England captain in 1924-25, under the chairmanship of P F Warner. The last time Australia had toured England, in 1921, the selectors had found it necessary to try out thirty players. This summer they required the services of only seventeen. Warner much appreciated the assistance of the professionals: ' Both these eminent players were of the greatest help. Playing day after day they were in the closest touch with cricket and they brought a long experience to our task.'

Writing as early as in February of that year Hobbs had high hopes of a change for the better in his country's fortunes: 'Ever since I returned from the last cricket tour in Australia I have in every utterance in public preached the gospel of hope and cheerfulness for English cricket.'

There was a sense in the country that this might be England's year. For the first game of the series at Trent Bridge about 18,000 were present on the first day but frustrated and disappointed to see only fifty minutes' play. The rain which delayed the start by three-quarters of an hour set in for much of the second and third days. The gates were not opened on either of them. No further play was possible. The signs, however, had seemed propitious for England when the toss was won enabling Hobbs and Sutcliffe to continue their now well-established partnership. They made only 32 in the time available, mainly because of the superb fielding, but they did so easily and with confidence. They also showed all their old understanding in running between wickets.

Fortunately, the barometer was set fair for the second Test at Lord's.

Hobbs had limbered up for this trial of strength by polishing his skills against Oxford University. With Sandham he established a Surrey record for the first wicket: 428 (Hobbs 261, Sandham 183).

England, in the person of Arthur Carr (Nottinghamshire), lost the toss. Australia, in the person of Warren Bardsley, seized the opportunity. 338/8 on the first day was a good score after some misadventures en route. Fred Root disposed of the Australian captain Collins: 11/1. The dangerous Charlie Macartney fell to Harold Larwood, in his first Test (84/2) before lunch was taken at 112/2 with Bardsley 52*, Woodfull 8*. By tea the former had advanced to 128* but Woodfull, Andrews, Gregory and Taylor were all out. The score then was 249/6. Arthur Richardson had 20* but he and Ryder departed before the close. By then Bardsley, who was dropped by Strudwick on 6, on 112 (both chances were given off Tate) and 172 (off Woolley) had scored 173*. He was to be put down on the second day by Kilner, a caught-and-bowled chance on 177, but carried his bat for 193*.

At 12.20 Hobbs and Sutcliffe set off in pursuit of 383. They did not let the bowlers have the initiative. While it would be an exaggeration to say they threw all caution to the winds, they did launch a quite splendid attack, 45 was up in half-an-hour, 50 five minutes later. Richardson slowed down the scoring with a leg-side attack to a leg-side field but the 77/0 at lunch had come in 70 minutes: Hobbs 50*; Sutcliffe 21*. 'A more confident start I seldom saw,' wrote M A Noble in his book *Those Ashes*. Sutcliffe brought up their fifth opening century partnership against Australia with a rasping square cut for four off Mailey.

Hobbs' innings lost momentum in the later stages, having taken but 2 hours and 10 minutes to reach 88. Only 104 were added in the two-and-a-quarter hours of the afternoon's play. There was no collapse. The partnership had reached 182 when Sutcliffe (82) was bowled by Richardson. Hobbs was accused of playing 'six-days cricket' in a three-day match. Sutcliffe's dismissal came in a period when his partner was bogged down. It is one of the very rare occasions when it was alleged that Hobbs played for himself not for his side. Noble, who, in many ways, was the most friendly of Australian critics, put the case against him strongly:

That hour which was wasted while he went from 88 to a hundred definitely put an end to any chance there might have been of England forcing a win. To be sure Richardson and Ryder pegged away steadily and the bowling looked very good but by that time Hobbs must have been seeing the ball as big as a hayrick and it really seemed that getting his century was uppermost in his mind. Only Hobbs himself can say but to us who were watching it seemed that for that period the interests of his side were a secondary consideration.

Macartney was in agreement. Hobbs

took an interminable time to run from 90 to 100. This waste of time on the second day went a long way towards robbing England of a win as the pace should have been forced to enable Carr to close his innings earlier.

Wisden shared this view:

Admittedly the leg-theory was very accurate and the fielding keen, yet it is difficult to think that, whatever the nature of the attack on a good wicket Hobbs could not have pushed along more vigorously...Batting for five hours (he, towards the end) played like a tired man.

Arguably, at the age of 43 Hobbs had every right to feel tired after scoring 119 out of 219/2; but *Wisden* also spoils its case by getting an important detail wrong. Hobbs batted not for 5 hours but for 4 hour and 7 minutes in all.

Arthur Gilligan, however, was less stringent in his comments in his tour account *Collins' Men* when referring to the partnership but he did say Hobbs had 'an exceptionally slow period' in the nineties and Sutcliffe had a 'a long quiescent period' in the middle of his innings which has received less attention. Perhaps the bowling was not as mediocre as history, with the benefit of hindsight, might lead us to suppose. After all, Gregory, Mailey, Richardson and Ryder had all been bowling when England were convincingly defeated in 1924-25. P F Warner was more sympathetic to Hobbs:

After lunch he was kept very quiet by the accuracy of the bowling but there can be no doubt that remembering the lessons of past Tests, he fully realised his responsibility, and, moreover, it should be recorded that he is no longer a young man. It was a great innings.

Hobbs put his own point of view in *Playing for England*:

Richardson bowled 'leg-theory' and I really did not see why I should oblige him by taking risks. Also Ryder bowled wide on the off side to keep me from making runs. The critics took the attitude that I ought to have taken the risks. A characteristic British trait is it not, that in order to be fair to others we cause our own to suffer...had we not seen an England collapse more than once in previous innings after Sutcliffe and I gave the side a substantial send-off?

He has a fair point: he was, after all, in the best position to make the right decision about the quality of the Australian bowling. Since he was a man of integrity he would have had the courage to admit it if he felt he had been in the wrong. As it was, he believed the criticism to be unjust and refuted it. Even so, his critics may have had a point, especially in view of the brilliance of his early assault. Nevertheless, his innings was a chanceless one and contained ten 4s. He was finally caught at third man by Richardson off his old adversary Macartney just before 5.30. Oddly, although it was Hobbs' tenth century against Australia, it was only his second against them in England.

Woolley (50*) with great splendour and Hendren (42*) with ebullience added a fine 78 in the last hour. The third day was also fine. The wicket remained firm and true. Their partnership of 140, which lasted only 111 minutes, was ended when Woolley (87) departed. Hendren had 127* by the lunchtime declaration by the enterprising Carr. Chapman with 50* had also joined in the fun. England's batsmen were at last in the ascendant. Their score of 475/3 was undoubtedly a great source of encouragement and confidence to them throughout the summer.

The Australians then lost five wickets for 194 but not that of Macartney who extemporised in a display of originality and flair. A fine innings of 133* bordered on the impudent. He seemed to have half-a-dozen different ways of playing one type of delivery, each one daring, imaginative and effective. He made 50 out of 67 and 100 out of 146. Simple statistics do sometimes go a long way to giving the extent of a player's dominance although they can say little about his style.

Hobbs now came into a rich seam of runs. In the games between the second and third Tests he demolished the Hampshire attack at Southampton for 200 before taking 70 off the Gentleman at The Oval. All seemed set fair for Leeds. In the interim, however, Macartney had not lost his touch.

At the time of the toss at Leeds the sun was shining fiercely on a damp, marled wicket which had been hastily prepared as the original was deemed unsuitable. Had that sun continued to shine and had a difficult chance stuck, Carr, who put Australia in to bat, would have been hailed as a captain of genius. Neither happened, however, and Macartney, on 2 when dropped by the unhappy English captain himself, took the England bowlers apart. He made 100 out of 131 in 103 minutes and at lunch was 112* with the score 153/1. His twinkling feet and apparently telescopic reach reduced the ambitions of the attack to dust. He was simply magnificent. He finished with 151 made at 53 runs per hour. His departure at 235/2 let in Andrews but briefly, before Richardson came to join Woodfull and was dropped on 23 by Geary off Tate. They took their side to 366/3 at the close: Woodfull 134*; Richardson 70*.

There was no early respite for England on the second day. The Australians' total, 494 (Woodfull 151; Richardson 100), reached at lunchtime meant that victory for England was out of the question and there was a distinct possibility of defeat for by the end of the day they had limped to 203/8.

Hobbs and Sutcliffe had begun solidly enough with a stand of 59 in 80 minutes before the latter was beaten by Grimmett. They had been somewhat leisurely between the wickets, failing to convert some singles to twos. Hobbs may not have been conscious of *The Times'* comment that he 'had been blamed, not without a show of reason, for the slowness of his score in the later part of his innings in the Lord's match'. With Woolley he took the score to 104 before he was caught for 49 at point by Andrews when trying to turn a short ball from Mailey to leg. By tea, England had slipped to 112/4 with Hendren and Woolley gone as well. Carr, Chapman and Tate contributed but little and although Kilner hit a useful 36 it was left to Geary (6*) and Macaulay (18*) to see out that day's play after the scoreboard showed 182/8.

The wicket was good on the third morning and the England pair responded with a sterling partnership of 108 for the ninth wicket. Macaulay's 76 was to give him not only his highest score in Test cricket but his finest hour in his country's service. Exactly 200 behind on the first innings, England followed-on.

There were twenty minutes before lunch which Hobbs and Sutcliffe successfully negotiated for 15 runs. Had either of them been dismissed early on then England would have been on the rack. The wicket was beginning to crumble under a hot sun. The high skills of the batsmen were tested to the full, in particular by Mailey and Grimmett.

Hobbs and Sutcliffe, each distinct, with a separate identity, were as a pair, a unit, Hobbs-and-Sutcliffe more than twice as strong as the sum of their parts. Their temperament must have been as exasperating as their technique. Their methods of making runs complemented each other's. This is a point that Arthur Gilligan makes well, showing that, while Hobbs tended to score more on the on-side, Sutcliffe favoured the off. It followed that:

it is impossible for any opposition to keep on changing the set of the field every time a stroke for an odd number of runs is made. It is not generally recognised that, owing to this characteristic of the batting of these two, their partnership almost amounts to that of a right-hander and left-hander in together. When they get set it certainly has that effect on the fielding side.

Their first major task was to save the game. This they did. They took no risks. Theirs was a chanceless partnership. Every ball seemed to meet the centre of the bat. Nothing was hit in the air. Anything loose, however, was properly punished and, although their methods were said to be defensive, the stand realised 156 in about two-and-a-half hours. On 77 Hobbs passed the record of the great Australian left-hander Clem Hill; that of 2660 runs in England v. Australia Tests. Hobbs and Sutcliffe had enjoyed their sixth century stand against the old enemy. It came to an end when Hobbs (88) cut a well-pitched up ball from Grimmett into his wicket. This happened in the last over before tea. All danger of defeat was past. At the close, 254/3 (Sutcliffe out for 94) was the fine result of a solid uphill fight.

Hobbs' heavy scoring sequence was sustained with 163 in the Lord's match against the Gentlemen where he shared with Sutcliffe (103) an opening stand of 263 which was a record for the fixture. In Surrey's game with Kent at Maidstone which followed, yet another century first-wicket partnership was provided. In this Hobbs (77) and Sandham (49) put on 128 together.

Hobbs, therefore, had every reason to feel happy with his touch when reporting to Old Trafford for the fourth Test. It was to be a unique occasion, in one respect, if not another. Rain at such a special event was no new phenomenon in Manchester. The first day saw just ten balls bowled and 6 runs scored. Nothing more was possible. On Sunday, Carr went down with tonsillitis. On Monday he was unable to continue playing. Hobbs was asked to take over. It was a great moment for a great player, the highest compliment that could be paid a professional:

Mr Warner came into the dressing-room before the day's cricket began. 'Jack' he said, 'we have talked things over and we would like you to lead the side.' 'You are doing me a great honour,' I answered, 'but Mr Stevens (an amateur) is in the eleven.' 'Yes, we know,' said Mr Warner. And he explained. 'We would like you to take it on, all the same.' 'I'll do my best,' I said... Unfortunate though the circumstances were, I was very proud.

Warner, whose decision it was, naturally found much to praise in Hobbs as captain:

Let me say at once that he carried out his duties to the satisfaction of all. He proved himself a good leader and his side worked very happily together under him.

A more objective, even critical view could be expected from Noble but, 'Hobbs was, in my opinion, quite adequate as captain. He changed his bowlers well with an eye to the necessity of contrast. He did not over-bowl his men.'

He had little joy as tactician, however, against Macartney or indeed Woodfull who were masters of his bowlers on a soft easy wicket. At lunch on the second day the score was 109/1. They were on 49 and 42 respectively. Difficult to separate though they were, steady, accurate bowling and intelligent field placing prevented them from running away with the game; even so they could not be stopped from adding 192 for the second wicket in three hours. Macartney (109) went first and Woodfull (117) followed at 252/3. The rest of the Australian batting did very little. They ended with 335 on the Tuesday morning.

Hobbs and Sutcliffe had ninety minutes' batting before lunch. The weather was good. The wicket was easy. The former was at his best. The latter could not establish himself. One reporter was surprised as he felt Sutcliffe was 'not at first allowed his fair share of the bowling'. It took them just over an hour to put on 58 which was by no means dilatory. Sutcliffe (20) was then caught at the wicket off Mailey. The score had reached 135 when

114

Hobbs (74) lofted Grimmett to be comfortably taken at deep extra-cover by Ryder having played an innings as valuable as it was artistic. Noble said:

He had played a fine game for his side and it must have been highly gratifying to him, on top of the responsibilities of captaincy to know that he had succeeded in building up an impregnable position and that he had been mainly responsible for frustrating the Australians' hopes...Hobbs' pluck, resource and judgement prevented it (the follow-on). His defence was rock-like but anything over-tossed or a little short was dispatched summarily. He filled the role of sheet anchor and had satisfaction of knowing that England was safe before his dismissal.

After Sutcliffe's departure, Ernest Tyldesley, who had been tentative at first, settled down, enjoying some luck to make 81, much to the delight of his home crowd. Woolley stroked his way a stylish 58 before the match petered out with England 305/5.

Much time was lost to rain in Surrey's second match with the Australians which followed the Test. Hobbs scored 9, a rare failure. In a run of nineteen consecutive innings a sequence commencing with the 261 v Oxford University (begun on 23 June) and ending with a remarkable score against Middlesex at Lord's on 9 August, it was the only occasion on which he did not reach double figures. Indeed, in a season of forty-one first-class innings he was dismissed only ten times for fewer than 20 runs. In his second benefit match, against Nottinghamshire, Hobbs was more successful, with 24 and 60. His final innings before the fifth Test was 176* v Middlesex. After that he wisely stood down from the Somerset game (feelings in Somerset must have been very mixed about this) to rest in preparation for what was to be, in fact, the first 'timeless' Test in this country.

To face Australia England did not pick Carr, Kilner, Root or Tyldesley. Chapman was the new captain, about whose elevation there was all manner of a brouhaha. There were elements of an anti-Chapman campaign (on grounds of his youth and inexperience in captaincy) as well as a pro-Carr one. Hobbs, one of the Selection Committee, was quite taken aback by this:

I really can't understand why all the fuss is made when a captain is superseded. I am one of those who consider that a captain must be worth his place in either batting or bowling like any ordinary member.

The selectors were unafraid of change. In came Rhodes (his first Test had been in 1899), Geary and Larwood. Each made a contribution. The wicket-keeper, Strudwick, would have departed in favour of Brown of Hampshire, had not the latter injured his thumb.

Chapman did his duty well. He won the toss. Then everyone forgot they were playing in a match that could last a fortnight if they so desired. Batsmen came and went with something approaching alacrity, apparently doing all in their power to assist the fielding side in its aspiration. Silly shots to long hops and full tosses, coupled with silly decisions about taking runs, accounted for about half the 14 wickets that fell on that full, fine first day. Of all the rum dismissals none was rummer than that of Hobbs who could almost be said to have set a pattern for the day's play. After Hobbs (37) and Sutcliffe had put on 53 for the first wicket, one reporter could scarcely believe his eyes:

He batted divinely for an hour and then missed a slow full pitch directed at his leg stump and was clean bowled. I know this thing happened because I saw it myself.

More than sixty years after the event one can sense the writer's bewilderment, his blank incomprehension that Homer could possibly nod. How did Hobbs react?

'Fancy missing a thing like that,' I said to myself as the stumps rattled. And Tommy Andrews at silly point flung back his head and murmured: 'Oh what a turn-up for the books!'

John Marchant in *The Greatest Test Match*, writing in the same month as the event, remembered the dismissal well: 'I don't know when I have seen so utterly flabbergasted a batsman as he looked for a moment - and then he burst out laughing.'

Mailey the bowler was probably just as amused but one would hazard the guess that Sutcliffe, say, was not laughing. Nor would he have laughed at the events which followed. Woolley (18) hit brightly but was beaten by Mailey's googly (91/2) and Hendren (8) dragged a ball from Gregory on to his wicket. Lunch: 108/3 (Sutcliffe 40*). Chapman in a typical innings of dash and enterprise brought new life to his side as a captain should, then, on 49, jumped out once too often to Mailey: 189/4. Stevens, recognised as a sound defensive player, decided to emulate his leader and banged away briefly. Overwhelmed by his temerity at depositing a ball from Mailey on to the pavilion awning he changed his policy to one of 'safety first'. Mailey's next ball he patted gently into the hands of Andrew at silly point. The partnership had produced 87 runs in seventy-five minutes: 213/5.

One run later the sixth wicket fell when Sutcliffe (76 - top scorer of both sides' first innings) was beaten by a perfect Mailey leg-break having played the previous ball on to his face. Rhodes (28) was as unflappable as ever but in a misunderstanding with Geary (9) the latter was run out: 231/7. Tate, a fine striker of the ball, made 23 very useful runs in a fifteen-minute stand with Rhodes which lifted the total to 266 before the Sussex all-rounder became Grimmett's first victim. In the same over Larwood became his second: 266/9. Strudwick was left on 4* when Rhodes succumbed to Mailey who finished with 6/138 in a total of 280. Lest it be thought that the vagaries of the wicket were responsible for this disappointing total, Marchant quotes Hobbs as saying: 'it was plumb, as good a wicket as he has ever played on.'

Wisden with masterly understatement commented: 'In a match unlimited as to time, the lack of restraint shown by several of the batsmen was difficult to understand.'

Fortunately for England, Australia had some fine players who also chose this day as one on which to demonstrate one or two of their own aberrations. Bardsley (2) snicked to the wicket-keeper a long hop from Larwood which he could have left alone: 9/1. Macartney (25) played dazzling cricket before obligingly helping 'the most atrocious kind of long-hop' from Stevens into his wicket: 44/2. Perhaps this one delivery may be cited as an example of how difficult it is to find out precisely what happened. The quotation is from Marchant. *Wisden* agrees with his assessment of the delivery. Gilligan calls it ' a shorter ball but not a long-hop'. Warner says simply it was a top-spinner and gives no indication of its length. Noble avers that the ball 'pitched just short of a good length (and) jumped a little'. Macartney, suitably chastened no doubt, makes no reference to the dismissal in his autobiography.

At 51 Ponsford (2) ran himself out while Andrews was genuinely beaten by Larwood's pace and break-back: 59/4. One run later came the close of play. It gave the spectators a welcome opportunity to ponder upon the wonders they had seen.

England fancied their chances when play began on the second gloriously fine day. They must have fancied them even more when Woodfull (35) was induced to play on to his wickets a good-length ball from Rhodes: 90/5. Thirty-two runs later, the same bowler ensnared Richardson (46) who drove him hard but in the air to wide mid-off where Geary sprang to his right to make an excellent catch: 122/6. Gregory joined his captain. By lunch they had added 44.

In the afternoon they did much to restore their country's fortunes. Gregory had seized the initiative from the moment of his arrival. His fine shots, which produced 73 runs, included ten 4s. It was spirited batting characteristic of his whole approach to cricket. With Collins he added 107 in 105 minutes. Tate finally had the all-rounder caught by Stevens (227/7). The brave Collins (61), who had been plagued by neuritis during the summer and had batted in pain, soon followed, well caught by Stevens in the gully: 231/8. After an invaluable 67-run stand between Oldfield (33*) and Grimmett (35), Tate removed the bowler and summarily dealt with his successor, Mailey, before he too could once more drive England to distraction with his by no means insignificant batting skills.

Australia led by 22 when Hobbs and Sutcliffe walked to the wicket with an hour to play on the second day. When stumps were drawn their respective scores were 28* and 20* in a total of 49. They impressed one correspondent who deemed their batsmanship to be 'masterly in its wisdom and in the execution of particular strokes'.

On the third morning they played themselves into cricketing

immortality. It may be thought that by 1926 both were well-established anyway, but it was this match in particular that is remembered as seeing the greatest of their partnerships. This is not only a judgement made with the benefit of hindsight, but the assessment of Hobbs' contemporaries. Thunderstorms on the Monday evening and early Tuesday morning gave the uncovered wicket a thorough drenching. At first the pitch was slow, dead and easy. Hobbs and Sutcliffe had the chance to re-establish themselves in conditions that were not especially demanding.

Grimmett and Macartney opened the bowling. Sutcliffe was unmoved, taking 40 minutes to add a run. Macartney was replaced by Richardson whose first ball Hobbs pulled high over the leg-side fielders for 4 and his 50. Collins soon directed the bowler to go round the wicket instead. The gods were with the batsmen as the sky remained overcast for the first hour of play. Hobbs and Sutcliffe knew that as soon as the sun came out they were done for. So ran the received wisdom. So their own experience told them. In most temperate terms Hobbs commented to his partner:

I remarked to Herbert as we patted the wicket at the end of the first over: 'Jolly bad luck, that rain. It has cooked our chances.' He agreed...And really at that juncture I thought we had precious little chance...I guessed that the great crowd felt what I was feeling for I heard their sigh of relief at the end of each over, especially the pavilion fans who could see Arthur Richardson turning the ball and knew why he had three or four short legs.

The view has been expressed that Hobbs, realising the left-armer Macartney would present the greatest danger as he turned the ball more sharply than his colleagues, treated Richardson's off-breaks with great respect in order to keep that bowler on. Hobbs discounted this, and not only because he took nine off Richardson's first over: 'the ball came so awkwardly I just couldn't get (it) away.' The spinner, however, was unable to find the crucial line. With seven fielding on the leg-side, he tended to pitch on middle-and-leg. As Hobbs stood a foot wide on the leg side, the bowler could not aim at his pads without giving the batsman a free hit. When the ball was delivered Hobbs either glided across or ran into the appropriate stroke. The sun came out at mid-day, fitfully at first and then with greater intensity. Its effect on the wicket caused the ball to jump and pop and squat. Each ball was predictable only in its unpredictability. The surface of the pitch had little bits cut out of it by the spinning ball. To say that it was important no wicket fell before the strip dried out is to err on the side of understatement. In the ninety minutes from noon, the match and the series was truly in the balance. No bowler in favourable conditions had the power to enable him to master these batsmen. *The Times* marvelled at their skill: 'Their artistry in manipulation of the bat was consummate, their judgement infallible, their patience inexhaustible.'

At lunch England's score was an unbelievable 161/0: Hobbs 97*;

Sutcliffe 53*. That the Yorkshireman's 50 had taken just over three hours mattered not a jot. When the wicket was at its worst they had survived. Indeed, by doing so, they had taken a match-turning initiative. Shortly after the interval a two and then a daring short single brought Hobbs to a century he must have greatly coveted, not only for his country but also for his own supporters. It was his only Test century against Australia made at The Oval. The jubilation of the crowd was equalled by his own. As Marchant observed:

When he reached home safely at the end of that utterly impertinent run, he was waving his bat in the air. Then he waved his cap. Then, as the riot continued, he waved his bat and cap at once.

Three formal cheers were roared round the ground. It was not an anti-climax for him to depart in Gregory's next over. The ball broke back sharply, grazed his pad and just (only just, but it was enough) flicked off his off bail. 100 out of 172 in three hours forty-one minutes. No chances.

Few people could speak with more authority than Gilligan. He applauded both the partnership and Hobbs' innings unreservedly:

I do not consider either did such a big thing at any time on my tour of Australia as they did at The Oval in 1926...This must be regarded everywhere as one of the greatest innings Hobbs has ever played and, therefore, naturally, one of the greatest in the history of cricket.

An Englishman might be expected to make a partial assessment. But the praise of the Australians was equally unstinted. Noble, the onlooker:

On a rain-affected pitch he showed all the resource of a great player, getting right back to dangerous breaking ones or waiting for those there were over-tossed beating the break, making scoring strokes. It was an innings worthy of the great batsman he is and it put England in a winning position.

Macartney, the participant, adopted exactly the same attitude:

Hobbs played the best innings he has played in any cricket. That innings was responsible for winning the rubber for England. He had some very nasty bowling to take and he undoubtedly sacrificed himself in many cases to keep Sutcliffe away from the bowling.

This particular point was not accepted by Sutcliffe who was aggrieved that he was not given full credit by the press for his share in the stand:

I was a little surprised next day to read that Hobbs had nursed me during Richardson's opening attack. I had at least an equal share of Richardson's bowling, when the wicket was at its worst and I make this claim because I am proud of the part I played in that anxious fight.

Be that as it may, the partnership had opened all of England's seven innings in 1926 and achieved a magnificent average of 118 in so doing.

Woolley entered the arena. He at once began to display his beautiful strokes, making 27 attractive runs before being lbw (some thought unluckily) to Richardson: 220/2. Hendren (15) never found his touch but stayed while 57 were added. He was out in a curious fashion. Originally, and to his bewilderment, adjudged bowled by Grimmett, he was later said to have been caught by Oldfield: 277/3. During this stand, Sutcliffe reached his fifth hundred against Australia after five hours at the wicket. He had moved up a gear and was now hitting the ball hard. Chapman was with him for a while but he made only 19 before Richardson beat him with his faster ball: 316/4. The fifth wicket fell 57 runs later when Stevens (22) lashed Grimmett in the air to Mailey at cover. In the last over of the day Sutcliffe himself was injudicious enough to let Mailey get a ball past his vigilant bat. 161 out of 375/6 in seven hours eight minutes. No chances. Sixteen 4s. A great innings.

Little remains to be said about the rest of the England innings which resumed after a shower on the fourth morning. Tate (33*) was the exception as he struck about him merrily to lift the tail and the total to 436 which was reached, after a further break for rain, at 3.15pm.

Australia, therefore needed 415 to win. They never looked like getting there. Two good catches in the slips by Geary off Larwood removed both Woodfull and Macartney to leave them at 31/2. On the same total, as if to keep himself warm, Larwood took a fine low catch in the gully off Rhodes who compelled Ponsford to poke ineptly at the spinning ball. The veteran finished with 4/44, Larwood with 3/34 and Australia with 125. Shortly after six o'clock Geary passed Mailey's defences and for the first time in fourteen years England held The Ashes.

The Times gave expression to everyone's struggle to come to terms with what was happening:

...as the news of the last day's play was flashed from The Oval to the ends of the Empire (the impression) was that it was almost too good to be true.

Perhaps the last word on this famous triumph should be left with Warner. A former player and captain, now selector, he could take a broad view. In *The Cricketer* he wrote:

This victory means everything to English cricket. Had we been beaten, despondency would have crept over the land. As it is our cricket will be fortified and refreshed...To my mind, the Australians lost the match on Tuesday and Hobbs and Sutcliffe won it for us by their incomparable batting...That they did not fail us at a time of most desperate crisis was only in keeping with their reputation. Never has English cricket known a more dauntless pair: the greater the task, the greater their endeavour.

120

Hobbs' achievements that year did not end there. 102 against Yorkshire in a tough draw at The Oval would certainly have pleased him. Then, after a quiet match against Leicestershire, he went to Lord's.

He carried his bat though the Surrey innings of 579/5 declared in six hours forty minutes, hit forty-one 4s, took part in three three-figure stands and was on the field throughout the match in which Surrey beat Middlesex by an innings and 63 runs. His 316* was not only the highest score of his career, it was (and is) the biggest total made by an individual on that ground.

In 1926, he scored ten centuries (no one made more), 2949 runs (no one made as many) and an average of 77 which no one could surpass. For the second successive year he was at the top of the first-class list.

10 Further Triumphs, 1926-29

In 1927 Surrey were sixth in the Championship, as they had been in 1926 and were to be again in the following year. In all three seasons, Hobbs missed a number of his county's games. In 1926 this had been because of the demands of representative fixtures. In 1927 there were no Tests but illness and injury reduced the number of his first-class innings to 32, the fewest he played in any season, apart from 1921, when he had appendicitis.

Having scored two hundreds in the Hampshire match, he missed five weeks' play after the meeting with Yorkshire at the end of May, having contracted an unpleasant skin complaint. He next appeared against the Gentlemen at The Oval where he made a sound 43 before he went to Blackheath for Surrey's game with Kent. There Hobbs, with 121, completed a hundred hundreds for his county. It was the 142nd century of his career and thereby hangs a tale which shows just how sensitive, even at this stage, this tough batsman was: 'Just after I started playing again the team was picked for the Gentlemen v Players match at Lord's, and I was omitted. This was a grief to me because somehow I thought that I ought to have been asked whether I was fit.'

He wanted that hundred against Kent, not so much because his side needed it on this occasion, nor because it was a personal record, but because he had a point to prove. 'Perhaps this sounds a trifle spiteful but I am only human,' Hobbs wrote.

Other highlights included 105* before lunch against Nottinghamshire; 150 in Sandham's rain-ruined benefit v Yorkshire and 146 taken from the touring New Zealanders whom he met for the first time. Although he was twelfth in the averages with 1641 runs his average was 52.

The following year, 1928, he once more leapt up the list. Thirty-eight innings were not so very many but they brought him 2542 runs at 82. Only his county colleague, Jardine, with fewer than half Hobbs' innings and runs, finished ahead of him with an average of 87.

Much was expected of the visiting West Indians not least because in Francis, Constantine and Griffith, they had three genuinely fast and hostile bowlers. The side's catching, however, was inconsistent and, as the rain seemed to follow them round the country, their batsmen struggled to find form. They were playing Tests for the first time.

Hobbs (123*) and Sandham (108*) had an unfinished stand of 253 in Surrey's second innings in the match with the tourists. In it Constantine demonstrated his all-round prowess which was to be such a feature of the summer, outside the Tests. He was concerned in the fall of six Surrey wickets, dismissing four and catching two more. His 50 was the top score in his side's first innings and he saved the game with 60* in the second.

In Hobbs' first ten matches he scored four centuries and three other innings of more than 50, so that when he captained the Players at The Oval at the beginning of June, he was comfortably in runs. But in that match, while chasing a ball to the boundary, he tore a muscle in his thigh. *Wisden* reported: 'Not much was thought of the matter at the time but it so happened that the strain prevented Hobbs getting any more batting for about six weeks.'

The next match was a Test Trial. The selectors for the summer were Leveson Gower, Douglas and Gilligan with Hobbs and Rhodes again co-opted. Hobbs was selected. Presumably he agreed; but on the first day his injury, which needed proper rest, so encumbered him that, 'I was compelled, acting on the advice of a doctor present, to refrain from fielding again after tea.' Indeed, he took no further part in the contest or any first-class game until Surrey met Kent at Blackheath at the end of the second week in July. One run in the first innings promised little but 69* in the second was enough to confirm his fitness for the England team to meet the West Indies in the second Test.

In the match immediately preceding the Test, while Fender was away playing for the Gentlemen at Lord's (where Hobbs doubtless thought he should be too, Hobbs captained an all-professional Surrey team to victory at Northampton. He contributed 117.

In the first Test at Lord's the West Indies had been crushed by an innings and 58 runs. One report, however, echoes down the years: The West Indies 'gave the impression that their batting strength is not sufficient to give them any real chance of beating England under equal conditions. The deficit is of temperament rather than of technique and will be less apparent as their experience grows.'

The West Indies now won the toss to gain first use of a soft and easy wicket. They lost one wicket in the morning, that of Challenor when he had made 24 and the score had reached 48. The athleticism and anticipation of a great fielder was responsible for his downfall. In the opinion of the onlookers, the fielder had started to move before the stroke was completed and as *The Times* reported: 'Mortal man could not be expected to guess that his cricket sense would enable him to stop and return the ball as he did.' Hobbs was back and he expressed his delight:

A ball played by Roach came to me at mid-off on my left side. I crossed the ball with my feet, picked up and threw with a single action. Elliott accepted in fine style and swept Challenor, Roach's partner, out by yards. I felt pleased to know that I could still field in that manner - a manner that grows more difficult as the years pass.

92/1 at lunch gave a solid base but despite Roach's excellent 50 the West Indies were unable to build on it successfully. Hobbs considered that 'they could play the fast stuff all right, but only too obvious was their inability to cope with slow bowling, especially the googly which they had not hitherto encountered.'

Freeman, of Kent, a master of the leg-break and googly, was in his element. He took 5 for 54 as the West Indies slipped to 206 all out. In the remaining hour, Hobbs (32*) and Sutcliffe (39*) 'gave a characteristic display of batsmanship against the notoriously dangerous fast bowling of the West Indies', and took their side to 84/0.

On Monday, Francis, Constantine and Griffith all continued to bowl with great fire, but they were poorly supported by their fielders. Hobbs tried to turn Constantine round the corner. Challenor, a fine opening bat but now aged forty and past his best, at short leg was too slow to take the opportunity. On 53 Hobbs edged Francis to first slip where Browne put down a straightforward chance. This was not a costly error. With no addition to his score he jumped out to a slow in-swinging delivery from Browne and hit it high into the deep where St Hill took a good running catch at long-on: 119/1. Sutcliffe (54) soon followed (124/2) and E Tyldesley did likewise (131/3). England were momentarily embarrassed but Hammond (63) and Jardine (83) put matters right. Although Chapman pulled a muscle when sprinting a single which put him out of the game, the side had little trouble in reaching 351.

The West Indies slid to 71/4 before bad light ended play for the day. In the morning there was no recovery. Freeman's mastery was at its peak - it was in this summer that he captured his record number of 304 wickets. In this innings he took 5/39 which brought him to 10/93 for the match. The batsmen totalled 115. England had again won by an innings, plus a margin of 30 runs.

Following the 117 against Northamptonshire and the Test 53, Hobbs continued a productive sequence: 65, 6 and 109, 93 and 85, 2 and 200*. The last two innings were played at Edgbaston against Warwickshire in the Championship. Hobbs batted nearly six hours on 10 August. Next day the Test began. By the end of it, Hobbs had added a further 89*.

The first day was hot, the wicket easy. The pattern of the second Test to a large extent repeated itself. The West Indies won the toss. The openers Challenor (46) and Roach (53) did the side no small service. 112 was on the board before the second wicket fell. Tate (4/59) then enjoyed most success with the ball. Chapman excelled himself in the field with four catches, two that were brilliant in the slips, a brave one at short-leg and a skyer at mid-on. 238 was a disappointing total.

There were over two hours' play remaining when England batted. Hobbs and Sutcliffe (63) had little trouble in putting on 155 for the first wicket. Sutcliffe did not 'make' many of his runs but he took full toll from the loose deliveries that were on offer. He did not find his touch but he was, as ever, adept at productive survival. Hobbs was more nearly his real self but, as one press report said: 'It was plain, in spite of the greed with which he sought for sharp singles, that he was a tired man and lacked energy to drive. But his forcing strokes on the leg side were as vigorous and exquisitely timed as usual.'

In the first half-hour on the second day, Hobbs was missed twice. A caught-and-bowled chance to Francis went down when the batsman was on 95. Four runs later Nunes, keeping wicket, could not hold on to an edge offered off the same bowler. Nevertheless, Hobbs and Tyldesley pressed on at a run-a-minute. This time it was Hobbs' physical as well as his moral stamina that impressed. It was clear that he was not properly rested after Sunday, for he was most restrained in his driving. It was equally clear that he was not going to throw in his hand. Rain intervened at about 12.20. On his return to the pavilion, 'he looked pale and haggard as if bed was the proper place for him'. Yet he had scored twice as quickly as Tyldesley who was himself no slouch at the wicket. Nor had any short singles been missed. Nunes was driven to 'chase the ball' in his field placing, yet Hobbs' control was such that he could steer the ball into the positions which the fielders had just vacated.

On their return just before 2.30, both batsmen attacked briskly, adding a further 49 in half-an-hour. Hobbs by now was chancing his arm recklessly. After two slashes over the slips, each of which brought four, he pulled a short ball from Francis to short-leg where Small clung on to the chance. One suspects that the batsman may well have been relieved: 284/2; Hobbs 159; twenty 4s.

Hobbs' quality was underlined by the failure of England's middle order. Once he was out, it was said, several of his successors played as if they did not relish the pace of the bowling. Griffith finished with his best Test analysis of 6/103, of which five distinguished wickets came in a splendid afternoon spell at a personal cost of 21 runs: Tyldesley, Hammond, Leyland, Hendren, and Chapman. England staggered to 333/7 before Tate (54) and Larwood (32) played a recovery partnership of 61 in less than half-an-hour. The final total of 438 left the West Indies an hour's batting during which they reached 61/4.

Larwood at his sharpest (3/41), Tate cutting the ball effectively (3/27) and Freeman at his most guileful (4/47) shared the wickets in the second innings' score of 129 which was completed after seventy-five minutes on the third morning, leaving England victors, once more, by an innings and 71 runs.

Hobbs did not quietly fade from the first-class scene this summer any more than he ever did. In the eight matches remaining his scores included 96 v Gloucestershire; 105 v Yorkshire; 101 v Leicestershire; 119 for Leveson Gower's XI v the West Indies and, in his last innings, a magnificent 150 for the Rest of England against the Champion County, in this case, Lancashire.

Long before this, however, the touring party to visit Australia in the winter had already been selected. There were three amateurs including the captain, Chapman, D R Jardine (Surrey) and J C White (Somerset) who had not been to Australia before. Among the professionals, Hobbs, Sutcliffe, Hendren, Mead, Tate and Freeman had had experience of an Australian tour. The new travellers were E Tyldesley and G Duckworth (both Lancashire), H Larwood and the unlucky S Staples who had to return home early (both Nottinghamshire), L E G Ames (Kent), G Geary (Leicestershire), and W R Hammond (Gloucestershire).

The first Test was the first Test ever played at Brisbane, at the Exhibition Ground.

Up to this point on the 1928-29 tour, Hobbs had been used carefully by Chapman who gave the Surrey man an opportunity to find his land legs and spared him the game against Western Australia which began only two days after the ship had docked. He failed (26) in his first innings, against South Australia, but made amends with 64 in the second when he and Sutcliffe put on 131 in seventy-five minutes. This was another high-scoring draw, as was the match with Victoria in which Hobbs scored 51 without ever really finding his form. Rested from the New South Wales fixture, he may have watched with interest a young fellow called Bradman make 87 and 132*. If he did so, he would not have worried unduly as Jardine (140) hit his third century of the tour, and Hammond (225) and Hendren (140) their second. As this was also a draw, the victory gained against an Australian XI (Hobbs 38 and 67*) would have been most welcome. Queensland were also defeated: Hobbs, 30. There was fierce competition among the Englishmen for the batting places in the first Test but those of the openers were secure.

It was a good toss to win as the pitch was perfect, the day hot and the light excellent. Hobbs and Sutcliffe settled in when Chapman had called correctly. The former hooked Gregory's fourth ball to the boundary and at once seemed established. Sutcliffe, as was his wont, was more circumspect but their batting in tandem had such as easy mastery that the possibilities seemed immense, despite one flaw, noted by that shrewd observer P G H Fender in his book *The Turn of the Wheel*. In his opinion, they ' had not run between the wickets anything like as well as we are used to seeing them do. There were several misunderstandings, nearly a dozen in the period, though none were of such a nature as to cause one to fear the loss of a wicket.' They put on 85 in a fraction under one-and-a-half hours before Sutcliffe (38) hooked Gregory to fine-leg where Ponsford took a very good running catch. Lunch 85/1.

After the interval came a sad and uncharacteristic blunder. Mead cut Grimmett through the covers, for an easy two and even a comfortable three had they been decisive. But, as Fender repeated, 'Hobbs ran his second run slowly, turned, both hesitated, then Jack said "Yes" and failed to make his ground.'

The score was now 95/2. Hobbs' 49 had taken ninety-five minutes and contained six 4s. Apart from the running it had been an excellent innings, and it was only the first time in seventy-six Test innings that Hobbs had been run out. When Mead went quickly, however, (108/3), the innings needed to be rebuilt by Jardine and Hammond, who brought their team safely to 160/3 at tea. Their 53-run partnership was broken after the interval, having taken eighty minutes in all and blunted the edge of the bowling. Hammond (44) fell to Gregory at 161 and Jardine (35) at 217/5. Both men had been barracked but no further wicket fell on the first day which ended with England under less pressure but by no means secure: 272/5 (Hendren 52*; Chapman 39*).

The captain departed at 291 on the next morning having arrived at a flamboyant 50. Tate, not easily disconcerted with a bat in his hand, smote 26 out of the next 28 before being snared by Grimmett: 319/7. Hendren by now was on 61. Larwood then began an all-round performance of high class and made the first of his two 50s in Test cricket. 30,000 present after lunch can hardly have failed to appreciate his sparkling 124-run stand with Hendren which finished with the fast bowler out for 70 (seven 4s, a five and a 6) after just under two hours' batting. The partnership was, and remains, a record for the eighth wicket for England v Australia. The Middlesex man carried on to his highest Test score against Australia, 169, before being last out at 521 at 4.40pm. He had batted for 5 hours and 8 minutes and was at the wicket while 360 runs were added.

An hour's batting faced Australia. Larwood was in form. The fourth ball of his first over found the edge of Woodfull's bat; Chapman took a superb one-handed catch to his left in the gully: 0/1. The last time England had dismissed an Australian in Australia before a run was on the board had been in the second Test at Melbourne in 1911-12. The psychological lift this breakthrough gave to the fielding side cannot be over-stated, any more than can the demoralising effect on the batsmen. In Larwood's third over he yorked Ponsford: 7/2. Tate, not to be denied his share caught-and-bowled Kippax: 24/3. After fifty-two minutes' batting Australia were 40/4, Larwood having plucked out Kelleway's off-stump. Thus far his three wickets had cost him 9 runs. Four runs later, while the sun was still shining and there was not a cloud in the sky, the surviving batsmen appealed successfully against the light.

On the third day Australia plumbed the depths. They were all out for 122 but could only bat ten men as the great Gregory broke down with a recurrence of cartilage trouble and was thus compelled to bow out of all cricket in wretched circumstances. Over the years he had made a magnificent contribution of spirit and zest. Larwood's figures were 14.4-4-32-6. In a timeless game Chapman was not disposed to take any risk whatsoever despite an apparently impregnable lead of 399. He batted again.

With Gregory incapacitated (he had bowled forty-one overs in the first innings) and Kelleway (thirty-four overs) indisposed with food poisoning the Australians were sorely stretched. Neither man took any further part in the match.

Hobbs and Sutcliffe scampered along to 25 runs in fifteen minutes before Hobbs played back to the tweaked turn of Grimmett and was trapped in front of his stumps, lbw for 11. Sutcliffe (32) was dismissed just before tea was taken at 74/2. Poor light and a shower of rain led to an early close by which time England had lost no further wicket and had gained a lead of 502. On the fourth day, Mead (73) and Jardine (65*) were the principal scorers although everyone made 20 or more before the declaration, the first in a Test in Australia, came at 348/8.

The home side, needing 742 to win, reached 17/1 at the end of the day and lost their remaining seven wickets quickly for a final score of 66.

40,000 people came to Sydney for the first day of the second Test, doubtless hoping for some better form from their compatriots. They had a beautiful wicket. It was a glorious day. Australia won the toss. England had made one change. In order to strengthen the bowling the all-rounder Geary replaced Mead.

Woodfull and Vic Richardson (27) opened successfully, putting on 51 before Larwood bowled the South Australian. At 65 Kippax, a fine sportsman, could not quite believe that he too had been bowled - by Geary - off his pads. He stood stunned. Hobbs immediately appealed. The fielders sat down. The crowd accused the wicket-keeper, Duckworth, of sharp practice but he could not possibly have broken the stumps and was in no position for the ball to have rebounded from his pads. Hobbs saw exactly what happened: 'there was not the least doubt that the ball went direct from Kippax's pad on to the wicket. Things were quite unpleasant for a time.' The square-leg umpire, in the best position to see, decided in favour of the fielding side.

The lunch score was 69/2 (Woodfull 26*; Ponsford 1*). Larwood may well have undermined the latter's confidence when dismissing him cheaply twice in the first Test, for Ponsford's cup indeed ran over when the Nottinghamshire man's speed caused him to turn away, only to have his left hand broken. He retired hurt, did not bat in the second innings and missed the rest of the series. Woodfull (68) and Hendry (37) both became victims of Geary before tea which was taken with the total at 163/4. Ryder made 25 but there was no substantial recovery by the time stumps were drawn, although Oldfield contributed a valiant 40*: 251/8. Geary had most impressive figures: 18-5-35-5.

After a swift ending to the Australian innings next morning, which left them with 253 on the board, Hobbs and Sutcliffe batted slowly during the hour before lunch. A record crowd in excess of 58,000 watched the play on a sultry day with thunderstorms in the offing, but since the Australian attack was not especially formidable the openers came under criticism. M A Noble wrote: 'both batsmen were always on the defensive and made only 36 during the period in which, with perfect safety, they could have scored double the number...Hobbs was not sighting the ball well.'

Fender agreed:

Neither batsman had made an attempt to attack the bowling in the way we are used to seeing them do and one rather felt that this was probably because they were trying to make certain of a restart together after lunch though, at the same time, we felt it rather dangerous as a policy to let the Australian bowlers settle down so comfortably for they were bound to bowl better in consequence.

At the interval Hobbs was 25* and Sutcliffe 11*. Afterwards Sutcliffe was caught at slip off Ironmonger without addition to his score: 37/1. Hammond came out but just under half-an-hour later at approximately 2.50, light rain compelled them to leave the field. Hobbs had reached 36* and Hammond 12*.

During the break which lasted until 4.45, there was a happy and memorable ceremony, one day in advance of Jack Hobbs' forty-sixth birthday. A 'Bobs for Hobbs' fund organised by *The Sydney Sun* had had great success. As a result, Monty Noble presented to the batsman a wallet containing forty-six sovereigns and a gold-mounted boomerang with the appropriate inscription: 'To John Berry Hobbs on his 46th birthday from friends and admirers in NSW.' In his book Noble has a special section in which he conveys what Hobbs meant to his friends, 'the enemy':

The hero of yesterday walks scantily clothed, in the threadbare garments of a 'has been'! Not so Hobbs. He is as necessary to England as salt is to a boiled egg...No English cricketer could have been assured of a more cordial welcome. His heroic deeds on behalf of the Mother Country were legion. Sincerity was the keynote of the receptions accorded to him as he took the field from State to State.

After the presentation, the crowd sang, 'For He's a Jolly Good Fellow' and Hobbs did a tour of the ground with Noble to acknowledge the tumultuous applause. On his return to the pavilion gate, he was hoisted aloft and carried shoulder high to the dressing-room.

In an interview Hobbs said, 'I never dreamed that people would do such a thing for a visiting cricketer. I cannot imagine it happening in any other part of the world.'

The kindness of the reception and the generosity of the crowd not surprisingly affected him. He was able to add just four more runs before Grimmett made him edge the ball to Oldfield who achieved the unusual feat of catching and stumping him simultaneously. An hour later, at the close, England were 113/2: Hammond 33*, Jardine 23*.

So much rain fell on the Sunday that observers could push their fingers an inch into the ground but then hot sun made the surface as hard as a board once more. On Monday England moved into control, especially in the person of Hammond who batted throughout the three sessions with a combination of steadiness and dazzling off-side strokes. Jardine (28) soon left but Hendren joined Hammond in the major partnership of the innings, 145. It only took them a very few minutes more than two hours before Hendren (74) was caught off Blackie. 86* at lunch, 150* at tea, Hammond had reached 201* by the evening. Chapman had hit a fast 20 but Larwood, 30*, gave steadier support. England closed at 420/5.

They continued remorselessly on the following day to the record score of 636. Hammond, after completing a superb 251, finally departed at 496/7, having helped to add 459. Larwood (43) and Geary, having a fine all-round match (66), made useful contributions but every batsman reached double figures, something which had not happened since 1895. Before the end (39/1) Larwood had at once dismissed Richardson thanks to a brilliant short-leg catch by Hendren.

A brave fight back by Woodfull (111) and Hendry (112) was mainly responsible for taking Australia to 339/4 during Wednesday but Ryder's staunch 77* was only increased by 2 on the sixth day. The innings ended at 397. Tate, with economical figures of 46-14-99-4 was the main wicket-taker. Left with 15 to win the England batting order was juggled curiously by Chapman. Geary and Tate were elevated to the post of opening pair, but both were dismissed so that what should have been a ten-wicket victory appeared on paper as 'only' an eight-wicket one.

The third Test at Melbourne provided another excellent wicket - after the lively first hour. Chapman failed to win the toss, but when Australia lost Woodfull, Richardson and Hendry for 57 he may even have been pleased he had done so. There was no further dramatic success for the English bowlers before the end of play, however, by which time Kippax had made an elegant 100 and Ryder was 111*. His runs were robustly made but he quickly departed on the morrow, after adding only 1. Bradman, a mere twenty years of age, batted over three hours for an invaluable 79 but the rest did little with the exception of a'Beckett (41) in his first Test.

It was a slow day. Only 168 runs were made in a full four-and-a-half hours. The 121 added by Australia took them 3 hours and 20 minutes. They were all out at 4.30. The crowd, in excess of 60,000, had had nothing from which they could take unalloyed pleasure. The last hour, however, did give them one moment. Hobbs, having swept Grimmett to bring up his 3000th Test run and having scored 20 in thirty-five minutes, went after a'Beckett outside the off-stump only to edge him into Oldfield's receptive gloves. *The Times* wrote dismissively:

Hobbs was out to a poor stroke when England went in and he is clearly nothing like the Hobbs of four years ago either in his fielding or in his batting.

From the overnight 47/1 England moved comfortably onwards. Hammond was impervious to all that a'Beckett and Hendry (both medium-pacers), Grimmett (leg-breaks), Blackie (slow off-breaks), Oxenham (medium off-breaks) and Ryder (fast-medium) could bowl and sauntered to 169*. During that time he lost Sutcliffe (58) with whom he shared a partnership of 133, Chapman and Hendren, both cheaply, before Jardine (21*) saw out the proceedings with him. 312/4 became 368/5 when Jardine's solid 62 came to an end on Wednesday. The tail was disappointing as was a final score of 417 after a promising position when stumps were pitched. Hammond's 200 was the centrepiece. That the Australian attack was never collared is shown in the fact that they bowled in all 195 overs (England had bowled 180 overs in Australia's 397) and especially in Blackie's commendable figures of 44-13-94-6. There is much evidence, of which this is but one small example, that batting in timeless Tests in Australia in the 1920s often lacked speed, dash and spectator appeal; but, of course, there were giants in the earth in those days.

Only 20 behind on the first innings, Australia soon established themselves second time around. They reached the evening with a most satisfactory 118/2: Woodfull 64*, Kippax 34*. Next day, the New South Welshman soon left for 40 and Ryder failed but Bradman took his place to great effect. Lunch was taken at 168/4: Woodfull 90* and Bradman 9*. Larwood pulled a muscle and only managed 16 overs in the entire innings all of them below his normal pace. The heat was intense. Tate and Geary bowled with great spirit, however, and admirable though the Australian batting was, it was never able to dominate totally. Woodfull (107) and Bradman (112) were the mainstays. The close saw a score of 347/8.

That night the rain fell. In the morning it was still falling. A traditional Melbourne 'sticky' wicket was in the offing. Play began late, at 12.30. The last two wickets did nothing of any significance. White's match figures were a tribute to his stamina and accuracy: 113.5-50-173-6. England required 332 to win. It was a forlorn hope. Hobbs and Sutcliffe faced two overs before lunch. The sun was out and the wicket was going to be at its worst until tea. Opinion was unanimous. The following comments give the picture:

The Melbourne sticky wicket is a nasty affair; the ball not only turns but gets up almost straight and like a flash. Indeed it may be said to do everything but keep straight. (*The Times*)

The Melbourne wicket under these conditions can be the worse in the world. (Noble)

Our friends came to the pavilion to commiserate with us, saying what a pity it was the rain came. We thought so too. We considered we didn't have a chance of getting the runs. (Hobbs)

The only speculation was whether England would get over or under 100; no one dreamt she would get any more and the game was counted as being all over bar shouting. (Fender)

The batsmen needed a slice of good fortune. Immediately after lunch, Hobbs, on 3, was deceived by a lifter from a'Beckett; the ball lobbed from the shoulder of his bat into the slips where Hendry missed the chance. England could have been, should have been, 10/1 and beginning the slide down the greasy pole. There were 1 $\frac{3}{4}$ hours between lunch and tea which had to be endured. The batsman's dead bat techniques and allied defensive skills, however, thwarted all that the opposing captain, Ryder, could bring to bear upon them with the varied attack at his disposal. In Noble's opinion the bowlers did not capitalise on the conditions as they should have done. This is something of a backhanded compliment to the batsmen. It is after all a maxim of the game that bowlers can only bowl as well as batsmen allow them to. While the openers had no intention of hitting them off their line, the ability of Hobbs and Sutcliffe to leave the sharply rising ball alone - and their courage in letting it hit them obliged the bowlers to drop shorter - and then the batsmen pulled them hard. Fender has left a vivid account of what happened:

The wicket behaved as badly as it possibly could, brought out every trick in its bag, yet England's opening pair fought on without flinching in the face of tremendous odds. About three balls in five hopped up head or shoulder-high, some turning as well and all stopping almost visibly as they hit the ground. The batsmen were hit all over the body from pads to shoulder, and in two or three cases even on the neck and on the head, all from good or nearly good-length balls.

Scoring runs was not their main business but their dispatching of the bad ball coupled with their excellent running between the wickets enabled them to add 75 runs in this period of 105 minutes. About this stand *The Times* was uncharacteristically enthusiastic especially in so far as the older man was concerned:

To Hobbs must be awarded the palm...He could not be caught by any tricks; his footwork was superb; and he showed younger and possibly more active players how it was possible to change the stroke almost at the last minute and still make it technically correctly.

By tea, Hobbs had 36 and Sutcliffe 32. The hundred came up in two-and-a- quarter hours. Just before it did, Hobbs signalled for a fresh bat, tried it out, settled for the old one, and sent a message to his captain that Jardine should come in at 3, instead of 6, as he knew his Surrey colleague temperamentally and technically to be the least likely of the remaining batsmen to lose his wicket in difficult circumstances. Chapman took the

132

advice when at 105 the first wicket fell. Hobbs (49) played forward to Blackie and as the ball pitched short of his outstretched leg he may have been unlucky to have been adjudged lbw in view of the generally unpredictable nature of the pitch. But the job had been done - and done well - as Jack Fingleton, later a fine opening batsman for Australia (as well as a distinguished journalist) remembered:

The two Englishmen that day demoralised the Australian bowling, their fielding and the captaincy of Ryder. They gave their usual superb lesson of running between the wickets. One never let the other down.

The worst of the devil had gone from the wicket. Sutcliffe, 42* when Hobbs left, was still there in the evening, 83*. Jardine 18* had fought his way through and England, if by no means home and dry, were well on their way: 171/1.

The pitch was not without its problems on the seventh day but Sutcliffe continued with massive, unflappable authority to his century before lunch when he was 105*. Jardine (33) had gone and England at the interval were 222/2. On 257 Hammond (32) was run out. Hendren attacked con brio and finished with 45. Sutcliffe finally nodded. After a chanceless innings of 135 (six hours, twenty five minutes: nine 4s) he was lbw to Grimmett: 318/4. Although three more wickets fell, 332 runs were duly made for a great victory which won the series and retained The Ashes.

The Prime Minister, Baldwin, sent the team a message of congratulations, and over 262,000 people had seen a remarkable match. No less remarkable was the Reuter's report, published on 7 January 1929, that followed:

Hobbs stated today that the question as to whether he had played his last Test Match was not one for him to decide. (He wished to stand down after the win in the third contest to give others a chance.)...If selected, the would naturally have to concur.

This slight element of dissension was happy resolved by the time teams met again at Adelaide for the fourth Test where England fielded an unchanged side. Hobbs had been rested for the visit to Tasmania but, returning to the team for the fixture with South Australia which immediately preceded the Test, had scored a handsome double of 75 and 100 although troubled to some extent by the heat, especially in the second innings.

Chapman won the toss. On a cool, overcast day, Hobbs and Sutcliffe moved out to make good use of another hard, true wicket. They batted with their customary ease and confidence. The fifty stand came in just over an hour. Brisk, safe singles were the main reason for their progress. Hobbs hit the first boundary after sixty-five minutes. By lunch they had put on 77: Hobbs 41*, Sutcliffe 31*. A reporter concluded: 'Hobbs, who now seems to tire very quickly, played a master's innings.' One stroke revealed his genius with the bat. He shaped to play a leg-side ball to the on; the ball swerved late in flight; with an effortless shift of his feet, he played a perfect stroke through the covers. He came to his 50 out of 94 in 1 ^{3}/4hours. The hundred partnership was completed after 113 minutes. It was their ninth century stand against Australia. On 143 Hobbs (74) was out to a good, low, slip catch by Ryder off Hendry. At the same score went Sutcliffe (64) and, as Jardine soon followed, tea was taken at 149/3. Hendren did not last (179/4) and England were in trouble. Chapman (39) shared in a crucial 67-run stand with Hammond who finished the day on 47 with England 246/5. Much of the advantage of the excellent opening stand had been lost.

The next day was a very hot day. The wicket was fast. Conditions were ideal for batting. It may be fairly argued that neither side made the best use of them. Hammond (119*) held the rest of the innings together, scoring 72 of the last 88 before the total of 334 was reached. Grimmett had a fine analysis: 52.1-12-102-5.

When Australia batted, they were rapidly reduced to 19/3. Woodfull, Hendry and Kippax were out. Tate, Larwood and White had each enjoyed a success. But the immensely talented nineteen year-old Archie Jackson, who was making his debut having replaced Richardson as Woodfull's opening partner, batted attractively for 70*. Ryder kept him company to make a sound 54*. Close of play:131/3.

After Sunday's rest, Jackson began shakily and lost his partner (63) at 145. At lunch he was 97* while Bradman, with some luck, was 34*. The first ball after the interval was delivered by Larwood and dispatched by Jackson to the boundary. Thus it was he joined an elite company who have scored a century in the first innings of their first Test. This restored his touch and he performed with a delightful artistry until he was sixth out at 287. By the end of the last session Australia had reached 365/9.

They finished next morning with a lead of 35. Both England's openers failed. Hobbs tried to glance Hendry, did not make solid enough contact and Oldfield moving to his left took the catch easily. England 1/1; last ʳ..an 1. Sutcliffe reached 17 but was then also caught behind the wicket: 21/2.

Such a double failure was extraordinary. During their fourteen-match association as openers against Australia, Hobbs' and Sutcliffe's stands had previously been: 157 and 110; 283 and 36; 126;0 and 3; 32 unfinished; 182; 59 and 156; 58; 53 and 172; 85 and 25; 37 and 8; 28 and 105; 143 and 1. It is indeed a splendid sequence. Only in the fourth Test of the 1924-25 season had both of them been out by the time the score had reached 50.

Hammond, continuing to enjoy his greatest series, was 105* at the close while Jardine, possibly underestimated as a Test batsman by cricket historians, had again proved his worth with 73*.

England's recovery to 206/2 was sustained on the fifth day. Their partnership eventually realised 262, a record for the third wicket for

England v Australia which still remains. The only disappointment was Jardine's failure to make a century. He scored 98. Another very hot day slowly sapped Hammond's stamina but not until he had made 177 out of 327 was he out, the seventh wicket to fall. In the match as a whole he batted 11 hours and 43 minutes. The only other English pleasure was provided by Tate's bright, hard-hitting 47. The total of 383 meant that Australia needed 349 to win.

24/0 overnight, they fought hard down the next day, at the end of which Oxenham and Bradman remained to carry on the battle and the score was 260/6. Ryder (87) and Kippax (51) had given grounds for hope.

The final twist of a memorable match came when Bradman was on 58 and well on the way to winning the match. Only 41 runs were required and there were three wickets in hand:

Oldfield played a ball from White fairly hard straight to Hobbs' right hand, not very deep, at cover and called Bradman who responded. That ought to be enough to convey the result.

So says Fender. Actually, the throw was not very straight but Duckworth took it well and did what was necessary. A tense victory by the small margin of 12 runs was finally secured when Larwood caught Blackie off White. It was most fitting that the Somerset left-arm spinner had the satisfaction of this wicket as he had bowled magnificently throughout with an astonishing accuracy, steadiness and penetration. The figures say it all: 1st innings - 60-16-130-5; 2nd innings - 64.5-21-126-8.

In the month between the fourth and fifth Tests, Hobbs did little of note but there was no real possibility of his not playing in the final game, especially as Sutcliffe was unable to take part because he had thrown his arm out a fortnight earlier, against New South Wales. Chapman stood down reportedly because of influenza but curiously fit enough to act as twelfth man. White assumed the captaincy, Leyland replaced Chapman as batsman, Tyldesley took Sutcliffe's place and Jardine moved up the order to partner Hobbs. Australia gave their side a younger, fresher look by dropping Hendry (aged 33) and Blackie (46). a'Beckett disappeared as well. In their stead came Fairfax, only 22, and all-rounder who bowled fast-medium, Hornibrook (29), slow to medium left-arm spin, and Wall (24), the first fit fast bowler Australia had used in the whole series.

At Melbourne once more, White won the toss. The new England opening partnership did a sound job for their side in the hour-and-a-half up to lunch, but it was not stirring stuff. The first hour produced just 31 and only 51 runs were made in all (Hobbs 36*; Jardine 12*), but, more to the point, no wickets were lost to the vagaries of a first-morning Melbourne wicket. Although the sun was shining, it was a cool day for the participants and a cold one for the spectators. The wicket was hard, offering some encouragement both to the batsmen and the faster bowlers. Wall had his first success at 64. Jardine (19) deflected a pull on to his cap whence it flew high to give Oldfield the opportunity of a high running catch. In Fender's opinion the conditions were in Hobbs' favour:

He was showing no signs of either fatigue or anxiety. It was apparent that he was in his best form and we all anticipated big things.

Hobbs' 50 was made out of 73 in 1 $^3/_4$ hours. The only chance he gave was when he was on 77. Fairfax induced an edge to Hornibrook in the slips. In his delight, the tall Queenslander tried to throw the ball up before he had secured it. Down went the ball. On went Hobbs. Hammond (38) left before tea when the score was 159/2: Hobbs 89*.

At 4.39pm, with a single, he completed his twelfth and last century against Australia. It was his fifth at Melbourne. It took 3 hours and 28 minutes. In Noble's view it was:

a fitting climax to a great career. Thunderous cheers greeted its accomplishment and after they had subsided the crowd on the 'Hill' broke out again into a spontaneous chorus of three more cheers. His form had been far superior to that in his previous innings during the tour.

He was not troubled by the bowlers and did not look like getting out. He was at the wicket another 70 minutes, adding a further stylish 42 before he was bowled by Ryder: 235/3. Fender wrote:

Hobbs had played a grand innings. He was always sound and master not only of the bowling but of himself in every way and he played with the utmost ease and freedom. He was never really pressing for runs but took full advantage of anything approaching the loose while he showed all his old ability to force runs here and there, as and when he wanted them without taking the faintest shadow of a risk.

5 runs later Tyldesley (31) was dismissed by Ryder so two new batsmen had to contend with the Australian attack on the second day which began with England 240/4. After the nightwatchman, Duckworth's departure (260/5), Leyland, in his first Test v Australia, joining Hendren, had the good fortune, on 13, to be missed off Ryder just before lunch. The batsmen stayed together through the afternoon until Hendren (95) was out to the last ball before tea when Leyland was 54*. He dominated the last session with 45 of the next 69 runs and, although he became stuck on 99, reached 110* by the close: England 485/9. Australia had missed Grimmett who injudiciously but helplessly had stopped one of Hobbs' drives with his knees.

On the third day only 187 runs were scored, yet fewer than fifteen minutes were lost. England ended on 519, Leyland 137. Australia reached 152/2. A dull affair - but not altogether unexpected in the context of timeless Tests.

136

The fourth day produced another 215 runs. Another two wickets, one of which was Woodfull's for 102, were lost. The fifth day saw Bradman reach 123, Fairfax 65 and Australia 491. They had needed 271 overs to score their runs. England's 519 had taken 215. The hero of England's bowling was Geary with a record number of overs: 81-36-105-5.

Jardine was out first ball to Wall before the close. The fast bowler also soon yorked Larwood on the sixth morning. Hammond, no doubt jaded by now, made 16 (75/3) but at lunch Tyldesley was there with Hobbs: 111/3. 'The fast scoring was due to Hobbs' versatility and enterprise.' (Noble). When he was fourth out at 119 he had made a brilliant 65. In both attack and defence his footwork had been quick, his scoring strokes had been as fluent and as stylish as ever. The ending was an anti-climax, sadly. He tried to play a gentle cut off Grimmett but the ball kicked unexpectedly and he only succeeded in giving Fairfax an easy catch at short third man.

So Hobbs left the wicket at Melbourne for the last time. His record there was remarkable:

1907-08	83	and	28	;	57	and 0
1911-12	6	and	126*	;	178	
1920-21	122	and	20	;	27	and 13
1924-25	154	and	22	;	66	
1928-29	20	and	49	;	142	and 65

Matches	Innings	Not Out	Runs	100s	50s	H.S.	Average
10	18	1	1178	5	4	178	69

Leyland (53*) and Tate (54) did most to take England to 257 in the face of some genuinely quick and hostile bowling from Wall, 5/66. With half-an-hour left that evening a new Australian opening partnership was formed which must have been a quiz-master's delight ever since: Oldfield and Hornibrook. They did more than could reasonably have been expected by staying until just before lunch next morning and while doing so put on 51 of the 286 needed for victory.

Tenacious play by both sides limited the runs to 158 and the wickets to 4. And the evening and the morning were the seventh day...

England had their moments on the eighth morning but Duckworth missed an easy stumping of Bradman who finished on 38* and Ryder, who was to make 57* was ruled not out in the same over when he was run out by a distance. As Noble described it: 'It seemed that Ryder was well out. He had failed to ground his bat but the appeal was disallowed.' That was really the last excitement. Australia reached 287 in the afternoon thus winning by five wickets.

The Times' assessment of Hobbs' performances was unenthusiastic:

Hobbs has palpably been suffering nearly all the tour from 'anno domini'. He has tired easily and early and the strong Australian light has affected his sight of the ball.

Yet it seems surprising that such a decrepit and ailing cricketer should be able to score 451 runs, average 50, in the Tests, and 962 first-class runs in all on the tour at an average of 56!

In 1929 Hobbs was once more at the top of the English first-class averages (2263 at 66) and would doubtless have played in all five Tests against South Africa had it not been for a mishap at Lord's in the Test Trial in early June. In prime form he had struck a delightful 59 for 'England', often dancing down the wicket to the spinners. When 'The Rest' batted it was his county captain and friend Percy Fender who gave him half a chance to take a catch: 'Hobbs seemed to hold the ball for a moment, but fell heavily and did not complete the catch.' It was announced later that he had torn a ligament in his right shoulder.

Hobbs missed Surrey's next seven matches and two Tests. He returned for Sutcliffe's benefit at Leeds where he made 11 and 43. He then went to Blackheath for the meeting with Kent which coincided with the third Test. He was upset by a report in a Kent newspaper which wondered whether he would choose to play for England or improve his average by turning out against Kent:

This was a very unkind way of putting it and quite unjustified [he scored 5 and 150* in the draw]...The fact was that I was fit to bat and Surrey could hide me or nurse me in the field; moreover, I could go careful myself, so that Surrey were willing to play me with all my disadvantage. To play for England, however, is a very different matter; one cannot there be a passenger in the field. The Selectors knew the position and were not prepared to play me. I dare not let my arm come over or attempt to throw at any pace.

His full fitness gradually returned. Bowley (Sussex) and Killick (Middlesex) each had two Tests as Sutcliffe's partner but neither did enough to make his place secure. Hobbs, therefore, returned to the England team for the final Test at The Oval. He had shown himself to be in good touch. His previous three innings had been 97, 134 and 48.

On the first day, the Test wicket was said to be 'grimy and spiteful' in one report, although *Wisden* implies it was 'splendid' throughout the match. There was plenty of sunshine pouring on to a rain-soaked ground. Deane, the visitors' captain, put England in to bat. There was 3 hours and 40 minutes' play; 166 runs were scored for the loss of 4 wicket. One observer noted thoughtfully of Hobbs:

We who have watched him long and often have established telepathic sympathy with his moods - we were not quite comfortable. When he stepped in to drive and merely stunned the ball we wagged apprehensive heads at one another. When he missed a slow full pitch on his pads, we felt pretty sure that his eye was temporarily out.

At 1.25 Hobbs (10) mistimed a hook at a short-pitched leg-break to be well caught at short leg by Quinn off the leg-spin bowling of McMillan: 38/1. Hammond failed and although Woolley (40) flourished for a time before he trod on his wickets, Wyatt only made a few.

Sutcliffe remained 84* and continued to 104 on the second day when South Africa were batting before lunch in pursuit of 258. The slow left-arm spinner Vincent earned his figures of 45-10-105-5: Sutcliffe, Hammond, Woolley, Wyatt and Leyland were an impressive haul.

The wicket still favoured the bowlers. Before South Africa quite knew what was happening they were 20/3. That they reached a highly creditable 283/5 by the close was due almost entirely to the veterans Taylor (131) and Deane (93). On the third day there was an ideal batting wicket which both sides utilised to the full. South Africa made a further 207 in the two-and-a-half hours before lunch before the declaration at 492/8: Cameron 60, Morkel 81, McMillan 50.

England had no trouble in playing out time and they did so most entertainingly. The opening partnership of 77 lasted only seventy-five minutes. Hobbs' share was a sparkling 52. After spending about ten minutes playing himself in he

began to play as he sometimes does when he has made Surrey safe and is prepared to let somebody else bat. He then shows us all the strokes brilliantly executed for a longer or shorter period and finally gives away his wicket by one for attempting which a schoolboy receives a serious lecture from the games' master. This time the period of brilliancy lasted exactly one hour during which it was almost impossible to place the field for him. (*The Times*)

The fun ended when he tried to pull a straight ball from Vincent over square-leg but, beaten by the spin, skied it to Mitchell at slip. Sutcliffe completed his second century of the match (109*) and Hammond (101*) hit with great power in a total of 264/1.

At the end of this season, during which he made ten centuries, Hobbs, in his 47th year, showed that he was by no means finished either as a Test player or as a maker of centuries.

11 Indian Summer and Final Years, 1930-34

In 1930 Hobbs headed his county list again but was eighth in the first-class table. His 2103 runs were scored at an average of 51 per innings. Of these his contribution to Surrey was 1142 at 54. There were his last Test matches but occasionally he stood down for a rest. Yet, as *Wisden* 1931 pointed out, 'For Surrey to lack the assistance of Hobbs, however, is no new experience. Indeed, owing to the calls of representative games and at different times to injury from which he has been suffering, Surrey in fifty-three Championship matches out of 136 during the past five seasons, have had to take the field without their great batsman.'

This was a year in which he kept free of illness and injury. It began brightly with 137 and 111 in the opening game against Glamorgan. There were ten more matches for him before the first Test against Australia at Nottingham. Of the fourteen innings Hobbs had, half of them were over 50 and all but one were in double figures. 1930 was an unusual season in that at least twice Hobbs clearly disagreed with a fielder's appeal. The Test Trial saw the first of these 'incidents'. Batting for 'England' v 'The Rest', Hobbs played Worthington into the slips were Duleepsinhji took the ball very low down. The batsman thought the ball had touched the ground. One reporter observed, 'He had some conversation with Duleepsinhji and eventually an appeal was made to the umpire' who supported the fielder.

For the first time, in an effort, no doubt, to avoid the draws which had been so much a part of Australia's last tour of England in 1926, four days were allocated to each of the Tests with the exception of the fifth which, if the series were undecided before it began, was to be played to a finish.

There was much excitement at Trent Bridge during the cricket which had many attractive features. Chapman won the toss. England batted. Hobbs and Sutcliffe had by no means perfect conditions in which to display their skills, as the wicket retained a little moisture which gave bowlers Wall, Fairfax, Grimmett, Hornibrook and McCabe (fast-medium) some assistance. The first hour produced 41 runs but shortly after the 50 was registered, Sutcliffe (29) was caught in the slips: 53/1. Grimmett then enjoyed some magic moments: Hammond lbw (63/2), Woolley, leaning too far forward to his first ball, stumped (63/3) and Hendren's off stump shaken by a googly. England were in disarray at 71/4. 'The Australians were then quite naturally chuckling with joy,' one reporter noted. The captain then joined the old hand who had 'played the great man's part' and 'batted as if he were the only good cricketer on the side'. Lunch was taken at 91/4: Hobbs 37*, Chapman 8*.

In poor light they continued but this did not prevent Chapman from peremptorily striking Grimmett for three 4s in an over thereby raising his own and the side's morale. Nearly half an hour was lost to the weather from 2.35. On their return the batsmen made the most of the bowlers' difficulty with the slippery ball. Hobbs went to his 50 with a splendid hook for 4 off Wall. Chapman continued to hit fiercely for 52 out of 82 in sixty-five minutes: 152/5. Shortly after Larwood came out, with Hobbs on 55*, rain drove everyone off again for an hour and three-quarters before it was possible to play once more at 5.30pm. Grimmett bowled Larwood: 188/6. At 6.15pm Hobbs, on 78, was caught by Richardson in the slips off McCabe: 218/7. His had been a most important contribution as Warner wrote in his account of the tour, *The Fight for the Ashes in 1930*: 'Hobbs was once again the backbone of our batting. He batted with his usual skill and judgement and England would have been in sorry plight but for him.'

The Times correspondent said Hobbs 'had never shown the slightest sign of a poor stroke'. Tate stayed for a little while but played the last ball of the day into his wicket to make the score 241/8, with Robins, in his first Test against Australia, 28*.

The Middlesex all-rounder personally added 22 next day, after play began at 2.15pm and was mainly responsible for the total of 270 at three o'clock. There had been overnight rain and by the time Australia went in to bat, the sun was doing its work - and the visitors could not cope with the treacherous conditions.

Tate soon had Australia in disarray, dismissing Ponsford, Woodfull and Bradman at a personal cost of 7 runs. The score: 16/3. The visitors did well to recover 144 all out early on the third morning. That they did so was largely thanks to a valiant 64* from Kippax who alone played the leg-spin of Robins (4/51) well.

England's 126-run lead was swiftly built upon by their openers in a stand of 125 in 113 minutes. Hobbs was at his best making his runs at speed and with complete assurance before being stumped off Grimmett for 74, five minutes before lunch. As Fender reported:

Hobbs played one of the most brilliant innings which I have ever seen him play. He gave the bowlers no rest, and though he did not take many risks, he introduced an ingenuity and versatility into his batting which soon had Woodfull and his bowlers at their wits end. No one could keep him quiet and whenever he found runs difficult to get in the orthodox way he would step in front of his off-stump, for instance, and sweep a ball from outside that stump to the leg boundary with precision and confidence.

England went into lunch with a lead of 251 and nine wickets in hand. All did not quite go according to plan after the interval. Sutcliffe (58) had his thumb split by Wall and had to retire with the score 134. Hammond and

141

Woolley both failed again. After a shaky start Hendren (72) held the rest of the innings together until Australia was left with 429 to win. In less than an hour before the close, after the early dismissal of Woodfull, Ponsford (21*) and Bradman (31*) attacked to reach 60/1.

The fourth morning saw Sutcliffe and Larwood (gastritis) out of the match. There were two substitute fielders; Duleepsinhji, the twelfth man, and one Sydney Copley of the Nottinghamshire ground staff who had never even played in a first-class match. The Australians pressed on vigorously and although Ponsford (39) and Fairfax (23) perished in the morning, McCabe was at his best while Bradman went from strength to strength before lunch: 198/3 (Bradman 88*; McCabe 33*). By three o'clock they had moved comfortably enough to 229. Bradman had his century. McCabe was on 49. Victory for Australia was by no means out of the question. Tate was tiring. He bowled a slower ball to McCabe who drove it hard but slightly uppishly. Copley at mid-on flung himself forward and to his right to take a brilliant one-handed catch as he crashed to the ground. It was the turning point.

When Bradman, after a fine 131, was deceived and bowled by a googly from Robins, who finished with seven wickets in the match, the back of the resistance was broken. The end came at 5.35. England, thanks largely to Hobbs' batting (he top-scored in both innings) and good fortune with the weather, were the victors by 93 runs.

In the next match, the visitors might have hoped for some respite from Hobbs but he struck 146* in the second innings for Surrey in a drawn game. *The Cricketer* was enthusiastic:

He began rather slowly for him but he later played in characteristic fashion and without punishing him severely clearly showed that he was, on the day, Grimmett's master. Already with the season only about half over he has done enough to prove that he is still absolutely indispensable for England's best eleven even when his splendid fielding is not taken into account.

This gave the Australians a foretaste of what they could expect at Lord's in the second Test.

There, however, the luck turned. Sutcliffe had not recovered. Oddly, instead of playing Hobbs' regular county partner, Sandham (who had been asked to go to the ground and with whom Hobbs shared 66 century opening stands) the Selectors opted to retain Woolley, pushing him up the order to open. Larwood too was unfit. In his place, G O Allen, who had played little cricket that year, made his debut.

Despite these changes, England made good use of perfect weather and an excellent wicket when Chapman won the toss. There was, nevertheless, a subdued start. Hobbs with a new partner (and their combined age was 90) had no opportunity for the short singles in which he took so much delight and with which he normally confounded his opponents. He failed to establish himself, played back to a well pitched up ball from Fairfax, snicked it to Oldfield and was out for 1: England were 13/1. Woolley flamed with contemptuous fire which brought him 41 before a startling catch by Wall in the gully meant a score of 53/2. After only forty-five minutes this was, to say the least of it, an unusual start. When Hammond (38) left at 105/3, England were not best placed. The rest of the day, however, belonged happily to Duleepsinhji. In his first Test against Australia he maintained a family tradition when he did what his uncle Ranjitsinhji had done. 'Duleep' batted with great style and flair. Ably assisted, first by Hendren (48) and later by Tate (54) he scored 173 in 4 $\frac{3}{4}$ hours and, although he was put down twice, he never looked to be in trouble. Finally dismissed (387/9) just before the close, he had been at the wicket while 334 were added. A score of 405/9 at the end of the day must have left the 28,000 crowd with a sense of comfort, optimism and well-being.

But that sense was not justified because, after England added a further 20 runs, Australia proceeded to score with ease, speed and authority, 404/2. Statistics tell the story: Ponsford (81) shared an opening partnership of 162 with Woodfull. This was an excellent platform on which Bradman was then able to display his prodigious talents in all their glory. After he and Woodfull had put on 231 in 154 minutes, the Victorian (155) was out but there was no relief. 96/0 at lunch had become 244/1 at tea. At the close Bradman's perfection had brought him 155* off only 171 balls.

The third day saw Bradman make the (then) highest Test score in this country: 254. Kippax (83) was his principal assistant. Australia declared at tea with a new record score: 729/6. England needed 304 to avoid an innings defeat. The loss of both openers by the time the total had reached 53 was a disappointment as was the manner of their going.

At 45 Hobbs, on 19, made an uncharacteristic error. He walked across his wicket to play a Grimmett half-volley to leg, missed, and was bowled round his legs. The crowd was no more stunned than was the batsman. A reporter commented on Hobbs' apparent bewilderment as he looked at the wicket: 'He could hardly believe it.' Woolley compounded England's misery by treading on his wickets when trying to pull Grimmett to square leg. 93/2 was the score when stumps were drawn.

When Hammond, Duleepsinhji and Hendren were all back in the pavilion and the runs on the board were only 147, England looked well on the way to humiliation. Chapman and Allen then joined in a spirited stand which put on 115 in ninety minutes remaining before lunch to restore hopes of saving the game: Chapman 52*; Allen 54*. Ten runs later however, Allen (57) was lbw to Grimmett. Chapman, undismayed, hit ever more boldly, going from 69 to 93 with five scoring strokes: 4, 6, 4, 4, 6. Dismissed at 352/8 he had made 121 in 152 minutes.

Australia, eventually left with 72 to win in ninety minutes, had a few early shocks which reduced them to 22/3 but won easily enough by 7 wickets.

Grimmett took 8 wickets in the match and, although they had cost him 272 runs, they were not, in the context his batsmen had provided for him, expensive.

England had retrieved some honour in the game but by now most people realised that they had new phenomenon to counter. Any lingering doubts were dispelled by the end of the first day of the third Test at Leeds. Australia were in complete command thanks to the greatness of the 21-year-old New South Welshman. Lunch: 136/1 (Bradman 105*). Tea: 305/2 (Bradman 220*). Close of play: 458/3 (Bradman 309*). England did well to confine the visitors to 566 all out on the second morning: Bradman was finally out for 334 made off only 448 balls.

Half an hour before lunch was successfully negotiated by Hobbs and Sutcliffe, and 17 runs were acquired. Their 50-partnership came in ninety minutes and both seemed well settled when a controversy exploded. Hobbs (29) in attempting to turn Grimmett to leg edged the delivery into the air and a' Becket dashed in from silly mid-on for the ball. Percy Fender saw what happened:

As he reached for it he fell and with hands outstretched rolled over to his right and sat up clasping the ball in both hands. Hobbs seemed quite certain that the catch had not been made and he and Oldfield were in the best position to see... Oldfield made no appeal at any time.

Hobbs was indeed uncertain that catch had carried:

I stood my ground, not quite sure what had happened. If I had been sure I was out I would not have stayed for a moment. I would much rather be in the pavilion if I knew I was out. It may be news to some people who have criticised me for not leaving straight away that the first thing I did was to say: 'Did he catch it, Bertie?' to Oldfield at the wicket. 'No,' he answered. So we waited...when, after the delay, I was eventually given out, I accepted the decree without a word. If Oldfield had said I was out, everything would have been different.

In a recent conversation with the author, Maurice Allom, the former Test player and colleague of Hobbs in the Surrey side at that time, said that Hobbs was always trusted implicitly: 'He was the 'arch-gentleman' on the cricket field. He would never do anything underhand or take advantage of a situation or a player.'

Hobbs was out. England were 53/1. Sutcliffe left 11 runs later and when Duleepsinhji was dismissed at 123 embarrassment threatened. Leyland (44) hit positively, however, to accompany Hammond to 206. Two wickets then fell and the evening's score of 212/5 (Hammond 61*, Duckworth 0*) gave little room for confidence. Rain and bad light came to England's rescue on the third day limiting play to just fifty minutes. 30 runs accrued; no wickets were lost.

Although Hammond's 113 and Duckworth's resistance for 33 runs were both ended before lunch, England had reached 355/7 by the interval on the last day. The innings ended at 2.50pm with a deficit of 175. The follow-on was enforced.

The openers came out in very poor light. After quarter of an hour they appealed successfully against it. They were booed by the crowd (which did not happen to either of them very often) and criticised in the press. Hobbs believed this to be quite unjustified:

The manner in which the newspaper critics denounced our action was, in my opinion, deplorable...Herbert Sutcliffe came down the pitch to me and said, 'What do you think about the light?' 'Not very good,' I answered, 'and if Clarrie Grimmett goes on again at the dark end we will appeal...' (Grimmett had a low trajectory. His arm tended to get lost in the dark background at one end of the ground)... If he had gone on at the other end, we would not have said a word for there was no big shadowy stand facing us there, and no stormcloud above it. Let it be noted that our critics were sitting in that big stand, looking on the bright side of things!

As the light immediately improved, they were only off for about five minutes which no doubt made the critics more caustic than they otherwise might have been.

Matters did not improve for Hobbs. On 13, he was run out for only the second time in his Test career. With Sutcliffe he had put on 24 when his partner played Grimmett to deep mid-off and called. They set off for what seemed to be simply another one of those innumerable singles with which they teased and frustrated the opposition, but Bradman had other ideas. As Fender wrote:

The fielder picked up and returned so quickly and accurately that the ball hit the top of the leg stump towards which Hobbs was running and he was just out. It was a magnificent piece of fielding and to be remembered by all who saw it.

England lost two more wickets before bad light brought an end to play forty minutes before the official close: 95/3.

At Manchester, for the fourth Test, there were a number of changes. England's battered bowling was reshaped. Out went Geary, Tyldesley and Larwood. In came Peebles (leg-breaks and googlies), Goddard (off-spin) and Nichols (all-rounder, fast bowler). For Australia, Ponsford and Fairfax returned in place of Jackson and a'Beckett.

The tourists won the toss on a slow and easy wicket which, although damp, had on the day little sun to bring it to life. At lunch Woodfull (37*) and Ponsford (30*) had 75/0 on the board, and, of the bowlers, only Peebles looked dangerous. One small incident recalled in Ian Peebles' auto-biography *Spinner's Yarn* tells much about Hobbs as a human being. When Peebles was preparing to bowl for the first time in a Test against Australia:

Jack Hobbs made a detour in his journey from cover to cover to give me a word of encouragement. What he said, in essence, was that this was just the same as any cricket match and to bowl as I would in the ordinary way. It was a characteristically thoughtful gesture and started me off on just the right note.

In the afternoon, the picture changed. The openers continued until 106 when the captain (54) was caught. In came Bradman. 32 runs later, having been beaten more than once by Peebles and missed by Hammond, of all people, off that bowler, he was caught at slip for 14, off Peebles. Kippax joined Ponsford but their partnership lasted only until the total reached 184. Hammond then asserted himself by bowling the latter for a durable, well-made 83 and, after Peebles had confused McCabe into being lbw (189/4), bowled Richardson: 190/5. 2 runs later tea was taken and England were on top.

They were unable to dominate the last session, however, when the Australians were at their most tenacious. Kippax made a fine 51 and although Oldfield did not last (243/7), Fairfax (21*) and Grimmett (21*) were there in the evening: 275/7.

They finally completed a most useful 87-run stand for the eighth wicket, finishing respectively with 49 and 50; this was the leg-spinner's only half-century in Tests. The innings closed at 345 leaving Hobbs and Sutcliffe thirty-five minutes' batting before lunch. Although they were not parted and scored 29 between them, it was in this period that a vicious break back from all Wall beat Hobbs for pace and struck him in the groin. This delayed the game for several minutes as he was in acute discomfort.

After lunch Hobbs, still feeling groggy, batted with less than his usual zest and his timing was awry. Sutcliffe, on the other hand, was at his very best and took the major responsibility for maintaining the momentum of the scoring. By the time he had reached his 50, Hobbs, grimly hanging on with typical courage, had made 13. They stayed together for two hours to reach 108. It was their eleventh hundred partnership against Australia. At that point Hobbs (31) chose to cut a rising ball from Wall only to flick a thick edge to Oldfield. The wicket-keeper, standing back, had to make some ground to his right to make a fine catch. Hammond quickly played on to Wall. Sutcliffe shortly afterwards (119/3) was dismissed by the same bowler after hitting an exciting 74 which had contained one 6 and ten 4s. Tea was taken at 136/3. Duleepsinhji (54) batted delightfully but Leyland with 35 was the only other batsman to make any impact in what became a score of 251/8 by the end of the third day. This was when only about three-quarters of an hour's play was possible because of rain. During that time England had lost three wickets while adding 30 runs to their Saturday total of 221/5. McCabe, with his fast-medium deliveries, picked up his best bowling figures in Tests against England: 4/41. The fourth day was washed away.

Hobbs had two very special moments in the matches which followed the fourth Test. *The Cricketer* analyses the matter well:

Hobbs' faultless 106 against Sussex at Hastings must have occasioned him considerable pleasure...it caused him to have made at least one three-figure score in both home and away games against each of the other first-class counties. Incidentally it was also his 125th hundred in all matches for Surrey, his 152nd in England and his 174th altogether...Although The Oval is undoubtedly his favourite ground, as many as fifty-nine of the 125 large scores referred to have been obtained whilst playing on his opponents' grounds or only six fewer than the number made at Kennington where the excellence of the wickets provided has generally been proverbial.

This match was followed by a 'friendly' game with Middlesex at The Oval. Although it was not part of the County championship, it was an important part of cricket history. Hobbs made 40, and with his sixteenth run he passed the record aggregate of W G Grace, against whom he had played on that long ago day of his debut in 1905. At the end of this innings their figures were respectively as follows:

	Innings	Not Out	Highest Score	Runs	Average
W G Grace	1493	105	344	54896	39
J B Hobbs	1187	95	316*	54911	50

As the Test series was level, and England were fortunate to find themselves in such a position, the final match at The Oval was to be played to a finish.

More changes were made: one by Australia, Jackson in for Richardson; Whysall and Larwood replaced Goddard and Nichols in the England side which prompted relatively little comment. What did cause a flutter among the dovecots was the dropping of Chapman as captain in favour of R E S Wyatt who thus captained the team in his first Test against Australia. Hobbs comments:

It was indeed the bombshell of the season. As a member of the Selection Committee I must take my share of the responsibility...the Selectors' decision was unanimously against the continued appointment of Chapman...And now let me make an admission. As I look back I think we made a mistake in leaving out Chapman...But the sole idea of the Selectors was to stiffen the England batting.

Wyatt won the toss on a beautiful day and took first use of a pitch which was characteristic of The Oval: flat, firm, consistent, a batsmen's delight. In a timeless Test the batsmen were not going to be in a hurry. By the end of an hour 24 runs had been acquired. It was at this juncture that Hobbs drove McCabe through the off-side for a lovely four. It was Hobbs too, who brought up the 50 with a delightful square-cut for 4 off Grimmett. He also glanced Hornibrook to the long-leg boundary for another four. When he hooked Wall for yet another four, he moved to 47 made out of 68 just before lunch. The crowd's delight turned to dismay, however, when the next ball was bowled. It may have been a fraction faster. It encouraged the same shot but Hobbs mistimed his stroke and lifted the ball directly into the hands of Kippax who was fielding at short-leg.

Whysall, Hammond and Leyland all failed. Although Duleepsinhji made an attractive 50, England were very much on the back foot when Wyatt entered the arena to join Sutcliffe (64*) at 197/5. He received a warm reception from he crowd. Two runs later came tea. After the interval the batsmen did much to restore their side's fortunes by carrying the score to 316/5 by the close: Sutcliffe 138*; Wyatt 39*.

On Monday morning the pitch was still easy. After fifty minutes' further resistance, Sutcliffe (161) was dismissed with the total 367. The partnership of 170 was at that time a record for England's sixth wicket against Australia. Tate soon departed (379/7) to be followed by the captain who had fought splendidly for his 64 over three hours. The tail did not wag. 405 all out at 12.45 meant that the last five wickets had gone down for 89 runs in 105 minutes.

Woodfull and Ponsford put on 39 in the half-hour remaining before lunch. They had moved to 159 by tea: Ponsford 110*, Woodfull 40*. Ponsford, a good job well done, was out immediately on the resumption in poor light. The fielding side were pleased to see the back of his partner for 54 at 190/2, but Bradman 27* and Kippax 11* saw that there was no further loss before six o'clock: 215/2. The third day was much spoiled by rain but when it ended there was no doubt of the strength of the Australian position: 403/3; Bradman 130*; Jackson 43*. The latter did not make a confident start, however, as Fender describes:

In trying to get off the mark he took the risk of playing the ball to Jack Hobbs' right hand at cover. Hobbs fielded the ball and bowled underhand at the wicket, and as I afterwards ascertained, the ball going along the ground, was slightly deflected at the last moment by the rough ground round the bowler's foot-holds and missed the wicket by a hair's-breadth.

The partnership, which eventually reached 243, was then a record for Australia for the fourth wicket against England. 506/4 (when Jackson was out for 74) was far from the end of the matter though. Bradman, accompanied by McCabe, who was to make 54, went on to a magnificent 232 before he was caught at the wicket off Larwood by Duckworth who most unusually, had had a poor match behind the stumps, missing Woodfull on 6, Ponsford when 23 and Bradman himself on 82. Fairfax finished 53* while Oldfield contributed 34. The innings eventually came to an end at 5.30 when the total had reached 695.

Forty-five minutes remained for England to bat. Wyatt thoughtfully invited Hobbs to stand down from opening in order that he might be fresh for the following morning. This offer Hobbs declined, with thanks. As was his custom, he went out with Sutcliffe. The welcome from the crowd took the form of a great roar of appreciation as everyone now knew that this would be his last Test innings. When he reached the wicket, he was moved by Woodfull's warm gesture in leading his team in three cheers - for Hobbs the cricketer; Hobbs the man; and for his achievements. 'I shall never forget it as long as I live,' Hobbs wrote. 'It went right to my heart. It still goes to my heart whenever I think of it.'

What followed is best described by Ian Peebles, who was present. Hobbs made his way quietly to 9, then

in trying to cut Alan Fairfax, he got a bottom edge and nicked the ball on to his wicket. He paused sadly for a moment, then walked quietly back to the pavilion and out of Test match cricket. He took with him much of England's hope of recovery in the current match, and a quarter of a century of glorious memories. A great sense of anti-climax descended upon the scene, and the large crowd seemed quiet and subdued in the realisation that a unique era in English batsmanship had just ended.

England, 24/1 when night fell, had to sit out an entirely blank rain-ruined fifth day. By 3.50 on the Friday, when the sun had shone, it was all over. Hornibrook (31.2-9-92-7) returned his best Test figures. Six of those wickets came after lunch for 66 runs. Sutcliffe (54) and Hammond (60) lasted longest but a total of 251 meant a deserved innings and 39-run victory to the better side which took the series by two matches to one. At the end of the match a crowd gathered in front of the pavilion and called for the players. In the words of *The Times*: 'It took them quite a while to get Hobbs on to the balcony. His reception when he did appear was becomingly affectionate.'

* * *

The end of Hobbs' Test career was not a signal for a rapid winding-down of his involvement in the first-class game however. In the next four seasons he was to stroke his way to twenty-two centuries which, by most standards, is no mean performance: 10 in 1931; 5 in 1932; 6 in 1933 and, finally, just one in 1934.

In the winter of 1930-31 Hobbs played in India for the Maharajah of Vizianagram's XI. This is worth mentioning, for two reasons in particular. In the first place he quietly but firmly declined to play on a Sunday because of his principles: 'My early religious atmosphere brought me up to respect Sunday, to remember the Sabbath Day and keep it holy, to make it a day of rest for mind, body and spirit.' His views were respected and the necessary alterations to the tour programme were made.

Secondly, had Hobbs, or the authorities, regarded the matches in which he played there as first-class, then he might have been tempted to appear more often in 1934 or even to have played 'one more time' in 1935. Had the Indian matches been ruled first-class then, as some would have them ruled today, he would have ended 1934 on 199 centuries instead of 197.

I was very anxious not to go on too long and become an object of sympathy as so many of us do...I knew better than any of the critics could tell me that I could not perform as well as formerly. The only urge to go on was to be the first to score 200 centuries and thus to delight my friends and wind up on a good top note.

In 1931 there was little sign of muscles' atrophy as he finished seventh in the national averages (2418 runs at 56). It was the last and seventeenth season in which he passed 2000 runs. There were centuries in the Championship against Somerset (twice), Sussex, Warwickshire (his old whipping boys; this was his fourteenth and penultimate hundred against them), Derbyshire, Glamorgan and, perhaps most gratifying of all, 133* v Yorkshire who were to be the Champions while Surrey finished eighth. This time Hobbs carried his bat.

Curiously, although he made eight centuries against Yorkshire, this was the only one which came in a year when the Northern side won the Championship and they did so twelve times in Hobbs' career. What is even more of an oddity is that the only other years in which he took a century off a side which eventually headed the table were 1913 (Kent; Hobbs 115); 1928 (Lancashire; 101) and 1934 (Lancashire; 116).

By contrast, a sign of his stamina (and the tiredness of bowlers!) was his ability to score a hundred in his last innings of the season. This feat he accomplished on seven occasions: 1906; 1914; 1919; 1920; 1925; 1928 and 1932. In 1931 he went one better.

Earlier in the year at The Oval he and Sutcliffe had put on 203 for the first wicket against the Gentlemen. At Scarborough in early September their stand against the same opponents produced 227. It was the twenty-fifth time they had put on a hundred for the first wicket. Hobbs was at the crease nearly four hours, scored 144 (his only chance was given on 135) and stayed until 304 runs had been posted. As if this were not enough, in the very next match that same week, they made their last big partnership, 243 in 3 hours and 10 minutes, at which point Hobbs was out for 153. Tom Lowry, the captain of the New Zealanders who were so summarily put to sword, said Hobbs' century was the best innings played against them during the tour.

The following year Surrey moved up to fifth place. Hobbs, by now 49, although free from injury, chose not to play in seven Championship matches but no one scored more for the county in the competition or had a better average than his 1460 at 54. The spirit was still willing. In May against Worcestershire he was stumped when jumping out to drive. In August, with Sandham, against Middlesex, Hobbs (111) ran up 203 in a 150 minutes. A sequence in June, which proved he was not merely pottering about in pads, should not be forgotten: v Warwickshire (away) 83; v Essex (away) 75 and 34*; v Derbyshire (home) 67 and 11; v Essex (home) 113 and 119* - two centuries in a match for the sixth time and, in the second innings, a 232-run partnership with Barling took only 145 minutes; v Somerset (away) 123. The opening stand then with Sandham, who went on to 215, raised 264 at about a run a minute. Altogether this sequence produced 542 runs at an average of 90.

1932 was also the year which celebrated his last hundred against the Gentlemen. Fittingly it was at Lord's, a ground which was a personal favourite. The Players were 129 runs behind the Gentlemen when their second innings began. They had a strong batting line up but Sutcliffe, Woolley, Hammond, Hendren and Paynter managed only 85 between them. It was left to Hobbs carrying his bat for the seventh and last time in his first-class career, to stave off defeat with 161*. *Wisden's* tribute shows that this was no stodgy, back-to-the-wall display:

Hobbs from the start showed himself in splendid form...[and despite the loss of quick wickets] continued to play delightful cricket...Batting in masterly fashion for five hours, Hobbs gave no chance and but for slight lameness would, no doubt, have scored many more.

Jardine, captaining the Gentlemen, called it 'a great personal triumph'. Of that there can be no doubt. It also took him past another of 'WG's' records. 'The Great Cricketer' had scored fifteen centuries for the Gentlemen. 'The Master' had now made his sixteenth for the Players.

By the end of the following summer, 1933, Jack Hobbs had played in twenty-five English seasons. In twenty-four of them he had scored more than a thousand runs, the exception being his summer of sickness, 1921. It was this year, however, that, at last, he moderated the demands on his admittedly still trim physique. The strain had taken its toll over the years:

All my life I have suffered a great deal from severe headaches and sometimes I have taken the field or batted when I hardly knew how to hold up my head.

Even so, although he only turned out in a dozen matches, he did the county some service with half-a-dozen centuries. 1105 runs at 61 earned him fourth place in the first-class figures.

1934 saw him bow quietly out of the game without fuss or flamboyance although the Surrey Committee honoured him with the opening of the Hobbs' Gates at The Oval. His last century, 116, top score of the match, was against Lancashire at Old Trafford. A special effort this; a promise to an old friend, George Duckworth, that he would play in his benefit and thereby increase the 'gate' and the beneficiary's funds, was fulfilled.

A last match at The Oval produced 15 runs; his last appearance for Surrey was in Glamorgan, out for a duck. His final first-class game was for the Players at Folkestone. He finished, as he had started in 1905, with 18.

12 Afterword and Retrospect

In February 1935 Hobbs wrote formally to the Surrey Committee informing them of his intention to retire. Although he was then 52, this decision was received with great and genuine regret. Everyone knew he could not go on for ever but, in their hearts, many no doubt hoped he would. The Club honoured him with Life Membership as indeed the Marylebone Cricket Club was also to do in 1949 when he was one of twenty-six professionals who were accorded honorary membership.

He did not desert the game which he had served so nobly for so long. He appeared in charity games and occasionally for Surrey Club and Ground. An old friendship with the headmaster of Kimbolton School gave him the opportunity to play his last innings in 1941 when he turned out against the boys. Appropriately enough, it was a century - 116 for the Father's XI. He never played again but he later served on the Surrey Committee and he put in a cheerful appearance as umpire at The Oval in 1946. This was on the occasion of the celebration of Surrey's Centenary and a hundred years of The Oval as a cricket ground. The county played Old England and in the 1947 *Wisden* there is a photograph of Hobbs and his old friend Herbert Strudwick, the umpires, pictured with the Old England side.

Both his family (the Hobbs had three sons and a daughter) and his business flourished. For some people his greatest moment came, and not before time, in 1953 when he was the first professional sportsman to be knighted, at the age of seventy. It was an honour to the game, to professional cricketers in general but very much to the man himself. Freddie Brown (Cambridge, Surrey, Northants and England) wrote to the author:

He always made you feel as though you were the one person he wanted to see when you met him. I feel very privileged to have known him. A great example to all cricketers - never was a knighthood more deserved.

He remained devoted to his wife Ada, whom he nursed lovingly through her last illness until her death in March 1963. There was nothing more he felt he had to do and he slowed down until he himself passed quietly away on 21 December of that year.

* * *

Just how good was Hobbs, this batsman who has passed into cricket legend? Who better to ask than those who knew him personally and had a deep understanding of the game?

In his warmly appreciative analysis in *Profile of the Master* John Arlott, a close friend of Jack Hobbs, wrote:

His cricket has three distinct peaks of performance. In his early days his stroke-play had all the heady prodigality of richly endowed youth. In maturity he was the most completely rounded batting technician the game has ever known...In what was by cricketing standards, old age...his profound understanding of his craft compensated to an amazing degree for the deterioration of eye, mobility and muscle.

This brooks no argument. But how did he compare with other giants such as Bradman and Hammond? E W Swanton, who has probably seen as much first-class cricket at home and abroad during the last sixty years as anyone alive, wrote in a letter to the author:

He was the greatest of all professional batsmen. To compare him with Bradman is difficult because whereas Jack was a master on all pitches, fast, slow, fiery, sodden, dusty or of matting, Bradman played most of his cricket on plumb pitches, fast at home and almost always easy-paced in England, where all groundsman went out of their way to produce something pluperfect for the Australians. You cannot say that anyone was the equal of Bradman as a run-scorer of awesome concentration and stamina. Both had the full armoury of strokes.

Hammond was a superb player, at his best more *commanding* than either, but there were inequalities which prevent his being rated on an equality with Hobbs. He was a tremendous off-side player, but could be restricted by those who bowled at his legs - particularly O'Reilly.

Hammond was less confident and convincing than either against truly fast bowling.

This high opinion of Hobbs the batsman is shared by R E S Wyatt who captained England in Hobbs' last Test and who wrote in these terms to the author expressing as well his admiration of Hobbs the man:

His perfect poise when playing any stroke impressed me. On all wickets he was the greatest batsman I ever saw. A gentleman in every sense of the word, he was always courteous. Helpful and encouraging to the young player, he was a fine example as to how to behave at all times. He also had a good sense of humour.

One who played frequently with Hobbs in the late 1920s and early 1930s was Maurice Allom (Cambridge, Surrey, the Gentlemen and England). A former President of MCC and of Surrey, he gave the author an interview early in 1987:

Porter: What sort of man was he? Was he well-liked?

Allom: What I remember most about him was his genuineness and his kindness. He put one completely at one's ease. He was just a thoroughly nice man. He was fun and great company but you could talk to him about anything and get a serious answer. He was popular in the side. Everybody

held him in great esteem. He was frightfully good with the young professionals.

P: He is said to have had a great sense of humour?

A: He never let things get dull in the field and was always looking for
ways to keep us on our toes. A sudden shout of 'Mind your head' would
have us ducking and turning. Nothing would happen and we would look up
to see Jack chuckling quietly away at cover.

I remember once when Dennis Morkel, the South African fast-medium
bowler, was trying to get Jack to play him to his strong cover field. He
bowled him one well wide of the off stump. Jack moved lightly across and
with a twist of the wrists drove him all along the ground through square-leg
for four. Morkel looked astonished. As well he might. He tried again. The
next ball was further outside the off stump. Exactly the same thing
happened. Morkel persevered. The third ball was aimed at second slip.
Hobbs stood still. The umpire signalled a wide. Jack roared with laughter.

P: What impressed you most about his batting?

A: He was, of course, past his best when I first saw him. As a schoolboy
I had never seen him. In his stance at the wicket he was quite full chested
but by the time the bowler delivered the ball he was always sideways on, in
a perfect position. The most remarkable feature of his batting was his
footwork. Going forward or back, in attack or defence, it was exceptional.

P: How would you define his approach?

A: A great taker of initiatives, he was never waiting for things to
happen at the wicket. He made them happen. I remember how in the
Yorkshire matches, for example, he always went after the dangerous
medium pace of George Macaulay in the first over, to put him away for two
or three fours, and never let him settle.

P: How did he feel about the relationship between ' Amateur and
Professional?'

A: Jack was very aware of the distinction between ' Gentleman' and
'Player', although if any player were ever a gentleman it was he. The social
differences were ingrained. At 21 when I played for Surrey I was nervous of
this great man but he put me immediately at my ease. I knew him well for
a long time afterwards but only in the last few years of his life could he bring
himself to call me by my first name.

P: Did this affect his relationship with his captains?

A: In general Jack was very reluctant to bring any influence to bear on
a skipper. In fact, I don't ever recall him suggesting anything - be it about
bowling changes, fielding positions or tactics in general, when I was
captaining the side. On one occasion, I do recall asking his advice quite
specifically. Surrey had had a taxing week or more, leather-hunting. Came
the third day of a game against Lancashire when we could have made them
follow-on when there were about three hours left in the match. It had taken
us all morning and until 2.30 to get the last two Lancashire batsmen out. I

had been out with a serious illness earlier in the season and was not yet restored to full health. I said to him, 'Jack, our lads look absolutely whacked. I don't feel at all fit myself. Would it be an awful thing if we were to bat again?' It was the only time I asked him, but he wouldn't commit himself. Jack would not give me an answer, one way or the other. Extraordinary really, with the wealth of experience at his disposal. Anyway, we did bat again, and, I recall, I was hounded afterwards in the press.

P: Yet he had a fine tactical appreciation of the game?

A: At Melbourne in 1928-29 Jack made the pretence of changing his bat in order to advise Percy Chapman to send Jardine in at number 3 on that sticky wicket. This is well known. Less familiar to many may be his approach in that innings. It was a supreme example of his genius. He persuaded the bowlers, Ironmonger and Blackie, I think, to bowl the wrong line. When he knew the ball was not gong to hit the stumps he would deliberately flounder so they persisted with that line when they should have been taking a different approach entirely which would have given the batsmen much more trouble. Percy Fender told me about this, having discussed the matter with Jack. It was a remarkable exhibition of batting. Only a very great player could have done this.

P: Did he maintain his stamina in his later cricketing years?

A: Although he was said to be delicate in health, I never had any reason to suppose this to be so in the time I knew him. Indeed, one of the things I admired him for was the way he was so remarkably active. He kept himself very fit. I don't remember him suffering from migraine in his later years.

One of the reasons that Jack went on so long so successfully was that he became aware of his limitations and found it easier to play off the back foot.

* * *

Jack Hobbs' greatness lay not only in his supreme and splendid batting but in his admirable and likeable character. He had dignity, an awareness of his achievement and an understanding of its importance to cricket but he was never arrogant or conceited. His qualities as a man are praised by all who knew him, colleagues and opponents, captains and commentators, from England and abroad. It would be hard to find two such different temperaments and characters as Walter Hammond and Arthur Mailey, yet they both wrote of Hobbs in not dissimilar terms:

He was perhaps the greatest England batsman of my time and one of the most kindly, charming and unassuming men who ever graced the game. I do not believe he had an enemy anywhere. (Hammond)

We have all known batsmen who, although prolific scorers, were a 'pain in the neck', both to their comrades and their opponents. Some were selfish, some bad runners between the wickets; some opportunists at the expense of other players, some bad fieldsmen. Hobbs had none of these faults. (Mailey)

C L R James who has always been a shrewd, informed observer of character in cricket also had a very high opinion of Hobbs:

I found him very sympathetic, very friendly, conscious of his position and yet a simple man. He did not affect the style and manners of a gentleman as some professionals of the period did. He maintained his personality. He had to be respected because he respected himself.

Sir George 'Gubby' Allen (Cambridge, Middlesex and England), who was a friend and great admirer of Hobbs, told the author:

Technically he was perhaps the greatest batsman of my lifetime. Jack always seemed to get his feet in the right place which is the hallmark of the great player. So many of the modern batsmen go on to the front foot before the bowler bowls. This gets them into trouble with the short-pitched ball. Jack never had that problem.

He was a very good placer of the ball. I said to him once, 'You always beat the fielder, Jack.' His reply was simple: 'Well, that's one of the arts of batting, isn't it?' And, of course, he was quite right.

In his later years he was a marvellous leaver of the ball that he did not have to play. He knew exactly where his off-stump was.

He was a master of spin as he was of pace. I believe he told me that, when playing against leg-breaks and googlies, while he watched the hand, he played the ball off the wicket which showed he had remarkable speed of eye, foot and reflex. You didn't often see him prod forward. Jack looked so perfect in everything he did. Other players may have been almost as correct but they never looked so complete.

What are the qualities and skills that make a great batsman? Who is the greatest? Each generation will have its own answer to this impossible question.

For moderns, the completeness of Sunil Gavaskar, the power of Vivian Richards, the adaptability of Barry Richards, the defence of Geoffrey Boycott, the composure of Greg Chappell, the grace of David Gower, the consistency of Allan Border, the excitement of Ian Botham - all these would have to be considered.

For a slightly earlier generation the technique of Len Hutton, the authority of Peter May, the flair of Denis Compton, the class of Colin Cowdrey, the charm of Neil Harvey, the power of Clyde Walcott, the hitting of Everton Weekes, the ease of Frank Worrell, the zest of Gary Sobers, the obduracy of Hanif Mohammed would be in the reckoning.

Neither of these lists lays any claim to being all-embracing. Every individual will have his or her own favourites, but general agreement may be reached about two batsmen who, in all but stature, were head and shoulders above the rest: Jack Hobbs and Don Bradman. The latter in a recent letter to the author wrote warmly of his old opponent, whom he first met in the autumn of Hobbs' career:

By 1928 he was 45 and no batsman of that age has the flair and the drive and energy of his youth. But Jack still displayed superb and economical foot work, a complete range of shots all round the wicket and a splendid technique. In all those areas he was equal to the best.

As a man Jack was a thorough gentleman; extremely courteous and modest to a degree.

Of all the English professionals none enjoyed to a greater degree the respect, admiration and even affection of his colleagues.

This gentlemanly conduct did much to enhance the standing of English cricketers in the eyes of friend and foe alike. The game of cricket owes him a great debt.

In terms of run-getting, in the matches that mattered - and, after all, that is really what batting is about - Bradman is supreme. But few would argue that in variety of strokes, in timing, and in placement he was not equalled by Hobbs. Bradman was more relentless in his pursuit of runs, thus building a firm platform from which his side might launch a quest for victory. Hobbs, on the other hand, was more secure on rain-affected wickets, thus protecting his side against collapse.

Theirs was cricket of contrasting colours but they brought to the game a dedication and application which few have approached. In their different styles they both dominated the opposition. Both were technically assured. Both had an immense capacity to give pleasure to their supporters.

If Jack Hobbs never achieved the Test aggregate and average that Bradman acquired, it may be said of the Surrey man that he played with a freedom and charm that were uniquely his own as if he never forgot that cricket was a game. The words of Philip Trevor, who wrote an account of Hobbs' first tour, ring as true now as they did eighty years ago: 'So long as he was batting, he was always batting well; and wherever he went, there was only one opinion of him as a batsman.'

Supreme greatness transcends precise definition and analysis.
It is an impression. To dissect is to destroy.
It needs figures but it cannot be circumscribed by figures.
It needs manner but the manner is infinitely variable.
It raises an emotional response beyond the bounds of logical
argument.
It evokes inspiration without envy!

J M Kilburn *Overthrows* (1975)

APPENDICES

Key:
The roman numeral shows the number of the Test in each series:
G — Ground; S — Hobbs' score;
OP — Opening Partnership;
P — Partner; R — Result;
I — Innings

1. Jack Hobbs' Test record

Ground				S	OP	P	R
v Australia 1907-08							
1. II	Melbourne		b Cotter	83	27	Fane	Won
			b Noble	28	54	Fane	
2. III	Adelaide	c Carter	b Saunders	26	58	Fane	Lost
			not out	23	8	Fane	
3. IV	Melbourne		b Noble	57	58	Gunn	Lost
		c and	b Saunders	0	0	Gunn	
4. V	Sydney		b Saunders	72	1	Fane	Lost
		c Gregory	b Saunders	13	21	Fane	
v Australia 1909							
5. I	Birmingham	lbw	b Macartney	0	0	MacLaren	Won
			not out	62	105*	Fry	
6. II	Lord's	c Carter	b Laver	19	23	Hayward	Lost
		c and	b Armstrong	9	16	Hayward	
7. III	Leeds		b Macartney	12	8	Fry	Lost
			b Cotter	30	17	Fry	
v South Africa 1909-10							
8. I	Johannesburg	c Campbell	b Vogler	89	159	Rhodes	Lost
			b Vogler	35	36	Rhodes	
9. II	Durban		b Sinclair	53	94	Rhodes	Lost
		c Vogler	b Faulkner	70	48	Rhodes	
10. III	Johannesburg		b Faulkner	11		batted at 7	Won
			not out	93		batted at 5	
11. IV	Cape Town	c Faulkner	b Vogler	1	1	Rhodes	Lost
		c Campbell	b Snooke	0	0	Rhodes	
12. V	Cape Town	hit wkt	b Norton	187	221	Rhodes	Won
v Australia 1911-12							
13. I	Sydney	c Hill	b Whitty	63	45	Kinneir	Lost
		c Carter	b Cotter	22	29	Kinneir	
14. II	Melbourne	c Carter	b Cotter	6	10	Rhodes	Won
			not out	126	57	Rhodes	
15. III	Adelaide	c Hordern	b Minnett	187	147	Rhodes	Won
		lbw	b Hordern	3	5	Rhodes	
16. IV	Melbourne	c Carter	b Hordern	178	323	Rhodes	Won
17. V	Sydney	c Ransford	b Hordern	32	15	Rhodes	Won
		c Hazlitt	b Hordern	45	76	Rhodes	

v South Africa and Australia 1912 - *listed in chronological order*

18.	I	v South Africa								
		Lord's		b	Nourse	4	4	Rhodes	Won
19.	I	v Australia								
		Lord's		b	Emery	107	112	Rhodes	Drawn
20.	II	v South Africa								
		Leeds	c Ward	b	Nourse	27	20	Rhodes	Won
			c Nourse	b	Faulkner	55	46	Rhodes	
21.	II	v Australia								
		Manchester		b	Whitty	19	37	Rhodes	Drawn
22.	III	v South Africa								
		Oval	c and	b	Faulkner	68	4	Rhodes	Won
			not out			9	14*	Hearne	
23.	IV	v Australia								
		Oval	c Carkeek	b	Macartney	66	107	Rhodes	Won
			c Matthews	b	Whitty	32	7	Rhodes	

v South Africa 1913-14

24.	I	Durban		b	Baumgartner	82	24	Rhodes	Won
25.	II	Johannesburg	lbw	b	Newberry	23		batted at 3	Won
26.	III	Johannesburg	c Ward	b	Dixon	92	100	Rhodes	Won
			c Nourse	b	Dixon	41	4	Rhodes	
27.	IV	Durban	c Nourse	b	Blanckenburg	64	92	Rhodes	Drawn
				b	Blanckenburg	97	133	Rhodes	
28.	V	Port Elizabeth	c Nourse	b	Lundie	33	48	Rhodes	Won
			not out			11	11*	Rhodes	

v Australia 1920-21

29.	I	Sydney		b	Gregory	49	0	Russell	Lost
			lbw	b	Armstrong	59	5	Russell	
30.	II	Melbourne	c Ryder	b	Gregory	122	20	Rhodes	Lost
				b	Kelleway	20	36	Rhodes	
31.	III	Adelaide	c and	b	Mailey	18	25	Rhodes	Lost
				b	Gregory	123	20	Rhodes	
32.	IV	Melbourne	c Carter	b	McDonald	27	18	Rhodes	Lost
			lbw	b	Mailey	13	32	Rhodes	
33.	V	Sydney	lbw	b	Gregory	40	54	Rhodes	Lost
			c Taylor	b	Mailey	34		batted at 5	

v Australia 1921

34.	III	Leeds	absent ill - did not bat in either innings

v South Africa 1924

35.	I	Birmingham	lbw	b	Blanckenberg	76	136	Sutcliffe	Won
36.	II	Lord's	c Taylor	b	Parker	211	268	Sutcliffe	Won
37.	III	Leeds	c Pegler	b	Nourse	31	72	Sutcliffe	Won
				b	Blanckenburg	7	17	Sutcliffe	Won
38.	V	Oval	c Ward	b	Pegler	30	5	Sutcliffe	Drawn

v Australia 1924-25

No.	Test	Venue	Dismissal			Score	2nd	Partner	Result
39.	I	Sydney	c Kelleway	b	Gregory	115	159	Sutcliffe	Lost
			c Hendry	b	Mailey	57	110	Sutcliffe	
40.	II	Melbourne		b	Mailey	154	283	Sutcliffe	Lost
			lbw	b	Mailey	22	36	Sutcliffe	
41.	III	Adelaide	c Gregory	b	Mailey	119		batted at 5	Lost
			c Collins	b	Richardson	27	63	Sutcliffe	
42.	IV	Melbourne	st Oldfield	b	Ryder	66	126	Sutcliffe	Won
43.	V	Sydney	c Oldfield	b	Gregory	0	0	Sutcliffe	Lost
			st Oldfield	b	Grimmett	13	3	Sutcliffe	

v Australia 1926

No.	Test	Venue	Dismissal			Score	2nd	Partner	Result
44.	I	Nottingham			not out	19*	32	unfinished Sutcliffe	Drawn
45.	II	Lord's	c Richardson	b	Macartney	119	182	Sutcliffe	Drawn
46.	III	Leeds	c Andrews	b	Mailey	49	59	Sutcliffe	Drawn
				b	Grimmett	88	156	Sutcliffe	
47.	IV	Manchester	c Ryder	b	Grimmett	74	58	Sutcliffe	Drawn
				b	Mailey	37	53	Sutcliffe	Won
48.	V	Oval		b	Gregory	100	172	Sutcliffe	
49.	II	Manchester	c St Hill	b	Browne	53	119	Sutcliffe	Won
50.	III	Oval	c Small	b	Francis	159	155	Sutcliffe	Won

v Australia 1928-29

No.	Test	Venue	Dismissal			Score	2nd	Partner	Result
51.	I	Brisbane			run out	49	85	Sutcliffe	Won
			lbw	b	Grimmett	11	25	Sutcliffe	
52.	II	Sydney	c Oldfield	b	Grimmett	40	37	Sutcliffe	Won
					d.n.b.				
53.	III	Melbourne	c Oldfield	b	a'Beckett	20	28	Sutcliffe	Won
			lbw	b	Blackie	49	105	Sutcliffe	
54.	IV	Adelaide	c Ryder	b	Hendry	74	143	Sutcliffe	Won
			c Oldfield	b	Hendry	1	1	Sutcliffe	
55.	V	Melbourne	lbw	b	Ryder	142	64	Jardine	Lost
			c Fairfax	b	Grimmett	65	1	Jardine	

v South Africa 1929

No.	Test	Venue	Dismissal			Score	2nd	Partner	Result
56.	V	Oval	c Quinn	b	McMillan	10	38	Sutcliffe	Drawn
			c Mitchell	b	Vincent	52	77	Sutcliffe	

v Australia 1930

No.	Test	Venue	Dismissal			Score	2nd	Partner	Result
57.	I	Nottingham	c Richardson	b	McCabe	78	53	Sutcliffe	Won
			st Oldfield	b	Grimmett	74	125	Sutcliffe	
58.	II	Lord's	c Oldfield	b	Fairfax	1	13	Woolley	Lost
				b	Grimmett	19	45	Woolley	
59.	III	Leeds	c a'Beckett	b	Grimmett	29	53	Sutcliffe	Drawn
					run out	13	24	Sutcliffe	
60.	IV	Manchester	c Oldfield	b	Wall	31	108	Sutcliffe	Drawn
61.	V	Oval	c Kippax	b	Wall	47	68	Sutcliffe	Lost
				b	Fairfax	9	17	Sutcliffe	

2. The major opening partnerships in Tests

Year	Opponents	Ground	Test	Partnerships		

Hobbs and Rhodes

Year	Opponents	Ground	Test			
1909-10	South Africa	Johannesburg	First	159	and	36
		Durban	Second	94	and	48
		Cape Town	Fourth	1	and	0
		Cape Town	Fifth	221		
1911-12	Australia	Melbourne	Second	10	and	57
		Adelaide	Third	147	and	5
		Melbourne	Fourth	323		
		Sydney	Fifth	15	and	76
1912	South Africa	Lord's	First	4		
	Australia	Lords	First	112		
	South Africa	Leeds	Second	20	and	46
	Australia	Manchester	Second	37		
	South Africa	The Oval	Third	4		
	Australia	The Oval	Third	107	and	7
1913-14	South Africa	Durban	First	24		
		Johannesburg	Third	100	and	4
		Durban	Fourth	92	and	133
		Port Elizabeth	Fifth	48	and	11
1920-21	Australia	Melbourne	Second	20	and	36
		Adelaide	Third	25	and	20
		Melbourne	Fourth	18	and	32
		Sydney	Fifth	54		

36 partnerships 1 unfinished 2156 runs 8 centuries 5 fifties 61.60 average

Hobbs and Sutcliffe

Year	Opponents	Ground	Test			
1924	South Africa	Birmingham	First	136		
		Lord's	Second	268		
		Leeds	Third	72	and	17
		The Oval	Fifth	5		
1924-25	Australia	Sydney	First	157	and	110
		Melbourne	Second	283	and	36
		Adelaide	Third	63		
		Melbourne	Fourth	126		
		Sydney	Fifth	0	and	3
1926	Australia	Nottingham	First	32*		
		Lord's	Second	182		
		Leeds	Third	59	and	156
		Manchester	Fourth	58		
		The Oval	Fifth	53	and	172
1928	West Indies	Manchester	Second	119		

		The Oval	Third	155		
1928-29	Australia	Brisbane	First	85	and	25
		Sydney	Second	51		
		Melbourne	Third	28	and	105
		Adelaide	Fourth	143	and	1
1929	South Africa	The Oval	Fifth	38	and	77
1930	Australia	Nottingham	First	53	and	125
		Leeds	Third	2	and	24
		Manchester	Fourth	108		
		The Oval	Fifth	68	and	17

38 partnerships 1 unfinished 3249 runs 15 centuries 10 fifties 87.81 average

---

3. Hobbs' performances on each Test ground

	Ground	I	NO	Runs	HS	Score
In Australia	Melbourne	18	1	1178	178	69.02
	Adelaide	10	1	601	187	66.07
	Sydney	15	0	654	115	43.60
	Brisbane	2	0	60	49	30
In England	Birmingham	3	1	138	76	69
	Lord's	8	0	489	211	61.12
	Leeds	10	0	341	88	34.1
	Manchester	4	0	177	74	44.25
	Oval	11	1	619	159	56.27
	Nottingham	3	1	171	78	85.5
In South Africa	Johannesburg	7	1	384	93*	64
	Durban	5	0	366	97	73.2
	Cape Town	3	0	188	187	61.33
	Port Elizabeth	2	1	44	33	44

---

4. Test centuries

Year	Opponents	Ground	Test	Score	I
1909-10	South Africa	Cape Town	Fifth	187	1st
1911-12	Australia	Melbourne	Second	126*	2nd
		Adelaide	Third	187	1st
		Melbourne	Fourth	178	1st
1912	Australia	Lord's	First	107	1st
1920-21	Australia	Melbourne	Second	122	1st

		Adelaide	Third	123	2nd
1924	South Africa	Lord's	Second	211	1st
1924-25	Australia	Sydney	First	115	1st
		Melbourne	Second	154	1st
		Adelaide	Third	119	1st
1926	Australia	Lord's	Second	119	1st
		The Oval	Fifth	100	2nd
1928	West Indies	The Oval	Third	159	1st
1928-29	Australia	Melbourne	Fifth	142	1st

5. Hobbs' top scores in Tests

Year	Ground	Test	Score	Total
1907-08	Melbourne	Fourth	57	105
1909	Leeds	Third	30	67
1909-10	Johannesburg	First	89	310
	Durban	Second	53	199
			70	252
	Johannesburg	Third	93*	221/7
	Cape Town	Fifth	187	417
1911-12	Melbourne	Second	126*	219/2
	Adelaide	Third	187	501
1912	Lord's (v Australia)	First	107	310/7
	The Oval (v South Africa)	Third	68	176
	The Oval (v Australia)	Third	66	245
1913-14	Johannesburg	Third	92	238
	Durban	Fourth	64	163
			97	154/5
	Port Elizabeth	Fifth	11*	11/0
1920-21	Sydney	First	59	281
	Melbourne	Second	122	251
	Adelaide	Third	123	370
1924	Birmingham	First	76	438
	Lord's	Second	211	531/2 d
1924-25	Sydney	First	115	298
	Adelaide	Third	119	365
1926	Nottingham	First	19*	32/0
1928	The Oval	Third	159	438
1930	Nottingham	First	78	270
			74	302

6. Hobbs' centuries

Year	Number	Ground	Team	Opponents	Score
1905	1	Oval	Surrey	Essex	155
1905	2	Leyton	Surrey	Essex	102
1906	3	Worcester	Surrey	Worcs	125
1906	4	Leyton	Surrey	Essex	130
1906	5	Oval	Surrey	Worcs	162*
1906	6	Oval	Surrey	Middlesex	103
1907	7	Oval	Surrey	Warwicks	150*
1907	8	Southampton	Surrey	Hants	135
1907	9	Oval	Surrey	Worcs	166*
1907	10	Worcester	Surrey	Worcs	110
1907-08	11	Launceston	MCC	Tasmania	104
1907-08	12	Melbourne	MCC	Victoria	115
1908	13	Oval	Surrey	Hants	161
1908	14	Nottingham	Surrey	Notts	117
1908	15	Oval	Surrey	Oxford U	102
1908	16	Northampton	Surrey	Northants	125
1908	17	Blackheath	Surrey	Kent	106
1908	18	Oval	Surrey	Kent	155
1909	19	Oval	Surrey	Hants	205
1909	20	Oval	Surrey	Warwicks	159
1909	21	Birmingham	Surrey	Warwicks	160
1909	22	Birmingham	Surrey	Warwicks	100
1909	23	Bournemouth	Surrey	Hants	162
1909	24	Bristol	Surrey	Glos	133
1909-10	25	Cape Town	MCC	W. Province	114
1909-10	26	Durban	MCC	Natal	163
1909-10	27	Cape Town	England	South Africa	187
1910	28	Derby	Surrey	Derbyshire	133
1910	29	Oval	Surrey	Oxford U	119
1910	30	Leicester	Surrey	Leics	116
1911	31	Lord's	Players	Gentlemen	154
1911	32	Oval	Surrey	Lancs	117
1911	33	Leicester	Surrey	Leics	127
1911	34	Scarborough	MCC Australian XI	Lord Londes-borough's XI	117
1911-12	35	Melbourne	England	Australia	126*
1911-12	36	Adelaide	England	Australia	187
1911-12	37	Melbourne	England	Australia	178
1912	38	Nottingham	Surrey	Notts	104
1912	39	Lord's	England	Australia	107
1912	40	Manchester	Surrey	Lancs	111
1913	41	Northampton	Surrey	Northants	136*
1913	42	Oval	Surrey	Glos	113

1913	43	Oval	Surrey	Scotland	150*
1913	44	Southampton	Surrey	Hants	109
1913	45	Oval	Surrey	Middlesex	144*
1913	46	Oval	Surrey	Kent	115
1913	47	Birmingham	Surrey	Warwicks	122
1913	48	Worcester	Surrey	Worcs	184
1913	49	Bristol	Surrey	Glos	107
1913-14	50	Port Elizabeth	MCC	Cape Province	170
1913-14	51	Johannesburg	MCC	Transvaal	102
1913-14	52	Vogelfrontein	MCC	Transvaal	137
1913-14	53	Kimberley	MCC	Griqualand W	141
1913-14	54	Johannesburg	MCC	Transvaal	131
1914	55	Bradford	Surrey	Yorkshire	100
1914	56	Oval	Surrey	Warwicks	183
1914	57	Leyton	Surrey	Essex	215*
1914	58	Oval	Surrey	Hants	163
1914	59	Oval	Players	Gentlemen	156
1914	60	Oval	Surrey	Lancs	142
1914	61	Blackheath	Surrey	Kent	122
1914	62	Oval	Surrey	Notts	226
1914	63	Worcester	Surrey	Worcs	126
1914	64	Lord's	Surrey	Yorks	202
1914	65	Oval	Surrey	Glos	141
1919	66	Oval	Surrey	AIF	205*
1919	67	Oval	Surrey	Lancs	106
1919	68	Oval	Players	Gentlemen	120*
1919	69	Lord's	Players	Gentlemen	113
1919	70	Blackheath	Surrey	Kent	102
1919	71	Manchester	Surrey	Lancs	102
1919	72	Scarborough	Players	Gentlemen	116
1919	73	Oval	Rest of England	Yorks	101
1920	74	Oval	Surrey	Northants	114
1920	75	Oval	Surrey	Warwicks	122
1920	76	Oval	Surrey	Sussex	110
1920	77	Leicester	Surrey	Leics	134
1920	78	Birmingham	Surrey	Warwicks	101
1920	79	Sheffield	Surrey	Yorks	112
1920	80	Oval	Players of South	Gents of South	115
1920	81	Southampton	Surrey	Hants	169
1920	82	Oval	Surrey	Kent	132
1920	83	Scarborough	Players	Gentlemen	138
1920	84	Oval	Rest of England	Middlesex	215
1920-21	85	Melbourne	MCC	Victoria	131
1920-21	86	Sydney	MCC	N S W	112
1920-21	87	Melbourne	England	Australia	122
1920-21	88	Adelaide	England	Australia	123
1921	89	Leeds	Surrey	Yorkshire	172*
1922	90	Oval	Surrey	Essex	102

1922	91	Bristol	Surrey	Glos	139
1922	92	Nottingham	Surrey	Notts	151*
1922	93	Leicester	Surrey	Leics	145
1922	94	Oval	Surrey	Glos	143
1922	95	Birmingham	Surrey	Warwicks	168
1922	96	Lord's	Players	Gentlemen	140
1922	97	Oval	Surrey	Middlesex	112
1922	98	Lord's	Surrey	Middlesex	126
1922	99	Oval	Rest of England	Yorks	100
1923	100	Bath	Surrey	Somerset	116*
1923	101	Oval	Surrey	Lancs	104
1923	102	Oval	Surrey	Notts	105
1923	103	Oval	Surrey	Middlesex	136
1923	104	Scarborough	Players	Gentlemen	105
1924	105	Nottingham	Surrey	Notts	203*
1924	106	Oval	Surrey	Derbyshire	118*
1924	107	Lord's	England	South Africa	211
1924	108	Oval	Surrey	Glos	105
1924	109	Lord's	Players	Gentlemen	118
1924	110	Oval	Surrey	Notts	105
1924-25	111	Sydney	England	Australia	115
1924-25	112	Melbourne	England	Australia	154
1924-25	113	Adelaide	England	Australia	119
1925	114	Oval	Surrey	Glos	104
1925	115	Oval	Surrey	Glamorgan	109
1925	116	Oval	Surrey	Warwicks	120
1925	117	Leyton	Surrey	Essex	129
1925	118	Nottingham	Surrey	Notts	189
1925	119	Oval	Surrey	Essex	107
1925	120	Oval	Surrey	Cambridge U	104
1925	121	Oval	Surrey	Cambridge U	143*
1925	122	Oval	Surrey	Somerset	111
1925	123	Birmingham	Surrey	Warwicks	215
1925	124	Lord's	Players	Gentlemen	140
1925	125	Blackheath	Surrey	Kent	105
1925	126	Taunton	Surrey	Somerset	101
1925	127	Taunton	Surrey	Somerset	101*
1925	128	Scarborough	Players	Gentlemen	266*
1925	129	Oval	Rest of England	Yorks	106
1926	130	Oval	Surrey	Glos	112
1926	131	Oval	Surrey	Cambridge U	108
1926	132	Oval	Surrey	Oxford U	261
1926	133	Lord's	England	Australia	119
1926	134	Southampton	Surrey	Hants	200
1926	135	Lord's	Players	Gentlemen	163
1926	136	Oval	Surrey	Middlesex	176*
1926	137	Oval	England	Australia	100
1926	138	Oval	Surrey	Yorks	102

1926	139	Lord's	Surrey	Middlesex	316*
1927	140	Oval	Surrey	Hants	112
1927	141	Oval	Surrey	Hants	104
1927	142	Blackheath	Surrey	Kent	121
1927	143	Oval	Surrey	Notts	131
1927	144	Oval	Surrey	New Zealanders	146
1927	145	Oval	Surrey	Yorks	150
1927	146	Scarborough	Players	Gentlemen	119
1928	147	Lord's	Surrey	MCC	100
1928	148	Oval	Surrey	Glos	124
1928	149	Oval	Surrey	West Indies	123
1928	150	Nottingham	Surrey	Notts	114
1928	151	Northampton	Surrey	Northants	117
1928	152	Oval	Surrey	Kent	109
1928	153	Birmingham	Surrey	Warwicks	200*
1928	154	Oval	England	West Indies	159
1928	155	Oval	Surrey	Yorks	105
1928	156	Oval	Surrey	Leics	101
1928	157	Scarborough	H D G Leveson Gower's XI	West Indies	119*
1928	158	Oval	Rest of England	Lancs	150
1928-29	159	Adelaide	MCC	South Australia	101
1928-29	160	Melbourne	England	Australia	142
1929	161	Oval	Surrey	Hants	154
1929	162	Oval	Surrey	Essex	102*
1929	163	Blackheath	Surrey	Kent	150*
1929	164	Oval	Surrey	Somerset	204
1929	165	Oval	Surrey	Kent	118
1929	166	Weston-super-Mare	Surrey	Somerset	134
1929	167	Cardiff	Surrey	Glamorgan	128
1929	168	Oval	Surrey	Leics	115
1929	169	Lord's	Surrey	Middlesex	111
1929	170	Scarborough	C I Thornton's XI	South Africans	151
1930	171	Oval	Surrey	Glamorgan	137
1930	172	Oval	Surrey	Glamorgan	111*
1930	173	Oval	Surrey	Australians	146*
1930	174	Hastings	Surrey	Sussex	106
1930	175	Oval	Surrey	Leics	100
1931	176	Oval	Surrey	Somerset	128
1931	177	Oval	Surrey	Sussex	117
1931	178	Oval	Surrey	Warwicks	147
1931	179	Oval	Players	Gentlemen	110
1931	180	Chesterfield	Surrey	Derbyshire	105
1931	181	Oval	Surrey	Glamorgan	106
1931	182	Taunton	Surrey	Somerset	101*
1931	183	Oval	Surrey	Yorkshire	133*
1931	184	Scarborough	Players	Gentlemen	144

1931	185	Scarborough	H D G Leveson Gower's XI	New Zealanders	153
1932	186	Oval	Surrey	Essex	113
1932	187	Oval	Surrey	Essex	119*
1932	188	Taunton	Surrey	Somerset	123
1932	189	Lord's	Players	Gentlemen	164*
1932	190	Lord's	Surrey	Middlesex	111
1933	191	Oval	Surrey	West Indians	221
1933	192	Oval	Surrey	Warwicks	100
1933	193	Oval	Surrey	Cambridge U	118
1933	194	Blackheath	Surrey	Kent	101
1933	195	Oval	Surrey	Somerset	117
1933	196	Oval	Surrey	Notts	133
1934	197	Manchester	Surrey	Lancs	116

BIBLIOGRAPHY

General Reference
Cricket
The Times
The Cricketer
Wisden Cricketers' Almanack
Altham, H. S. and Swanton, E. W.   *A History of Cricket*   - 2nd edition (Allen & Unwin, 1938)
Bailey, P. et al   *Who's Who of Cricketers*   (Newnes/A.C.S., 1984)
Canynge Caple, S.   *The Cricketers' Who's Who*   (Lincoln Williams, 1934)
Dunstan, Keith   *The Paddock That Grew*   (Cassell, 1962)
Frith, David   *The Fast Men*   (Van Nostrand Reinhold, 1975)
Frith, David   *The Slow Men*   (Allen & Unwin, 1984)
Martin-Jenkins, Christopher   *The Complete Who's Who of Test Cricketers* (Orbis, 1980)
Morrah, Patrick   *The Golden Age of Cricket*   (Eyre & Spottiswoode, 1967)
Moyes, A.G.   *Australian Batsmen*   (Harrap, 1954)
Moyes, A.G.   *Australian Bowlers*   (Harrap, 1953)
Pollard, Jack   *Australian Cricket - The Game and the Players*   (Hodder & Stoughton, 1982)
Roberts, E.L.   *Cricket in England 1894-1939*   (Edward Arnold, 1946)
Ross, Gordon   *The Surrey Story*   (Stanley Paul, 1957)
Warner, P.F.   *Lord's 1787-1945*   (Harrap, 1946)
Warner, P.F.   *Gentlemen v Players, 1806-1949*   (Harrap, 1950)
Webber, Roy   *The Playfair Book of Test Cricket Vol. I 1877-1939*   (Playfair, 1952)
Wynne-Thomas, Peter   *England on Tour*   (Hamlyn, 1982)

On Hobbs
Arlott, John   *Jack Hobbs - Profile of the Master*   (John Murray, 1981)
Hobbs, J.B.   *My Cricket Memories*   (Heinemann, 1924)
Hobbs, J.B.   *My Life Story*   (The Star, 1935)
Hobbs, J.B.   *Playing for England*   (Gollancz, 1931)
Landsberg, Pat   *Jack Hobbs - Gentleman and Player*   (Harrap, 1953)
Lodge, Derek   *J.B. Hobbs - His record innings-by-innings*   (A.C.S. 1986)
MacLaren, A.C.   *The Perfect Batsman - J.B. Hobbs in Action*   (Cassell, 1926)
Mason, Ronald   *Jack Hobbs*   (Hollis & Carter, 1960)
Sparks, W.P.H.   *John Berry Hobbs*   (Fleetgate, 1926)

Tours and Tests
Barker, Ralph and Rosenwater, Irving   *England v Australia*   (Batsford, 1969)
Fender, P.G.H.   *Defending the Ashes*   (Chapman & Hall, 1921)
Fender, P.G.H.   *The Turn of the Wheel*   (Faber, 1929)
Fender, P.G.H.   *The Tests of 1930*   (Faber, 1930)
Frith, David (Ed.)   *England v. Australia - Test Match Records*   (Collins Willow, 1986)
Gilligan, A.E.R.   *Collins' Men*   (Arrowsmith, 1926)

Hobbs, J.B.   *Recovering the 'Ashes'*   (Pitman, 1912)
Marchant, John   *The Greatest Test Match*   (Faber & Gwyer, 1926)
Mason, Ronald   *Warwick Armstrong's Australians*   (Epworth, 1971)
Noble, M.A.   *Gilligan's Men*   (Chapman & Hall, 1925)
Noble, M.A.   *Those Ashes*   (Cassell, 1926)
Noble, M.A.   *The Fight for the Ashes 1928-29*   (Harrap, 1929)
Sewell E.H.D.   *Triangular Cricket*   (Dent, 1912)
Tebbutt, Geoffrey   *With the 1930 Australians*   (Hodder & Stoughton, 1930)
Wakley, B.J.   *Classic Centuries in the Test Matches between England and Australia*   (Nicholas Kaye, 1964)
Warner, P.F.   *England v Australia*   (Mills & Boon, 1912)
Warner, P.F.   *The Fight for the Ashes in 1926*   (Harrap, 1926)
Warner, P.F.   *The Fight for the Ashes in 1930*   (Harrap, 1930)

Biographies and Autobiographies

Bowes, Bill   *Express Deliveries*   (Stanley Paul, 1949)
Duckworth, Leslie   *S.F. Barnes - Master Bowler*   (Hutchinson, 1967)
Fry, C.B.   *Life Worth Living*   (Eyre & Spottiswoode, 1939)
Hammond, Walter   *Cricket My Destiny*   (Stanley Paul, 1946)
Hawke, Lord   *Recollection and Reminiscences*   (Williams & Norgate, 1924)
Hodgson, R.L.   *Cricket Memories*   (Methuen, 1930)
Leveson Gower, H.D.G.   *Off and On the Field*   (Stanley Paul, 1953)
Macartney, C.G.   *My Cricketing Days*   (Heinemann, 1930)
Mailey, Arthur   *10 for 66 and All That*   (Phoenix, 1958)
Murphy, Patrick   *'Tiger' Smith*   (Lutterworth, 1981)
Oldfield, W.A.   *Behind the Wicket*   (Hutchinson, 1938)
Parkin, Cecil   *Cricket Triumphs and Troubles*   (Nicholls, 1936)
Peebles, Ian   *Woolley The Pride of Kent*   (The Cricketer/Hutchinson 1969)
Peebles, Ian   *'Patsy' Hendren*   (Macmillan, 1969)
Peebles, Ian   *Spinner's Yarn*   (Collins, 1977)
Robertson-Glasgow, R.C.   *46 Not Out*   (Hollis & Carter 1948)
Rogerson, Sidney   *Wilfred Rhodes*   (Hollis & Carter, 1960)
Root, Fred   *A Cricket Pro's Lot*   (Edward Arnold, 1930)
Strudwick, Herbert   *25 Years Behind the Stumps*   (Hutchinson, 1926)
Wyatt, R.E.S.   *Three Straight Sticks*   (Stanley Paul, 1951)

Essays

Brodriff, Gerald   *Hit for Six*   (Heinemann, 1960)
Cardus, Neville,   *A Cricketer's Book*   (Grant Richards, 1922)
Cardus, Neville   *Good Days*   (Cape, 1934)
Fingleton, Jack   *Masters of Cricket*   (Heinemann, 1958)
Kay, John (Ed.)   *Cricket Heroes*   (Phoenix, 1959)
Kilburn, J.M.   *Overthrows*   (Stanley Paul, 1975)
Mason, Ronald   *Batsman's Paradise*   (Hollis & Carter, 1955)
Moyes, A.G.   *A Century of Cricket*   (Harrap, 1950)
Pollock, William   *The Cream of Cricket*   (Methuen, 1934)
Robertson-Glasgow, R.C.   *Cricket Prints*   (Werner Laurie, 1943)
Sewell, E.H.D.   *From a Window at Lord's*   (Methuen, 1937)
Thomson, A.A.   *Cricketers of my Times*   (Stanley Paul, 1957)

INDEX

174